THE LITERARY MIND

THE LITERARY MIND
Portraits in Pain and Creativity

Leo Schneiderman, Ph.D.

Eastern Connecticut
State University
Williamantic Connecticut

 **INSIGHT BOOKS**
Human Sciences Press, Inc.
72 Fifth Avenue
New York, N.Y. 10011-8004

Printed in the United States of America
987654321

Library of Congress Cataloging-in-Publication Data

Schneiderman, Leo.
  The literary mind.

  Bibliography: p.
  Includes index.
  1. Psychoanalysis and literature. 2. Literature,
Modern—20th century—History and criticism.
3. Creation (Literary, artistic, etc.) I. Title.
PN56.P92S36 1988   801'.92   87-17042
ISBN 0-89885-394-X (hard)
      0-89885-404-0 (paper)

CONTENTS

For Harriet,
with love

Chapter 1

"WHERE ID WAS, THERE SHALL EGO BE"

This is not the place to undertake a detailed summary of the voluminous literature that has sprung up on the relationship between psychoanalysis and literature since the appearance of Freud's pioneer study, "Delusions and Dreams in Jensen's *Gradiva.*"[1] Until recently, this vast literature, consisting of thousands of articles and scores of books, lacked a theoretical framework of its own, relying instead on basic Freudian assumptions of a clinical nature, with little reference to the creative or aesthetic side of literature. Starting with Ernst Kris' *Psychoanalytic Explorations in Art,*[2] which appeared in 1952, however, several ambitious attempts have been made to relate psychoanalysis to literature and to art on an independent theoretical basis. Kris' contribution, in particular, is of considerable historical and theoretical importance. His predecessor, Frederick J. Hoffman,[3] whose *Freudianism and the Literary Mind* had summarized the influence of psychoanalysis on twentieth century literature up to 1945, had set the stage for a critical overview of the theoretical assumptions underlying the application of psychoanalysis to literature. Kris set about to demonstrate that an id psychology was inadequate to explain the creative process. His theoretical orientation, which has been granted a commanding position by psychoanalytically oriented literary critics, is that of ego psychology. Kris shifts attention away from the unconscious, infantile, and irrational sources of creativity posited by earlier critics and focuses on conscious, preconscious, and rational thought processes. As applied to the genesis of fiction and poetry, Kris' approach generally diminishes the importance of repression and the defense mechanisms as explanatory concepts that can throw significant light on creativity.

Kris freely acknowledged his debt to Heinz Hartmann,[4] whose *Ego Psychology and the Problem of Adaptation,* published in 1939, had argued that behavior is not determined exclusively by sexual and aggressive instincts, but is influenced in decisive ways by the individual's striving for adaptation. In this connection, Hartmann had drawn attention to the role of the ego in mediating between the individual and the external environment. In highlighting the role of the ego in resolving conflict with the objective world, Hartmann was careful not to abandon the idea of the ego as a force for dealing with intrapsychic conflict. Hartmann's emphasis on the importance of perceptual and cognitive processes in one's coming to terms with reality pointed to the central role of the ego as a synthesizing force, and to the person's ability to adapt creatively to the demands of life. Thus, Kris' adoption of ego psychology as an explanatory framework for his investigations of artistic creativity acknowledged the relative autonomy of the creative artist in relation to his unconscious fears and evasions. Such autonomy implies, as Hartmann indicates, that the ego is capable, despite the pull of regressive forces, of testing reality and resolving conflict among the various ego functions. The effect is to produce a feeling of "full control and discharge of tensions." Kris sums up his position as follows: "The integrative functions of the ego include self-regulated regression and permit a combination of the most daring intellectual activity with the experience of passive receptiveness."[5] The reference to passivitiy is based on Kris' view that problem-solving, with its fruitful integration of id impulses with ego energies, is accompanied by the feeling that somehow the solution came from without and was passively received. Kris, in effect, grants the ego an active role in the creation of insightful solutions, but recognizes the special character of the subjective experience associated with creativity.

The innovations in psychoanalytic theory introduced by ego psychologists such as Hartmann and Kris focus on cognitive processes, rather than on personality development or structure. For this reason it is necessary to turn to the contribution of Erik Erikson,[6] an ego psychologist with a special interest in the problem of ego identity. As interpreted by Erikson, the individual strives throughout his life for environmental mastery. The sense of identity develops out of the ego's interaction with the social environment. Erikson sees the individual as powerfully motivated to develop a sense of self that is based on a clear perception of who he is and what he is competent to do. The crisis of identity diffusion during adolescence is of paramount concern to Erikson and forms the basis of his psychohistorical studies of the personalities of Martin Luther and Gandhi. By extending ego psychology into the domain of personality analysis, Erikson raises many questions about the connection between the search for identity and the process of creative adaptation to the environment. The adolescent crisis of role confusion posited by Erikson is central for understanding Luther's eventual rebellion against the Church and his creation of a new theology. Gandhi's career as the creator of a revolutionary ethos is similarly analyzed as emerging out of a series of crises centering around his identity. Erikson does not have much to say about the role of stress in generating creative solutions to problems. However, his life-cycle perspective, with its emphasis on crisis resolution at each of life's stages, is extremely valuable for charting the creative strategies of writers and artists, not only in their early search for identity, but in their lifelong efforts to impose symbolic meaning on experience under changing conditions as well. Perhaps the most important implication of Erikson's work, with its departure from orthodox psychoanalytic assumptions, is that a new metapsychology is called for, with special emphasis on clearly defined interactionist constructs.

Roy Schafer's *A New Language for Psychoanalysis*[7] examines the terminology of classical psychoanalysis and draws up a new set of language rules based on what Schafer calls *action language*. Action language seeks to substitute verbs and adverbs in place of nouns and adjectives for the purpose of eliminating "physico-chemical and biological" modes of thought from psychoanalysis. Without altering the basic assumptions of psychoanalysis about the importance of formative influences, unconscious motivation, the psychology of dreams, and so forth, Schafer applies the conceptual tools of phenomenology and existentialism to mental phenomena in the interest of linguistic precision and objectivity. With reference to the study of literature, Schafer's linguistic focus has a number of important theoretical implications. First, it brings into question an entire class of key "spatial" terms, such as id, ego, and superego, which psychoanalytic critics have invoked to explain an author's thought processes—particularly the motives underlying the choice of symbols, characterizations, and themes. Second, Schafer's analysis of "self" and "identity," with special regard to the process of separation-individuation, leads him to the conclusion that adolescent experience consists, in part, of the reification of feelings and relationships (not unlike the reifications represented by the spatial terms employed by psychoanalysis and criticized by Schafer). The adolescent struggle for autonomy and identity leads to the magical attempt to get rid of emotions and identifications, as if they were objects—rather than processes—leading to the experience of "emptiness, deadness, and desolation."[8]

The implications of this mode of analysis for understanding the autobiographical novel are obvious and compel a recognition of the saliency of primary-process, reified thinking in adolescence, as well as in childhood. The psychoanalytically oriented critic who wishes to benefit from Schafer's analysis is alerted to the need to approach the autobiographical novel in terms that emphasize "representational and behavioral differentiations from the parents of infancy," rather than references to concretized feelings and threatening influences.[9] In line with this reasoning, an analysis, for example, of J. D. Salinger's Catcher in the Rye would stress the protagonist's tendency to perceive his feelings and actions as "things," and the confusion and suffering that result from this archaic mode of thinking. The more complex works of James Joyce and Marcel Proust can be approached in the same manner, thereby revealing new layers of meaning.

A third dimension of Schafer's metapsychology has to do with the processes of *internalization* and *externalization,* concepts that he rejects because of their spatial, metaphoric connotations. Instead, Schafer prefers to speak of actions based on increasing organismic complexity and independence from environmental control. In rejecting the concept of internalization, Schafer also explicitly denies the usefulness of externalization and projection for describing how the individual deals with his own impulses and with other people. At best, metaphors referring to the inside or outside of the body are viewed by Schafer as fantasies that people have about psychological events, and are not to be confused with cognitive processes, as such. Although Schafer seems to stop short of questioning the validity of projection in all cases, he maintains that spatial terms should be understood as infantile fantasies that people have about taking objects into the body or expelling them. He acknowledges that such fantasies are basic for understanding what transpires in the transference relationship, but Schafer is careful to distinguish between the patient's archaic mental processes and the terms of analysis that are most likely to be productive for the therapist, in this instance, nonspatial modes of conceptualization.

The significance of Schafer's recommendations for developing a rigorous metapsychology for analyzing literature is that, by implication, he raises serious questions about the relationship between an author's fantasies and his literary productions. If fantasies are archaic thought processes based on infantile metaphors such as *inside* and *outside,* how can the creative process lead to fresh discoveries about the self and others? Granted that cognitive processes should not be thought of in spatial terms, it remains that the creative writer sets out on a metaphoric voyage of exploration that leads him from one locus to another. Starting with his own images, fragments of memory, ideas and emotions, the writer moves "outward" in pursuit of his objective, which is to create a fictional world "out there"—in other words, a self-sufficient universe that transcends personal experience and can be entered by readers equipped with the proper maps and a compass, including their own apperceptive mass. The element of exploration, as Albert Rothenberg[10] argues in *The Emerging Goddess,* is crucial in creative writing, and involves, I would add, movement away from the center, from subjectivism, toward objectification. The success of the artistic means employed by the writer in objectifying his fantasies is measured by his ability to stir the imagination of the reader, that is, to enter the psychological "space" of another person. Thus, although Schafer is on solid ground in identifying depth-analytical constructs as spatial metaphors, he cannot escape a basic dilemma of psychoanalytic thinking—indeed, of metapsychology in general.

This dilemma is created by the psychologist's need to build, between the individual and his social and physical environment, a conceptual bridge that will account for a wide variety of interactions. The writer of fiction is under no compulsion, of course, to explain how his experiences are communicated to the reader; his task is to find the right metaphors or symbols for communicating his own thoughts. The task of the psychologist who wishes to understand the creative process is to try to conceptualize how the writer discovers the right metaphors. Heeding Schafer's admonition, can one say that the writer internalizes experience by reflecting on it (this does not preclude working over preconscious and unconscious experience in symbolic form), and then externalizes it by finding the most effective way to gain and hold the interest of his reader, and perhaps even awaken his feelings and understanding? As I will try to show in the ensuing chapters, the stresses to which the writer is exposed, including pathogenic experiences, play a significant role in determining how the writer processes events, chooses themes, and characterizes fictional protagonists; in short, how the writer moves from the subjective to the objective plane.

If Roy Schafer's semantic approach is rooted in phenomenology and the drive toward conceptual clarity in the analysis of fantasy, Jacques Lacan's[11] epistemology is no less concerned with the role of language in relation to the imagination. For Lacan, the use of metaphor creates the possibility of substituting and combining the elements of experience, especially concrete experiences that occurred in childhood. Like Schafer, Lacan views language as a system of meanings that has mistakenly been identified with static essences, rather than with the dynamic act of speaking. In the act of communicating, the individual reveals his earliest sources of mother-centered knowledge and anxiety; that is, his archaic, narcissistic identification. But this portion of the communication process is unconscious, according to Lacan, having been repressed by the very use of language, which represents a step beyond the experiential state. Lacan thereby identifies consciousness with language, and, by contrast, equates the imagination with the fusion of primordial images and words in the form of primary-process thinking. But for Lacan there is no absolute distinction between primary and secondary process, insofar as the act of speaking conveys unconscious, narcissistic fixations and aggressions at the same time that it strives for accurate meaning and conscious intentionality. In effect, Lacan's epistemology states that we know the world experientially as well as by the application of metaphor. The experiential way of knowing is a striving for fusion with others in a regressive manner, whereas the application of metaphor represents the need for symbolic order. Again, like Schafer, Lacan would get rid of all references to static structures and regions of the psyche and would substitute a psychology of situations.

It is Lacan's position that it is only in the concreteness of a social interaction that the unconscious is activated in the form of subjective interpretation, transference, or metaphoric association. In the act of communicating, the imagination has a chance to show itself, not as pure fantasy, but as the union of the experiential and the symbolic. As such, imagination carries a residual set of meanings and images and is—in classical psychoanalytic terms—overdetermined. Unlike ordinary language, which represses the richest layers of meaning created by the unique history of the individual, metaphorical communication permits a flow of meanings between consciousness and the unconscious. Of necessity, such linkage between primary and secondary thought processes is inconceivable without reference to the experience of the author and the reader. Within this personal context, unanticipated and surprising conjunctions of images and ideas are given representational meaning in the form of fiction or poetry. The literary critic must confront not only the text, but the identity of the person who speaks through the text, and who uses language as the "resistance" he has thrown up to conceal unconscious truth.

The contributions of Schafer and Lacan belong to meta-psychology and point up the need to conceptualize new and more rigorous modes of linguistic analysis. The effect of their systems is to add to the chorus of doubt as to whether classical psychoanalysis can be applied to the study of literature without significant modifications. Reflecting this spirit of revisionism is the work of a group of scholars at the University of Florida. I refer to the research of Norman N. Holland, Coppelia Kahn, Janet Adelman, and their associates, especially their psychoanalytically oriented interpretations of Shakespeare. Murray M. Schwartz[12] has summarized the main theoretical trends that provide a historical background for the work of this group. These trends include an awareness, above all, of the significance of neo-Freudian developments. In this context, fiction is regarded as a form of symbolic problem-solving that involves resolution of intrapsychic and interpersonal conflict. Emphasis on the adaptive significance of the written word is accompanied by a continuing recognition of the importance of unconscious influences and infantile fixations. There is no doubt, however, that an important shift in perspective has taken place, one "that does not grant infantile fantasies sole determining status in the creation of meanings."[13] Instead, the focus of the Holland group is on the interaction of the author's vision with the world, and with the reader's no less subjective interpretation of the text. Literary criticism does not cease to demand clarification of the author's conscious and unconscious intentions, but insists that these meanings can be discovered only in what D. W. Winnicott[14] terms "potential space," or the region between the writer and the reader, between one self and another. The work of literature becomes a "transitional object" reflecting the dual experience of writer and interpreter.

Norman Holland[15] notes that the psychoanalytic study of literature has progressed from a one-sided preoccupation with the writer's unconscious to an appreciation of the writer's ego functions or adaptive strivings, and ultimately, to an understanding of literature as providing reader and critic with symbolizations of themselves. His position is that psychoanalysis should no longer seek confirmation of its hypotheses in the insights of the writer, or use its own conceptual tools to try to understand what the artist has accomplished. Holland argues that a literary work cannot be viewed as merely symptomatic of the author's state of mind, but must be seen as an end in itself, an artificial creation that can communicate general meanings through its themes. Holland also calls attention to the relevance of self psychology and object-relations theory for understanding literature. He refers to the work of Lacan, Winnicott, and Heinz Kohut, and maintains that the latest innovations in psychoanalytically oriented literary criticism attempt to take into account the identity of the reader as well as the perspective of the writer. Holland's position is that there is no single definitive meaning to be derived from a work of art. The historically and culturally conditioned reader or critic brings a special set of concerns to his interpretation of a literary work, and these concerns reflect the never-ending search for self-discovery. Holland sums up his position as follows: "Just as self and object constitute each other in human development, so in the literary transaction the reader constitutes text so that text may constitute its reader."[16]

The idea of the internalization of a literary work is given concrete meaning by Holland in *Poems in Persons: An Introduction to the Psychoanalysis of Literature*[17] In this work, Holland addresses a problem of major importance to psychoanalytic theory, as well as to literature conceived as symbolic problem-solving. This is the problem of separation and fusion, viewed within the context of the reader's subjective recreation of a work of literature. The reading of a poem, for example, "involves a sense of the boundaries blurring between self and other, a feeling of merger which derives ultimately from a recreation of the same symbiotic at-oneness with the giving mother."[18] Holland views literature as an experience that writer, reader, and critic interpret in the light of their individual style of adaptation. There is no clear boundary line separating a work of literature from its creator or its reader, because a literary text is ultimately a meeting place for personal wishes and fears. Holland states that he started his career as a literary critic under the spell of the New Criticism, with its emphasis on the self-contained text. He provides a measure of how far literary criticism has evolved over the last few decades by affirming the centrality of the author's personal style, along with the identity of the reader for experiencing literature in all its richness. Psychoanalytic theory, viewed from the standpoint of ego psychology and self theory, no longer dwells exclusively on the symbolic interpretation of literature, or on unraveling the oedipal problems of the author, but seeks to discover the author's worldview by seeing it in relation to the reader's psychological needs. In this connection, special mention should be made of Simon O. Lesser's *Fiction and the Unconscious*,[19] which is devoted specifically to identifying the reader's psychological needs and how fiction meets these needs. Lesser's main argument, derived from Freud's analysis of the reality principle and its inherent frustrations, is that fiction satisfies the need to transcend the limitations of everyday experience. The literary text provides the reader with a disguised scenario for the gratification of repressed wishes. In this way, in keeping with Holland's emphasis on the reader as well as the author, the act of reading a literary text involves the collaboration of the myth-maker and the reader in overcoming guilt and anxiety by evading the censorship of the ego and the superego.

Accordingly, the direction of growth of psychoanalytically oriented literary criticism is from the microscopic to the macroscopic, embracing reader and writer alike. The development of theory has proceeded from the interpretation of isolated symptoms of the author's "pathology" to the identification of larger themes that can take on a variety of meanings within the personal frame of orientation of different readers. This is not to say that the stresses to which the author is exposed, and which may give rise to pathology, have no place in the analysis of literary creativity. I will try to show in the following chapters that severe stress is indeed an important ingredient in generating creativity, but Holland is surely right in affirming that literature is a confrontation of self with self, of writer and reader, and of each with his own demons.

Paralleling, but by no means duplicating the work of the Holland group of applied psychoanalysis are the investigations of Harry Slochower and the contributions to the journal *American Imago*, which Slochower has edited for many years. This group includes Mark Kanzer, Leon Wurmser, Leo Rangell, K. R. Eissler, and many others who have tried to apply the insights of psychoanalysis to understanding the creative process. Like

Slochower, these investigators are not wedded to a narrow interpretation of psychoanalysis and are able to bring to their inquiries a broad cultural and historical frame of reference. Also clearly discernible in the writings of Slochower and his associates is an appreciation of the influence of social philosophy on the interpretation of literature. The effort to clarify the nature of creativity has led Slochower to pay special attention to myths, which he views as mankind's vehicle for transforming the lessons of the past into symbols pointing toward the future. Slochower's *Mythopoesis: Mythic Patterns in the Literary Classics*[20] expresses his belief in the synthesizing function of myths through symbol formation. Slochower is especially concerned with the symbolic function of the mythical hero as champion of personal identity, and as rebel and catalyst for cultural renewal. *Mythopoesis* is of particular relevance for understanding the sources of the literary imagination because it examines the process by which myths are transformed into modern literature, with its characteristic concern for communicating symbolic meanings. Slochower's studies of Aeschylus, Dante, Cervantes, Shakespeare, Goethe, Herman Melville and other literary figures illustrate how psychoanalytic and sociocultural perspectives can be combined with traditional forms of literary criticism, especially consideration of aesthetic dimensions. Particularly noteworthy is that Slochower and the members of his circle were among the first critics in America to demonstrate the importance of the works of Thomas Mann and Franz Kafka from an aesthetic standpoint and as sociocultural documents. *American Imago* continues to be an important outlet for explorations of artistic creativity, and its studies of literature, as much as its papers on painting, sculpture, and music, demonstrate the applicability of depth-analytical psychology for the study of culture products.

Morton Kaplan and Robert Kloss, in *The Unspoken Motive: A Guide to Psychoanalytic Literary Criticism*,[21] have examined a perennial issue in the psychoanalytic study of literature. Commenting on Albert Mordell's *The Erotic Motive in Literature*,[22] a pioneer work first published in 1919, Kaplan and Kloss point to what they term the "biographical fallacy," that is, the tendency to analyze the author's emotional life instead of his literary work. Kaplan, who edits *Psychology and Literature,* a journal that is by no means limited to applications of psychoanalytic theory, represents a school of thought that is somewhat closer to traditional literary criticism than is Slochower. Although Slochower and his associates are emphatic in distinguishing between creative activity and pathology, they acknowledge the importance of biographical data for understanding a work of art. Thus, K. R. Eissler's *Goethe: A Psychoanalytic Study*[23] combines biographical information with an analysis of the creative process. At the same time, Eissler's "Psychopathology and Creativity"[24] is careful to draw a line between the abnormal and originality in the arts. In a sequel to this paper titled "Remarks on an Aspect of Creativity,"[25] Eissler concedes that there are certain similarities between the process of creativity and the paranoid mechanism of projection, but regards pathology as resulting from a regressive surrender to the pleasure principle. The creative act, by comparison, is regarded by Eissler as falling somewhere between the reality principle and the pleasure principle.

Eissler's position is clearly more clinical than that of Kaplan and his co-workers, who argue that one must not work *away* from the text by attributing experiences to the author that properly belong to fictional characters. Kaplan rejects Mordell's view that a literary text is based, among other things, on the author's repressed emotions. The issue raised by Kaplan is not only central, but continues to defy easy resolution. Mordell's id psychology, which reflects Freud's emphasis in the latter's early works, has been succeeded by an emphasis on ego processes in more recent psychoanalytic literary criticism, as I have noted. In commenting on this change, Kaplan and Kloss state that infantile fantasy and emotions "tell us little about the author, less about textual problems, and nothing about the nature of artistic creation."[26] In support of this position they cite the views of Frederick Crews, whose book, *The Sins of the Fathers*,[27] applies psychoanalytic concepts to the works of Nathaniel Hawthorne. It is Crews' understanding that literary creation and symptom formation are two different things, and that a truly creative work of the imagination impresses us by its respect for the reality principle, and is not distorted by the operation of ego-defensive needs. The formulations of Kaplan, Kloss, and Crews imply that society, in rendering its judgment as to which literary production is a true work of art and which is merely a symptom of psychic disturbance, will be able to tell them apart without difficulty. This approach places a heavy burden on the critic, who is required to make not only an aesthetic judgment, but a clinical one as well.

The critic's problems are not removed by the knowledge that some literary figures who have been widely hailed as geniuses, such as Edgar Allan Poe, Charles Baudelaire, Louis-Ferdinand Céline, William Faulkner, and others, have led very troubled lives. Can psychopathology be transmuted into art without revealing itself as a flaw in the finished product? Kaplan and those who share his predilection for normalizing literature argue for the aesthetic integrity of a literary text and its ability to appeal to the conscious mind. My position, as will be evident to the reader of this book, is midway between the clinical and the aesthetic. Admittedly, old-fashioned id psychology, with its emphasis on sexual symbolism and its penchant for body language, did not lend itself to a balanced interpretation of art. I would argue, however, that the psychoanalytic study of literature cannot dispense with Freud's id psychology and substitute an ego psychology that attributes complete rationality and conscious control to the artist. Such a view, in my judgment, is retrogressive, and tends to reify and isolate the work of art, taking it out of its human context. It is indeed difficult to say how a work of literary imagination, viewed as a human undertaking, differs from a factual document, a manifesto, or a critical essay. Perhaps there exists a continuum in literature from the purely objective—if there is such a thing—to the purely subjective. We have grown accustomed to looking for creativity and genius toward the subjective end of the continuum, where the idiosyncrasies of the author enjoy the widest latitude of expression, as in the modern novel or in modern poetry. But a social context exists for all written works, from impersonal business contracts to confessional poetry. If one carries the implications of ego psychology to their logical conclusion, the last veil is removed between the objective and the subjective planes, between purely instrumental communication and the expressive work, and between the prosaic text and the poetic composition.

It is necessary to think of the adaptive needs of the writer in the broadest sense if one is to avoid denaturing literary criticism in the name of purism. These needs produce a variety of defensive strategies as well as realistic means for solving personal and aesthetic problems. Under the right conditions, the author's response to the challenges of everyday life can result in artisitic productions of great virtuosity. What these conditions are remains as much a mystery as in Freud's day, and it is no solution to maintain that the infantile, the irrational, the unconscious, and the pathological have somehow been filtered out of a text of true literary excellence. One has only to read one page of any outstanding modern writer to be struck by the intensity of the personal vision and to sense that this intensity is generated by powerful intrapsychic forces, neither mysterious nor rational, but rooted in human experience, especially crisis and conflict.

The writers whose works I analyze in this volume were not chosen for their pathology, but for their vital presence in their literary works. Their works were chosen because they are representative of major literary trends in the modern period. Yet in every case—and this would be true of many great writers whose work is not discussed in this book—pathology is a contributing factor to creativity. Both the sytle and substance of modern literature reveal its pathological substratum, sometimes glaringly, as in the poetry of Sylvia Plath, and sometimes obliquely, as in the work of William Carlos Williams or Robert Lowell. It is conceivable that society's decision as to what constitutes a valuable work of literature has little to do with how much or what kind of pathology is contained in the work.

Similarly, it is useless to assert that creativity is somehow linked with healthy-mindedness. The impulse to create something new seems to be associated with those traits that are antithetical to facile "adjustment." Commenting on the poetry of Sylvia Plath, Hans Kleinschmidt[28] suggests that creativity is associated with angry rebellion, guilt, ambivalence, and a disturbing feeling of being "different." This interpretation is consistent with Slochower's concept of mythopoesis, which regards the artist as one who transforms society's myths into instruments for criticizing life and challenging the status quo. Leo Rangel,[29] in his essay "The Creative Thrust: A Psychoanalytic Theory," sees each new movement in art as a rebellion against the past and as a determined effort not to repeat the formulas of the past. To the extent that literary activity is a collective enterprise in which writers vie with each other to create new forms, it implies a solidarity of the disaffected. In this way, the frustrations and intrapsychic conflicts of individuals are translated into recognizable "movements" of artistic or literary innovation.

Whether one thinks of the creative writer as an isolated rebel or as a contributor to a well-articulated avant-garde movement, the common denominator is a sense of opposition to prevailing social and aesthetic norms. Such opposition is often based on deep feelings and may be associated with more-than-ordinary suffering, whether neurotically self-induced or inflicted by an indifferent or hostile society. I readily admit that this is a "romantic" theory of how literature is created, but I believe it is psychologically sound because it posits a fusion of cognitive and affective processes, rather than a one-sided emphasis on one or the other. Such a theory recognizes the connection pointed out by Ernst Kris between inspiration and creative activity, in which unconscious fantasy processes come under the domination of the ego for the purpose of sublimation. Kris states: "Thus inspired creation solves an inner contest, sometimes as a compromise between conflicting forces, and sometimes as a defense against one particularly dangerous instinct."[30] The adaptive function of the creative act places it squarely in the life struggle of the artist. Even when the artist or writer is being playful or frivolous, the finished product must be taken seriously as an expression of inner need, but a need that has been met by creating something that can be shared with others.

It is the act of communication that distinguishes the work of art from an incoherent cry of pain or joy, and it is the presence of pain or joy in the act of communication that separates literature from other forms of writing, such as journalism, or the preparation of technical reports. Whether what is communicated is evaluated as "great" or as a work of genius is in some measure culturally and historically determined, as I have indicated, because much depends on the receptivity of the audience. The primary task of literary criticism involves more than making value judgments about what is great art and what is second class.

The challenge is to understand the experiential core of art, and how private fantasy derived from this base is made over into something public that has the power to move audiences and to capture their imagination. In meeting this challenge the critic may find that distinctions between works belonging to the Great Tradition and those representative of popular art become blurred at times, insofar as they embody similar conflicts, hopes, and fears. This does not mean that psychoanalytic literary criticism requires the abandonment of standards of excellence; it means only that the evaluative function of criticism can be strengthened and enriched by a clinical approach that locates an author's work in the context of his life. This is a holistic strategy because it seeks to place a text back into the life process of its creator from which it has been abstracted. Does such a strategy pose the danger that the literary work will be subordinated to the case history? Yes—but it is a risk that has to be taken. To do otherwise is, in effect, to subordinate the author's life to his work—as if he had never lived apart from his writing, and had never endured pain or known happiness. Let the creative work speak for its author, but let the author's examined life bear witness that he created by the sweat of his brow.

WILLIAM FAULKNER

Ego Functions and Fantasy

The life and work of William Faulkner pose a number of questions centering on the link between ego functions and fantasy. In addition, Faulkner's symbolic solutions to his problems through the medium of writing are informative because they seem to define the self-limiting characteristics of the artistic imagination, especially against a background of narcissistic vulnerability. In Faulkner's case, art possessing a terrible beauty and great emotional power was produced by a young man who was self-centered and emotionally withdrawn. Ironically, as Faulkner grew in ego strength and emotional responsiveness in the second half of his life he lost the drive and the gift to be creative.

I will try to show that symbolic alter egos, cast in the form of idealized images of recent and remote ancestors, played an important part in Faulkner's formative years. By reverting to a fantasy world peopled by charismatic ancestors, Faulkner was able to escape the painful reality of parental rejection. Although his mother was outwardly supportive of her slight, withdrawn eldest son, her basic attitude was ambivalent and defensive. Faulkner's fictional portraits of brave, enduring women who do their duty but are hard, willful, and basically unloving—Addie Bundren in *As I Lay Dying* (1930), Joanna Burden in *Light in August* (1932), Rosa Coldfield in *Absalom, Absalom!* (1936), Drusilla in *The Unvanquished* (1938)—appear to have some of the mother's traits. Maud Faulkner, a fiercely independent, frugal, controlling woman, was perceived by her son as both victim and victimizer. She was patently the victim of her husband's loud, abusive behavior during his frequent drinking bouts; she was also the symbol of impulse control, of propriety, and cold practicality for her young son. Faulkner's mother encouraged him in his literary pursuits from an early age, perhaps in defiance of her husband's crudeness and "good-old-boy" provincialism. Compared to his three vigorous, outgoing, athletic younger brothers, Murry Jr., Dean and John, Faulkner was the most vulnerable child—undersized, sad, and uncommunicative. Perhaps, too, Faulkner's mother went along with his reclusive, somewhat unmanly (by rural standards) interests to conceal her distress, which must have communicated itself to the young Faulkner, affecting his self-esteem and contributing to his need to prove himself. It is not surprising that the short story "A Return" describes a dutiful son who keeps sending money to his self-reliant, undemonstrative mother only to find, after thirty years, that she has not spent any of it, carelessly tossing the bills into a shoebox.[1] In actuality, Faulkner's mother, who lived long enough to see her son win the Nobel prize in 1949, was proud of his accomplishments, but it can hardly be doubted that Faulkner had to prove to himself that he had been worthy of her support in the beginning.

Faulkner's father, Murray, rejected his bookish son, whom he could neither understand nor win over. Young Faulkner, in turn, dismissed his father as a dull man.[2] Emblematic of their relationship was the incident in which Faulkner's father offered him a cigar when Faulkner was about seventeen. The boy broke the cigar in half in his father's presence and stuffed half of it into his pipe. Faulkner recalled in later years that his father had never offered him a cigar again.[3] Although Faulkner identified with his father on some levels—in his dislike for formal schooling, his love of hunting, and his fondness for strong drink—he probably identified more closely with other male figures. These included his rich and powerful paternal grandfather, a banker who had owned a railroad; a paternal uncle who was an influential figure in Mississippi politics; and perhaps most important of all, his great-grandfather, a legendary leader in the Confederate army and a successful writer. From the time he was eight Faulkner repeatedly affirmed that he wanted to be a writer like the Colonel, his great-grandfather. In contrast to these charismatic figures, Faulkner's father seemed a remote, inarticulate man who could be violent at times, having thrown a man through a plate-glass window in a fist fight in the center of Oxford, Mississippi, Faulkner's hometown.

Faulkner felt his father's rejection deeply, all the more so because his father had a much closer relationship with the younger brothers, who were more likely to accompany him on hunting and fishing trips. Faulkner, too, learned to hunt and fish at an early age and developed a fondness for camping, but these activities did not bring him closer to his father. The father took much pride in the athletic prowess of his younger sons, cheering them on with great enthusiasm at baseball and football games; Faulkner did his best to compete in sports but was at a serious disadvantage because of his slight physique. Despite his outward participation in sports and games, Faulkner abstracted himself increasingly from his young contemporaries, usually standing on the sidelines watching the others, whether in the schoolyard, or later, at high school dances. At the same time, Faulkner early developed the ability to tell stories, some of them based on the books his mother encouraged him to read, and others freely invented, so that other children often did not know whether Faulkner was telling the truth or making something up.

As a fantasy-ridden child, Faulkner depended heavily on his symbiotic relationship with his unhappy mother, who, like him, was also very diminutive. Not unlike D. H. Lawrence's mother, Maud Faulkner regarded her quiet, sensitive son as one of her few links with the world of refinement and gentility, especially during the early years of her marriage when her husband ran a livery stable. Accordingly, Faulkner's mother encouraged him not only to read, but also to write poetry and to draw, and protected him against the father's barely concealed contempt. Faulkner's emotional dependence on his mother, as well as on fantasy alter egos in lieu of his father, could not make up for certain ego defects. These defects included impaired self-esteem due to paternal rejection and small stature, a serious disadvantage in a subculture that attached much importance to physical size and strength. Faulkner tried to overcome his negative self-image by constructing an idealized self that would someday produce works of literary genius. Even as a teenager Faulkner confided to a few intimates that he believed himself to be a genius. Supported emotionally and financially by his mother until his marriage in 1929 at the age of 32, Faulkner nurtured compensatory feelings of superiority fueled by alcoholism, which began when he was still in his teens.

To overcome his low self-esteem, Faulkner tried to fulfill his grandiose needs through compulsive writing. Unlike Ernest Hemingway, who chose the path of perfectionism as a writer, pruning his compositions carefully, Faulkner allowed his fantasies to spill out with a minimum of preliminary censorship. The result can be seen in Faulkner's vast productivity and unevenness as a writer. Faulkner was no less expansive in striving for a grand style of life, especially after he purchased an old mansion a year after his marriage to Estelle Oldham, a divorcée who had been Faulkner's sweetheart during their school days. Although Faulkner was heavily in debt for many years, he not only rebuilt his mansion, but purchased a plantation complete with tenant farmers, an airplane, expensive clothes, and other accoutrements of wealth and status. Faulkner may have been motivated in part by the need to impress Estelle's wealthy parents, who did not approve of Faulkner as a suitable husband for their daughter, whose first husband had been a career military officer and diplomat.

To support himself and his growing number of dependents, Faulkner wrote at a furious pace, turning out short stories for mass-circulation magazines and writing scripts for movies. Faulkner was not only very productive, spinning out complicated plots of a melodramatic character, but he also invented entire family genealogies for his fictional characters, introducing a bewildering variety of personages from all walks of like. Although Faulkner was much given to the use of symbols, he was in no sense a psychological writer, preferring to resolve conflicts between his characters by violence or other mechanical means. The lack of coherence that some literary critics have noted in Faulkner's writings, including his major works, was a product of long-standing ego defects. These defects were aggravated by Faulkner's humiliating experiences in Hollywood over many years, during which he was exploited and treated contemptuously by directors and producers because of his unreliability due to alcoholism.

Faulkner's need for fantasy gratifications through writing reflects serious difficulties in achieving independence on the material plane.Faulkner devoted himself to full-time literary production even though he was well aware that it would be impossible to support himself as a creative writer. Long after he had become famous—or notorious—upon the publication of *Sanctuary* in 1931, Faulkner continued to depend on the good will of his many creditors. At the same time, as noted, Faulkner maintained a style of life befitting a country squire, complete with a household full of servants. Faulkner had a strong aversion to working for a living in a conventional way and was fired from his job (obtained for him by family political influence) as postmaster of the tiny post office attached to the University of Mississippi (1921–1924).

I believe it is correct to say that Faulkner was not neurotically inhibited from dealing with workaday reality in an effective way. Instead, he appears to have lacked the structural integration to cope with the demands of a conventional career. It is even questionable whether Faulkner could have survived economically if he had not been protected by a number of concerned people. Included in this group—besides Faulkner's solicitous mother—was the young Faulkner's close friend and literary mentor, Phil Stone, a young attorney who encouraged Faulkner and even arranged to have Faulkner's manuscripts typed professionally and mailed out to countless magazines and publishers. Another important protector and sponsor was Sherwood Anderson, who with his wife took the youthful Faulkner into their home in New Orelans. Anderson gave Faulkner much advice about writing, including the important exhortation to write about his Southern background, counsel that was to influence decisively the entire direction of Faulkner's development. During the 1930s, when Faulkner was compelled by neccessity to write for Hollywood, the director and producer Howard Hawks not only tolerated Faulkner's drinking and unreliability but did his best to promote Faulkner's career, though with little success. Even some of Faulkner's literary agents, notably Harold Ober and Charles Haas, were devoted to Faulkner's welfare, sending him money at crucial times and shielding him from the consequences of his drinking. Ironically, during his middle years as his drinking problem grew worse, more and more relatives came to depend financially on Faulkner. The turning point in Faulkner's career came when he was awarded the Nobel prize at age 52 and his financial situation improved dramatically. By then Faulkner had already developed a degree of ego strength during his struggle to support his family as a hack writer. However, after he achieved the status of Nobel laureate, his need for fantasy gratification diminished accordingly, with important consequences for his writing.

One of the most important ego defects that crystallized during Faulkner's formative years went beyond low self-esteem and involved a pernicious "bad-me" self-concept. Insofar as his schoolwork was concerned Faulkner was a good scholar, quiet and well behaved, but he began to show a serious pattern of truancy at an early age. As an adolescent, Faulkner's pattern of noncompliance took the form of distancing himself from his provincial setting by adopting British-type clothes and mannerisms. Faulkner's peers responded to his superior airs by labeling him "Count no 'count." Equipped with such props as a pipe and a cane, the young Faulkner sauntered about the square in Oxford, resplendent in British tweeds and cutting a somewhat ridiculous figure. His mother, who had to borrow money from relatives to outfit her son, must have had mixed feelings about her role in abetting Faulkner's ideas of grandeur. Faulkner was well aware that he was acting like a nonconformist and that the public image of him as a teenage aesthete and poet carried the connotation of deviance. Starting in his mid-teens, Faulkner's exhibitionistic displays of drinking prowess may have been intended to foster the corrective impression that he was, after, all, a real man who could hold his liquor.

Faulkner's brief sojourn in Greenwich Village as a youth, and in New Orleans' French Quarter as a guest of Sherwood Anderson, represented a distinct departure from the male-bonding pattern (of hunting, gambling, etc.) that was the norm for his time and place. Faulkner was ambivalent toward his Bohemian role and its artistic and intellectual implications. This ambivalence was shown by his refusal to take his studies seriously at the University of Mississippi and his dropping out after a short period. Later, Faulkner exhibited an open aversion to intellectuals, pretending that he was a simple man of the people, in contrast to the elegant persona he had assumed in his late teens and early twenties. Faulkner's motivation in accompanying Phil Stone to Memphis' red-light district on several occasions may have been to prove, at least to himself, that he was a regular fellow. It was on one of these visits to Memphis that Faulkner got the idea for *Sanctuary*, after a bar girl related a bizarre sexual incident to him and some other men. It was in Memphis, too, that Faulkner heard about the real-life prototype for his fictional gangster, the murderous but impotent Popeye, who raped Temple Drake, the female protagonist of *Sanctuary*, with the assistance of a corncob. The character of Popeye—a puny, dwarflike figure with a receding chin—is surprisingly like a caricature of Faulkner himself.

The bad-me self-concept was acted out in real life in Faulkner's disturbed and sometimes violent relations with his wife. During their honeymoon in Pascagoula, Estelle tried to drown herself in the Gulf of Mexico.[4] The course of their married life was not smooth insofar as both Faulkner and Estelle were heavy drinkers, quarreled often, and occasionally hurt each other physically. Faulkner's mother had opposed the marriage, stating that she thought hard-drinking Estelle would be a bad influence on her alcoholic son. Faulkner's hostility toward Estelle was manifested by his protracted love affair with Meta Carpenter, an attractive Hollywood script supervisor.[5] Faulkner idealized Ms. Carpenter, but his attitude toward women is seen more clearly in his disturbed relationship with Estelle, in which hostile projections seem to have played an important part.

Similar negative projections account for Faulkner's fictional portraits of young women, whose sexuality is often presented in a context of amorality and destructiveness. Older women, like Miss Jenny in *Sanctuary,* or Addie Bundren in *As I Lay Dying,* often possess a stubborn strength born of bitter experience, and are reminiscent of Faulkner's mother, who had a sign hanging above her stove that read: "Don't Complain—Don't Explain."[6] Faulkner depicts his fictional young women as nymphomaniacs and punishes them harshly. Candace in *The Sound and the Fury* (1929) is thrown out by her husband and deprived of her baby as a punishment for adultery; the young wife of the Reverend Gail Hightower commits suicide in *Light in August,* thereby punishing herself for infidelity; Temple Drake is not only raped by Popeye in *Sanctuary* but confined to a brothel in Memphis—a chastisement visited upon her by the author apparently for the sin of being a sexually attractive flapper of seventeen; Joanna Burden, though not young, is slain by her lover, Joe Christmas, in *Light in August,* not only because he thinks she wishes to control him, but because he is repelled by her blend of sensuality and evangelical fervor. Faulkner's young male protagonists are also punished, though in their case the offense is one of oedipal rebellion. In *Absalom, Absalom!* Faulkner causes young Charles Bon to be rejected by his father, the ruthless power-seeker Thomas Sutpen, and ultimately to be murdered by his half brother; the protagonist of *Sartoris* (1929), young Bayard Sartoris, engages in a variety of suicidal, daredevil activities and finally, after causing the death of his grandfather in a car accident, manages to kill himself as a test pilot; Quentin Compson, in *The Sound and Fury,* drowns himself shortly after his sister's wedding, driven to desperation because of his incestuous attachment to her; In *As I Lay Dying,* Darl, one of Addie Bundren's sons, sets fire to the barn containing his mother's coffin, and is subsequently institutionalized by his father; in *A Fable* (1954), Faulkner's last ambitious work, the Corporal, a Christ-figure, is executed after his father, the General, pleads with him to abandon his pacifism.

Although the motives that underlie the behavior of each of these errant sons are different, they are destroyed by their confrontation with the stern world of their elders, which they will not accept though they are powerless to alter it. They are bad sons because of their rebellion, but Faulkner gives us to understand that the society they challenge is corrupt and hypocritical, that is, that the fathers are bad no less than the sons. If we think of Faulkner's fictional oedipal sons as failures, we obtain some clues to Faulkner's lifelong flirtation with self-induced disaster. For example, Faulkner became a licensed pilot in his mid-thirties, after pretending for many years that he had been a fighter pilot in World War I at the age of 20. Faulkner's pretense of having been in aerial combat was carried to the extent of his telling people he had been shot down and had a silver plate in his head, as well as a leg injury that left him with a permanent limp. In a very real sense, Faulkner's fantasy of the mutilated warrior, treated fictionally in *Soldiers' Pay* (1926), reflected his image as an oedipal loser. Prophetically, Faulkner's youngest brother, Dean, whom Faulkner had encouraged to learn how to fly, was killed in a plane accident while working as a flying instructor, thereby suffering the fate that Faulkner might have unconsciously wished on himself. Faulkner's alcoholism, which was never interrupted for more than a few months, and which resulted in numerous hospitalizations, was the most visible and dramatic expression of Faulkner's self-hatred and need to punish himself.

The composite symbol that Faulkner employs to denote the bad fathers who destroy their rebellious sons is the South and, by extension, all of society. Critics who have tried to cast Faulkner was a chronicler of the South's material and moral impoverishment, or as a sort of sociologist charting the struggle between burnt-out aristocrats and upstart Snopeses are wide of the mark. Faulkner does not describe Paradise Lost, nor are his characters' vices, including racism, peculiarly Southern. Faulkner's writings, for all their literary polish and undeniable power, are a direct expression of his psychic structure; in no sense is his fiction guided by abstractions or a carefully thought-out philosophy of life. To be mistaken on this point is to fail to understand Faulkner as a man and as an artist. Faulkner was a poet and an aesthete to begin with, so that even his prose can be seen as alternating between lyricism and morbid incantation. He was also an uninhibited storyteller steeped in a folkloric culture as archaic as that of the Rajputs of India, which it resembles so closely in its martial traditions, its caste system, its penchant for violence and strong drink, and its political passions. I mention the folkloric background because of its isomorphism with Faulkner's psychic structure, in which narcissism, grandiosity, and fantasy, fueled by oedipal guilt, combine to produce a make-believe world. But it is an unreal universe—in Faulkner's mind as well as in the mind of the South—whose underlying shame and fascination with cruelty are clearly in evidence.

It becomes somewhat easier to understand Faulkner's ease of access to his unconscious if we take note of Paul Federn's distinction between two kinds of ego boundary.[7] In relation to his mother's inner world, Faulkner's ego boundaries were highly permeable—so that her outlook became his. The result was a special kind of mother identification, as reflected in Faulkner's female protagonists in their earth-mother capacity, heavy with child, such as Lena in *Light in August* or the nameless pregnant woman caught in a flood in *Old Man* (1939). These women have the quality of passive endurance, like Faulkner's blacks, but they are mother figures whose efforts at nurturance are resented as revealed in this passage in *Light in August:*

> Once he had owned garments with intact buttons. A woman had sewed them on. That was for a time, during a time. Then the time passed. After that he would purloin his own garments from the family wash before she could get to them and replace the missing buttons. When she foiled him he set himself deliberately to learn and remember which buttons were missing and had been restored. With his pocket knife and with the cold and bloodless deliberation of a surgeon he would cut off the buttons which she had replaced.[8]

The reciprocal of Faulkner's imperfect differentiation from his controlling mother was his isolation from other people and his avoidance of painful reality through alcoholism. The close relationship between Faulkner and his mother gave him access not only to her value orientation but to aspects of his own unconscious, which remained ego-syntonic, despite his disapproving but incompletely formed superego. Thus even his most extravagant fantasies were easily incorporated into his ego structures while the outer boundaries became rigid during his formative years. This rigidity made it difficult for Faulkner to cope realistically with externally induced stress. It also prevented Faulkner from extending his ego boundaries, that is, sympathies, to other people so as to include them in his vital concerns. The major exception to this insular trend was Faulkner's love for his only child Jill; Faulkner's love affair with Meta Carpenter was effectively encapsulated from the rest of his life and from his psychic structure. This carefully concealed relationship was clearly subordinated by Faulkner to his literary ambitions and the need to maintain his status as a distinguished citizen of Oxford, a role that he affected to despise but valued greatly, as evidenced by his baronial lifestyle in later years.

The statement that Faulkner was unable to truly cathect others, with the exception of his daughter—who was obviously an extension of himself—needs clarification. Some might argue that *Intruder in the Dust* (1948) reveals Faulkner's great sympathy for the plight of blacks in the South. This novel deals, after all, with the efforts of a white 16-year-old boy and his uncle, a lawyer, to vindicate a proud elderly black man, Lucus Beauchamp, who has been unjustly accused of murder. As the critic Edmund Wilson has observed in a review of *Intruder in the Dust*: "Chivalry, which constitutes his morality, is a part of his Southern heritage, and it appears in Faulkner's work as a force more humane and more positive than almost anything one can find in the work of even those writers of our more mechanized societies who have set out to defend human rights."[9] Faulkner was undoubtedly a man of good will, but it is necessary to understand his conception of human relationships to define the limits of his sympathy. As Wilson sadly admitted, Faulkner believed that the fate of the South's blacks should be left in the hands of high-minded Southern whites, without interference by the federal government in the form of civil rights legislation. Faulkner's view of relationships between blacks and whites was fundamentally paternalistic. His conception of human relationships in general was based on the assumption that power relationships are basic. Although Faulkner's writings leave no doubt that he pitied Southern blacks, it is equally clear that he could not imagine blacks as autonomous human begins, that is, as having an existence apart from their historic relationship with dominant whites.

Faulkner's difficulties in making an empathic response to blacks were partly cultural or an expression of views widely held by white Southerners. But in Faulkner's case these difficulties had an additional source. I refer to Faulkner's poorly resolved oedipal conflict as reflected in his fictional portraits of blacks as oedipal sons who, by their very existence, pose a threat to their white fathers in the role of masters. Even Lucas Beauchamp in *Intruder in the Dust,* old as he is, is perceived by whites as an arrogant black rebel. Joe Christmas in *Light in August,* a defiant man who can pass for white but does not deny his alleged black ancestry, turns out to be a murderer and is lynched by an outraged community. These fantasies of racial conflict are more than reflections of social conditions in the South a few decades ago. They are also projections of negative paternal introjects in which blacks are cast in the role of the oedipal loser who is literally castrated, as in the case of Joe Christmas. When Faulkner uses the metaphors "black blood" and "white blood" in *Light in August* he refers to the destructive impulses of the son and the restraining and punishing superego of the father: "It was the black blood which snatched up the pistol and the white blood which would not let him fire it. . . . It was the black blood which swept him by his own desire beyond the aid of any man, swept him up into that ecstasy out of a black jungle where life has already ceased before the heart stops and death is desire and fulfillment."[10]

One of the keys to Faulkner's creativity was his ability to abstract himself from his surroundings while simultaneously imbuing them with magical qualities. Faulkner's word-presentations were, in fact, bonded to thing-presentations that could enliven his imagination only under special conditions. When these circumstances were removed as a result of marriage and the intrusion of major responsibilities, Faulkner was left only with empty words separated from their passional underpinnings and the magical thing-presentations they had once symbolized. Thus, Faulkner was finished as a writer of inspired fiction when he emerged from his sheltered, self-absorbed mode of existence and had to deal with the world on an instrumental basis. Expressed somewhat differently, the full development of Faulkner's executive ego functions interfered with his fantasy life. It is therefore only partially correct, then, to say that enforced hack writing and the tribulations of his unhappy married life prevented Faulkner from going on to new literary heights. Faulkner had already scaled the heights of his imagination before he entered the real world and became a husband and father. From then on Faulkner was reality-bound and confined by the strictures of secondary-process thinking, which not even alcohol could remove.

Another clue to the relationship between Faulkner's ego development and his literary creations is provided by his unsuccessful efforts to portray psychologically convincing fictional characters. On the surface it appears that Faulkner's tragic protagonists are destroyed by psychological forces within themselves, and that they will their own extinction unconsciously. Every demon of destruction is let loose and man is revealed in all his death-dealing fury, at times majestic in his corruption. Even Faulkner's women, great with suffering, bring forth out of their bodies the raw materials for fresh disasters, ever more egregious crimes. Faulkner's characters seem to struggle desperately against the fate that is their character, which is to say, they seem to struggle with the unconscious, apparently pitting their endurance and their conscious will to live against their overpowering unconscious propulsion toward death. Part of the problem is that Faulkner's characters are not complete people with intact ego structures, so that even when they appear to make choices their behavior is determined by external forces. Their will is shaped by inescapable historical necessity, the will of dead ancestors masquerading as characterological rigidity or stubbornness.

An essay by Carvel Collins, who has edited many of Faulkner's early works, throws much light on this issue, which is at bottom the question as to whether Faulkner has given his characters a mechanical destiny or has allowed them to develop psychologically.[11] Collins argues that Faulkner was familiar with Freud's basic ideas as they were popularly understood in the 1920s, and that he learned about Freudian concepts through his contacts with other young writers who were members of

Sherwood Anderson's circle in New Orleans. Collins reports that he was informed by Phil Stone, Faulkner's close friend and literary cicerone, that Stone and Faulkner actually discussed Freud's work. It is Collins' contention that each of the three main characters in *The Sound and the Fury* represents a different topological structure of the personality as described by Freud: "The monologue of Benjamin the idiot he drew from Freud's concept of the Id, that of Quentin the suicide from Freud's concept of the Ego, and that of censorious Jason from Freud's concept of the Super-ego."[12] Even if it is not literally true that Faulkner had Freud in mind when he wrote *The Sound and the Fury*, it is clear that his characters are essentially personifications of the components of a divided self. This is why Faulkner's work verges on melodrama. Faulkner mangles the integral self in his characteristic stage machinery of lynchings, pregnancies, house burnings, rapes, bloodhound pursuits, burials, car accidents, and beatings. In effect, the integrating function of the ego is not allowed to operate in Faulkner's work, so that his characters lack a center that can imbue their acts and relationships with psychological meaning. Faulkner, of course, cannot be denied the right to use his stage machinery, which is so much larger and more terrifying than Poe's delicate, infected instruments, but the effect is to try to create tragic lives out of what are really fatal circumstances.

Faulkner's ego defects resulted not only from developmental fixations but from the influence of repression. As a writer Faulkner came very close to breaking through the barriers of repression, perhaps because he drank heavily while he wrote, and perhaps, too, because he found escape through fantasy. The result was that images and affects that are normally repressed dominate much of Faulkner's writing. In commenting on Faulkner's lack of control over his materials, Alfred Kazin refers to the "looseness" and "passivity" of Faulkner's work.[13] Faulkner seemed to be aware that he was often at the mercy of his unconscious and that he was being carried along from sentence to sentence by destructive forces beyond his control. Perhaps this is why, after revealing the depths of his misanthropy and pessimism, Faulkner is obliged to utilize his familiar, triumphant symbolism of rebirth, forgetting momentarily that in his lexicon such symbolism means only that a new victim has arrived.

Faulkner's strategy is to present us with fictional characters who are menaced by life and whose self-destructive compulsions are a passive response to external forces. These characters are victims of a strict determinism that resembles psychic determinism but is really something more mechanical that leaves no room for the rational ego to function. In addition, Faulkner's protagonists are psychologically deformed from the start, victims of their situation; life toys with them, turning their infirmities into certain death. Faulkner cannot tell us how, with the help of the ego, the living can achieve an intensification of life or how obstacles can be overcome. He tells us only how the dead, driven by the black blood of the id or the white blood of the fanatical superego, can bury the dead. By denying his characters access to the reality-based problem-solving capacities of the mature ego and the creative resources of the unconscious, Faulkner denies them the right to find their own way. He places his characters in hell, rather than permitting them to find it for themselves, *in* themselves, and in their relationships with others. Nor does Faulkner allow his protagonists to escape their doom by means of human resourcefulness. These negative strategies have the effect of erasing the ego boundaries that separate the autonomous individual from his environment. The frightening contents of the unconscious become indistinguishable from the shadowy scenery and fill Faulkner's make-believe world with terror. But it is the terror of melodrama because Faulkner makes his psychically wounded characters bleed in our presence when he should make them bleed internally. He makes his characters suffer disasters and indignities when he should allow them to undignify themselves in keeping with the laws of their psychic organization; Faulkner fills his readers with the terror of external necessity when he should terrify us with the image of our betrayed freedom as autonomous beings.

If Faulkner's characters appear to act out of guilt it is because they have violated a superego that is not conditioned by the norms of any culture as much as by the requirements of brute nature. Their sins are transgressions against a mystical life force that requires deadly sacrifices from those who defy it, like the Reverend Hightower in *Light in August*, who drove his neglected wife to suicide and ruined his own life. Faulkner's protagonists are not engaged in a struggle with the evil forces of society but with the forces of the unconscious Faulkner has projected onto nature. These projections produce a fictional landscape peopled by creatures out of Darwin, predators out of Nietzsche. De Sade invented them by the power of the word, Byron made them flesh, and Faulkner elevated them to Holy Ghosts. If Joe Christmas seems to suffer from hunger while fleeing from the sheriff's posse in *Light in August*, he is nevertheless incapable of being starved out. Even after he is slain and mutilated, Joe Christmas "looked up at them with peaceful and unfathomable and unbearable eyes." Faulkner's protagonists are unbreakable because their forms have been cast in a brass foundry of the imagination. They are beyond the reach of the superego as we normally conceive of it because they were not born out of mortal women, but sprang forth out of the granite sides of mountains, or rose up like brazen whales out of the primordial waters. And yet they are driven by oedipal fear and rage in spite of everything, because Faulkner has not been able to keep himself out of his fantasies.

Overcoming the barriers of repression, Faulkner carries the Faustian spirit to its limit, beyond mortality, and beyond individualism, to the realm of the superhuman. Perhaps *Faustian* is the wrong word, in spite of the terrific energy that explodes in the pages of Faulkner's novels and tales. As Jean-Paul Sartre has noted, there is no forward movement in Faulkner's stories; there is no future, but only the obsessional recall of the past.[14] It makes sense to compare Faulkner with Proust, as Sartre does, because in each instance the artist has remained a prisoner of the past and has sought his liberation by a unique strategy of creation. Samuel Beckett might just as well have been speaking about Faulkner when he said of Proust that, like everyone else, the past had "deformed" him.[15] In each case, time itself is denied and distorted and human lives are preserved under glass, so that events and emotions are magnified out of all proportion. Insofar as Proust's work is based directly on his life, we know at least that a connection exists even when it is not obvious. Faulkner's work is based on the lives of others, real and legendary, so that connections between art and life are concealed. His private hopes and frustrations are forced to operate in a clandestine, unconscious way. This is unfortunate because art can also grow out of deliberate self-confrontation, producing a compromise between the discipline of the craft and the power of the wish.

Chapter 3

LILLIAN HELLMAN

The Uses of Rage

In this analysis of the interplay of biographical and fictional motifs, I intend to demonstrate that, in the case of Lillian Hellman, chronic rage resulted from maternal deprivation and led to diffuse hostility, self-righteousness, and aggression turned against the self. I also intend to show that guilt-induced depression and self-doubt alternated with self-righteousness. Part of the basis of Hellman's guilt feelings, in addition to her anger at her mother, was caused by her excessive attachment to the father. This attachment, which was not without incestuous overtones, resulted in frustration and disappointment when Hellman, at age thirteen, discovered that her father was having an affair with a neighbor. Another etiological factor that contributed to Hellman's rage was her conflicted attitude toward her femininity and her identification with powerful males, the reciprocal of her regressive attachment to females, some of whom (her nanny, for example) served as mother substitutes. My purpose is to reconstruct the process by which these largely unconscious determinants shaped Hellman's creative endeavors, resulting in a series of highly original plays by American's first major woman dramatist.

Describing masculine protest behavior, Alfred Adler[1] remarks that female neurotics long to become *complete* individuals and express this wish in various ways. Lillian Hellman's first memoir, *An Unfinished Woman*[2] (1969), attests to a similar yearning: "I do regret that I have spent too much of my life trying to find what I called truth, trying to find what I called sense. I never knew what I meant by truth, never made the sense I hoped for. All I mean is that I left too much of me unfinished because I wasted too much time." Hellman's search for truth and sense was less a quest for transcendent values than a lifelong effort to discover her identity. The means pursued toward this goal led Hellman to develop, in Adler's terms, a unique style of life, in which the motive of masculine protest played an important role. This motive was given concrete expression through her dramatic works and autobiographical writings, as well as the vicissitudes of her private life.

From her earliest years, Hellman, an only child, sought to dominate her parents and to affirm her autonomy in all of her relationships. As will become evident, Hellman identified the feminine role with inferiority and passivity. Her confused, inadequate mother was the model of a dependent woman, just as her lively, attractive father exemplified the powerful male. Hellman was driven by intense anger, mixed with guilt. At the age of fourteen, after being scolded by her father, she composed a prayer that she repeated conpulsively for the next five years: "God forgive me, Papa forgive me, Sophronia, Jenny, Hannah, and all others, through this time and that time, in life and in death."[3]. Hellman had refused to tell her father where she had obtained a lock of hair he found in her watch, a recent gift from him. The day after the scolding, Hellman ran away from home for three nights and wandered around in the New Orleans French Quarter and in black neighborhoods. It was during this flight that Hellman's menses started. During this fuguelike interlude Hellman's sexual interest was awakened (or reawakened, in light of her earlier knowledge of her father's illicit love affair): "I . . . discovered, for the first time, the whorehouse section around Bourbon Street. The women were ranged in the doorways of the cribs, making the first early evening offers to sailors, who were the only men in the streets. I wanted to stick around and see how things like that worked, but the second or third time I circled the block, one of the girls called out to me. I couldn't understand the words, but the voice was angry enough to make me run toward the French Market."[4]

The basis for Hellman's anger (if it is possible to trace it to its earliest source) probably had its origin in her first year of life. Hellman's mother appears to have played no significant role in her childhood, having turned her over to a black wet nurse, Sophronia, who subsequently became Hellman's nanny. Sophronia was a rather formidable, taciturn woman whom Hellman idealized throughout her life. Even the precarious security and ambiguous acceptance represented by Sophronia was undermined when the latter went to work for another family when Hellman was quite small. Hellman's father, who was extremely fond of his only child, was frequently away from home for extended periods in his capacity as a traveling sales-man. Another element of instability in Hellman's early life was the peculiar arrangment by which her family lived in New York six months of the year and the remaining six months in New Orleans, as guests in a rooming house owned by paternal aunts, Jenny and Hannah. This arrangement continued until Hellman was in her late teens. As I have mentioned, Hellman's faith in her father was seriously shaken when, at the age of thirteen, she saw her father meet a woman for a rendezvous in the downtown section of New Orleans. On this occasion, Hellman was so upset that she threw herself down from her tree house and broke her nose. Her former nanny, Sophronia, whom Hellman sought out for help with her injury, and in whom she confided her painful discovery, made her promise not to tell anyone what she had seen. This incident probably reinforced Hellman's existing pattern of temper tantrums and made her even more stubborn and rebellious than before. Hellman's behavior toward her parents, relatives, and her aunt's boarders was extremely rude, by her own admission, and she continued to show disrespect and intolerance toward her college teachers later on, when she was enrolled at New York University.

Hellman's chronic anger cannot be explained entirely in terms of early maternal deprivation. Hellman was determined, even as a young child, to "reverse" the consequences of her female identity, and to avoid the danger of being forced "below," to use Adler's terms. Hellman's "corrective" powers were considerable, insofar as she was able to elaborate a system of defense based on fiercely guarded independence and "masculine" activities, such as hunting, fishing, sexual adventurism, political radicalism, argumentativeness, and the free use of coarse language in an age when most women were still quite traditional.

Strangely, Hellman's work as a dramatist, which brought her international acclaim, does not appear to have come about in relation to her central goals in life, and was terminated once and for all when Hellman began to come under increasing attack by drama critics, who found her later work unsatisfactory. What, then, was the meaning of Hellman's career as a playwright? My intention is to show that, through her inventions for the theater, Hellman tried to work out symbolically her conflicts centering on masculinity/femininity, or strength versus weakness. These efforts at conflict resolution were unconscious, and differed from Hellman's deliberate pursuit of an unconventional, independent style of life based on the masculine protest principle. Hellman's personal life gives ample evidence that she was able to fulfill herself as an autonomous, creative, and self-assertive woman; her fictional creations, reveal, however that Hellman never overcame her ambivalence toward "masculine" assertiveness, which she unconsciously equated with ruthless, unprincipled behavior. It is for this reason that her powerful, manipulative male and female protagonists are almost always "bad" people, even though they triumph with ease over their weak, but "good" adversaries. The victories gained by Hellman's bold protagonists reflect her ambivalence because they are empty triumphs—the revenge of the unloved against the lovable—but Hellman has arrayed her strong, amoral characters on the side of the reality principle, and has relegated her fictional decent people to the status of life's victims and feckless escape artists.

Hellman does not appear to have been unduly troubled by these unconscious conflicts in her private life, but she made a series of conscious decisions in keeping with her goal of independence. As a young adolescent she aligned herself unequivocally on the side of a female cousin who was rejected by

Hellman's family because of her love affair with an Italian gangster in flight from the law. Hellman states that she admired her cousin Bethe's independence of public opinion and took her as a model for her own behavior. At the age of nineteen, finding herself pregnant, Hellman had an abortion without informing her parents of her situation. A half year later, she married the man who had gotten her pregnant, pleased that she had not acted under compulsion, but was in control of her life. A few years later, Hellman divorced her husband, Arthur Kober, a writer and press agent, having become involved with Dashiell Hammett, then at the height of his success as the author of *The Thin, Man, The Maltese Falcon,* and other popular works. When Hellman discovered that Hammett was unfaithful to her (she was one of many women in Hammett's life), she flew from New York to Hollywood (where Hammett lived in a house he had rented from Harold Lloyd) smashed up the furniture and bar and returned to New York the same day—breaking off her relationship with Hammett, at least temporarily. Not long after, Hellman made a decision to go off to Latin America with her once-rich-and-powerful great-uncle Willy, to be his mistress while he recouped his lost fortune. She decided against this venture only at the last moment, after Hammett reminded her over the phone that Willy was a "murderer" (Willy had been an executive of the United Fruit Company and had taken a hand in violently suppressing workers in Central America). In this instance, Hellman's reaction against her uncle's "bad" character outweighed her admiration for his former prowess as a leader of men and the personification of masculine virtues. Hellman's fabrications about smuggling money into Nazi Germany to ransom political prisoners similarly reflected her desire to behave in accordance with "masculine" traits of courage and resolution, which, in this instance, she could clearly identify with the cause of justice.[5]

When we look again at Hellman's relationship to Hammett and her reaction to the discovery that he was unfaithful to her, we discover still another side of her self-concept. Hellman already knew that Hammett was frequently involved with other women and that she was merely one of his many mistresses. Moreover, Hellman and Hammett had no marriage plans or any other kind of permanent commitment to each other. Indeed, it was one of the explicit conditions of their intermittent relationship that they would give each other the widest latitude in every sphere of life. Why, then, did Hellman feel that she had a right to half-destroy Hammett's rented house as an expression of her jealousy and rage? It is necessary to return to Hellman's earliest narcissistic wounds, sustained at the hands of her inadequate mother. Hellman's reaction to her detached mother was to develop a grandiose self, along with the desire to merge herself with archaic, omnipotent self-objects, such as Sophronia, or later her father and his sisters, her great-uncle Willy whom she idolized from adolescence onward, and finally, the rich and successful Hammett. The half-glimpsed protagonist of Hellman's final memoir, *Maybe*[6] (1980)—the beautiful and glamourous Sarah Cameron— can be seen as Hellman's alter ego, a vehicle for vicarious archaic exhibitionism and grandiosity. Although *Maybe* purports to be a nonfiction account by Hellman of her later years, and includes events from her youth, her atempt to interweave her life with that of Sarah Cameron, a woman whom she knew but superficially, points to frustrated narcissistic needs. Hellman's narcissistic self-objects were never replaced by autonomous ego functions. Consequently, Hellman's narcissistic rage never subsided because her narcissistic needs were never met. This is why Hellman's fictional characters are fundamentally destructive. Even her most conspicuous idealist, Kurt, in *Watch on the Rhine* (1941) resorts to murder for the sake of his ideals. Hellman's other protagonists show few traces of nurturance or forgiveness. Love relationships as such do not exist, in Hellman's works, except in a peripheral sense. This omission cannot be explained by saying that Hellman is a realist, since people do love each other in the real world, however ambivalently.

Hellman's angry, sarcastic characters are preoccupied with grandiose schemes of self-enrichment and with outwitting each other. These protagonists mirror the imaginative operations of an archaic, omnipotent self, often a self filled with rage at idealized figures who have failed them. Thus, Lily, in *Toys in the Attic* (1960), who imagines that her erstwhile lover Julian is unfaithful to her, betrays him to the sinister bad figure, Cyrus

Warkins, knowing that Warkins will destroy Julian, if not physically, then financially. Indeed, Julian is beaten and robbed of all his money by Warkins' henchmen as a result of Lily's vengeful act. In the sense that this play, like most of Hellman's plays, is all about people getting even with each other, it is a reflection of the author's narcissistic injuries. In addition, Hellman's punitiveness, so plainly visible in her memoirs, mars her political idealism and her dramas alike, leading her into moral absolutism at times, and preventing her from developing multidimensional characters as well. The continuity of aggressive and retributive motifs in Hellman's life signifies the persistent intrusion of uncontrolled archaic forces into ego functions. These forces were never integrated with the ego's objectives, but continued to exert irrational pressure for omnipotence and total control, resulting in fictional characters whose aggressive manipulations overshadow their humanity. Under these conditions, Hellman was unable to create psychologically complex characters, falling back instead on melodramatic plots in most instances. While it is true that in *The Autumn Garden* (1951) and *Toys in the Attic*, Hellman's last and most mature plays, her characters are forced to grow in self-knowledge, their motives remain obscure to themselves and to their audience.

Hellman can present us with crystallized characters, either good or bad, but the sources of their adult character are usually hidden. There are certain exceptions, such as Julian in *Toys in the Attic*, the spoiled baby of the family raised by his doting sisters and obsessed with grandiose fantasies of wealth and luxury to be obtained without effort. Julian is probably Hellman's truest creation because he resembles her in his need to justify himself in the eyes of his family and in his quasi-incestuous relationship with his older sister, not unlike Hellman's attachment to her father. Like Hellman returning to visit her aging and impoverished aunts in the first flush of her theatrical success and Hollywood prosperity, Julian is a bearer of unwanted gifts, eager to share his wealth with his sisters. The sisters are narcissistic self-objects upon whom he has projected his grandiose needs; they understand intuitively that his largesse is generated by his own emotional needs, rather than by their objective wants. In *Toys in the Attic*, Hellman's last original play, she had found herself at last. Now she could dispense with her usual fictional connivers and infantile power seekers, and could deal forthrightly with her own conflicts. Perhaps this is why Hellman ceased to write original plays at this point in her life, when she was only in her mid-fifties and at the height of her creative powers. From this point on, Hellman was content to do dramatic adaptations of other people's novels and to write her memoirs, commencing with *An Unfinished Woman* (1969), published nine years after the staging of *Toys in the Attic*. Hellman was indeed unfinished or unfulfilled in many ways, but she was finished as a creative artist, having finally confronted herself on the stage in *Toys in the Attic*, as she caused one sister to accuse the other of incestuous wishes toward their brother Julian. The accused sister responds: "You never said those words. Tell me I never heard those words. Tell me, Anna. You were all I ever had. I don't love you anymore." This is not a commentary on the cessation of love between two sisters, but on the fragility of self-love, and the persistence of narcissistic wounds.

Despite Hellman's growing insights, which contributed to the psychological complexity of her later plays, there is a remarkable consistency about her fictional characters, mirroring the rigidity of her defenses. Starting with the character of Mary in *The Children's Hour* (1934), Hellman's stage creations reflect her unconscious conflicts. *The Children's Hour* is about two young female instructors at a girls' school who are accused by Mary, one of their students, of involvement in a lesbian relationship. Although the play is based on a true story reported in the newspapers, the character of Mary is similar in a number of ways to that of the young Hellman: tempestuous, willful, domineering, and tuned into adult sexual secrets. Mary, who is motherless, is the embodiment of the "bad me" because she acts out her jealousy and rage, particularly in response to adult love relationships. Like Hellman the child, Mary can be both destructive and self-destructive, impelled by a deep sense of injustice. Hellman as an adolescent had identified herself closely with her cousin Bethe, as I have mentioned, when Bethe was ostracized because of her unconventional love life. The young Hellman empathized with Bethe's spirit of rebellion and admired her loyalty to her beleaguered lover. As a young woman, Hellman became furious with Hammett when she pointed out Bethe's importance as a role model and Hammett failed to understand what she meant. The adolescent Hellman projected onto the frightened, inarticulate Bethe all her own yearnings for love and intimacy at the same time that she felt the injustice of Bethe's ostracism. For the romantic young girl, Bethe clearly was a victim of middle-class hypocrisy. Bethe's seeming badness appealed immensely to the young Hellman, who set herself the task of discovering the hiding place of Bethe and her mysterious lover. Like mary in *The Children's Hour,* who possesses precocious sexual knowledge (she is right intuitively about the lesbian inclinations of one of the accused instructors), Hellman was fascinated by Bethe's forbidden sex life. Unlike her fictional creation, Hellman tried to protect Bethe from the consequences of her sexual indiscretions. Thus Hellman's superego, ever punitive and unrelenting, was also on the side of righteous rebellion. The fictional Mary has no superego and is depicted as a complete psychopath. For this reason she comes across as a caricature and as evil personified. Her one-sided portrayal reveals that the playwright's harsh superego has gained the upper hand over the artist. This moralistic strain, closely related to Hellman's conflict between her powerful aggressive drives and her superego, permeates her dramatic work and weakens it considerably.

There is a dimension of Mary's character that Hellman develops with special emphasis and which appears to be related to her own power needs. Mary is a manipulative, controlling child who bullies the other girls at school and takes advantage of her doting grandmother's credulity. Although Mary is a negative character, Hellman imbues her with a malign power that makes her the star of the play. This outcome must surely have been unintended on the conscious level. After all, the play ends with the suicide of its female protagonist—one of the accused young women—and Hellman refers to *The Children's Hour* as a protest against the injustice of denunciation and innuendo. Hellman undoubtedly succeeds in making her point, but she says something in addition—that the exercise of power is fascinating, and that the wielder of power is more impressive than ordinary people. The playwright's unconscious predilection has led her to express two conflicting needs. The result is that she communicates her unconscious admiration for Mary at the same time that she condemns her. *The Children's Hour*, Hellman's first play, begins a pattern in which fictional characters who are willfull and unethical possess more life than do virtuous characters, who are usually depicted as weak.

Why did Hellman chose to write on the themes of lesbianism and slander? It is necessary to summarize her life situation when she wrote *The Children's Hour*. Hellman was twenty-eight years old, had worked as an editorial assistant for Horace Liveright, the publisher, and had undergone an abortion. She had been married for a few years but had obtained a divorce after becomeing Dashiell Hammett's mistress. Like Hammett, she was already an alcoholic. The context within which Hellman wrote *The Children's Hour* was one of bohemianism and rebellion. Hammett was the perfect partner for Hellman's style of life. A former Pinkerton strikebreaker, he had deserted his wife and two children, abandoned Catholicism in favor of Marxism, and was launched on a life of hedonism made possible by his literary success. Hammett's alcoholism apparently went hand-in-hand with a profound pessimism. Hellman states in her memoirs that she regarded Hammett as a man of firm principle, a brave and honorable person in a world of opportunists. He was her ideal father figure, twelve years her senior, tall and handsome, tolerant of her abrasive personality, and less in need of her than she was of him. Describing her state of mind shortly before she met Hammett, Hellman wrote in *An Unfinished Woman*[7]: "I was rash, overdaring, certain only that any adventure was worth having, and increasingly muddled by the Puritan conscience that made me pay for the adventures. I needed a teacher, a cool teacher, who would not be impressed or disturbed by a strange and difficult girl."

Hellman's involvement with Hammett and her choice of a forbidden theme for her first play must have been painful to her parents, who were present at the opening night of *The Children's Hour*. Her mother's true feelings were scarcely concealed by her overdetermined words of reassurance to Hellman when the play opened: "Well, all I know is that you were considered the sweetest-smelling baby in New Orleans."[8] It is noteworthy that for many years before writing *The Children's Hour* Hellman had been convinced that she had an offensive body odor and had been in the habit of taking three baths daily. This compulsion apparently had started when she was nineteen, when Hellman's first lover after making love to her, had told her that she had a peculiar odor. It is apparent, however, that long before Hellman's bathing compulsion surfaced, she had come to think of herself as unclean, like her beloved Bethe whom Hellman's girlhood friend Christy Houghton had denounced as a "whore." Like Mary in *The Children's Hour* who twisted the arm of another girl in order to intimidate her, the adolescent Hellman had reacted to Christy Houghton as follows: "The third time she said whore I twisted her arm and held it firm as I forced her to repeat after me, 'Does love need a minister, a rabbi, a priest? Is divine love between man and woman based on permission of a decadent society?' "[9]

In light of the foregoing, the question concerning the theme of lesbianism cannot be answered by saying that Hellman intended to shock her audience, in keeping with her rebellious nature. Hellman's choice of subject matter can only be understood as the outcome of her identification with her father and her uncle Willy. On the occasion when Hellman ran away from home after being scolded by her father, and which coincided with her first menstruation, she would not agree to return home with her father until he apologized to her for the scolding. Hellman states: "From that day on I knew my power over my parents. . . . But I found out something more useful and more dangerous: if you are willing to take the punishment, you are halfway through the battle. That the issue may be trivial, the battle ugly, is another point."[10] The beginning of Hellman's womanhood therefore coincided with the discovery of the uses of anger—and power—and her identity as a woman acquired a strong masculine component. Her later reputation as a rough-talking, hard-drinking, aggressive, no-nonsense woman no doubt derives from her incorporation of her father's real or imagined traits, as well as her uncle Willy's flamboyance and reputation as a man of violence. Hellman's penchant for self-destructive behavior, as evidenced by her accident-proneness when she was angry, and by her compulsive drinking, is linked with her powerful aggressive drives and her tendency to act out in a distincly unfeminine manner.

Her choice of Hammett as a lover points not only to her masochism (besides being an alcoholic Hammett was singularly self-centered and insular), but also to her need to identify herself with a "man's man," namely one who was tough, stoical, familiar with violence, and a rebel against the system. Both Hellman's father and her uncle Willy were early prototypes of Hammett, love objects who had disappointed her the same way Hammett disappointed her when she discovered him with another woman (as an adolescent, Hellman had seen Willy with his Cajun mistress and had suffered intense jealousy). When Hellman learned from the family cook in New Orleans that her paternal aunts, Jenny and Hannah, had always been in love with her father and that most women fell in love with him, but she didn't know why, Hellman thought to herself that she understood very well why women fell in love with her father and had suffered because of this knowledge.

The Children's Hour ends with the suicide of a young woman, Martha, who was in love with another young woman, Karen. The latter thereupon broke her engagement to be married to a man who revealed that he had half-believed the charge of lesbianism against his fiancee. Why has Hellman caused Karen—aged twenty-eight like Hellman at the time— to turn away from the man she loves and to refuse to marry him? Perhaps it is because, in the playwright's lexicon, it is taboo to marry the man one really loves because he is the forbidden incestuous love object or his substitute. As for Martha, Hellman causes her to commit suicide not only for the sake of a dramatic climax, but also because she represents the masculine side of her own nature.

In *Days to Come* (1936), Hellman's second play, and ostensibly a drama about a strike in an Ohio town and how it was broken, Hellman was unconsciously trying to come to terms with her failed marriage to Arthur Kober, as well as to resolve inner conflicts about her identity. These two aims are, in fact, closely interwoven in the structure of *Days to Come*. The play portrays a gentle, humane man, Andrew Rodman, who has inherited the family business, a brush factory that is the main industry in a small town. His workers are on strike, and Andrew, on the advice of his cynical lawyer, Henry Ellicott, has called in strike-breakers. The upshot of his decision is that his wife Julie falls in love with the strike organizer, Leo Whalen, and reveals to her husband that she did not marry him out of love as much as passivity and aimlessness. Although the protracted strike finally collapses after a night of violence, Andrew's reputation as a benevolent industrialist is ruined. The play ends by affirming the importance of labor's struggle for fair treatment by management. Of equal or greater importance is Hellman's focus on Julie and her unsuccessful search for identity: "I want to make something for myself, something that would be right for me."[11] This desire led Julie to declare her love for Whalen, a man she scarcely knew. Hellman has given Whalen many of the idealized traits that she attributed to Hammett, insofar as Whalen is brave and is able to retain his idealism in a world that he perceives as corrupt.

The character of Andrew, a well-intentioned man, but weak and ineffectual, appears to have its roots in Hellman's dissatisfaction with her former husband. Kober may or may not have resembled Andrew Rodman, but Hellman apparently saw him as lacking Hammett's macho qualities, with which she could identify herself wholeheartedly. Reflecting Hammett's cool, take-it-or-leave-it attitude toward Hellman, Whalen does not want Julie in *Days to Come*, and leaves town when the strike is over. Once again, Hellman's female protagonist is not allowed to have the man she loves because her underlying oedipal conflict will not allow such an incestuous resolution, even on the symbolic level. Though *Days to Come* was an unsuccessful play critically and commercially, it points more clearly than does *The Children's Hour* to Hellman's increasing strength as a critic of society. *Days to Come* is also indicative of mounting superego pressure and an undercurrent of violence in Hellman's writing, a motif that reflected not only the violence of her times, but also her own preoccupations. Her next play, *The Little Foxes* (1939), reveals that Hellman had begun to give full expression to her moral indignation, a sublimation of her intense rage.

In contrast to *Days to Come*, in which an industrialist is depicted as a decent man, betrayed by his calloused lawyer and his own weakness, *The Little Foxes* focuses sharply on the cruelty and greed of the rich. Even so, *The Little Foxes* includes a character who embodies the humane instincts of Andrew Rodman in *Days to Come*. I refer to Horace Giddens, the ailing banker who is pitted against his selfish and manipulative wife, Regina, and her scheming brothers, Ben and Oscar. The plot is mechanical and centers on an attempt by Ben and Oscar to advance their business interests by unlawfully using Horace's securities to complete a transaction. When Regina learns of their plot, she blackmails her brothers into signing over to her the lion's share of their future profits, which promise to be vast, or at least large enough to permit the socially ambitious Regina to cut a handsome figure in high society. Although Regina is a bad woman, she is plainly the heroine of *The Little Foxes*. Hellman distinguishes sharply between characters who are good but weak (like the confused and dissatisfied Julie in *Days to Come*) and those who are bad but strong. In *The Little Foxes*, for example, Regina's sister-in-law, Birdie, is a frightened, bewildered woman with humane feelings that she is too weak to act upon. In addition, her husband Oscar terrorizes her. By contrast, Regina, the central figure, is a powerful woman, verbally aggressive and as unscrupulous as her grasping brothers. Hellman seems to be echoing the popular dictum that, to be effective, to be a winner, it is necessary to be tough, even ruthless, in pursuit of instrumental goals. In *Days to Come*, even Leo Whalen, manifestly a man of courage and integrity, is notably unmoved by the news that the child of one of the strikers—his closest aide—has been killed by strikebreakers. He prefers to think abstractly of the failed strike as merely one of many struggles that labor will have to face in days to come. Hellman's "strong" people, like Whalen and Regina, are devoid of sentiment; on an expressive–instrumental continuum, they are located at the instrumental end.

Why should Hellman's strong characters be unfeeling? The explanation for this deficiency throws light on Hellman's defenses against impulsivity. Hellman indicates in her memoirs that she was aware of how dangerous and potentially self-destructive her explosive behavior could be, and therefore tried to control herself, usually without success. Her alcoholism attests to the half-heartedness of her efforts at restraint, and her memoirs confirm the impression that she was especially bellicose when drunk. Like many alcoholics, Hellman evidently felt powerful and grandiose when she drank. On the unconscious level, then, Hellman embraced her destructive impulses, while trying to neutralize them on the conscious level. For this reason, her strong, acting-out protagonists are portrayed as bad, that is, unethical, selfish, unfeeling, but are the stars of her plays. In fact, Hellman's weak characters are ineffective in proportion to their sense of decency and their capacity for affection. Regina's tender-hearted daughter, Alexandra, in *The Little Foxes*, is powerless, for example, to prevent her scheming mother from bullying her stricken father Horace, who has only a short time to live. If Hellman's weak characters are defeated by their ruthless adversaries, they are at least more successful as rounded character studies. The powerful villains in Hellman's plays fail to convince us that they are psychologically valid portraits because they are one-dimensional. The result is a set of vivid caricatures. Her protagonists also lack the range of feelings necessary for communicating inner conflict, thereby eliminating the possibility of tragedy. Hellman's characters are either too good or too bad and remain unchanged from start to finish.

The rigidity with which Hellman clings to her one-dimensional portrayals carries over from one play to the next. Regina, in *The Little Foxes*, who deliberately withholds medication from her dying husband, is nothing but the spiteful Mary of *The Children's Hour*, now grown up. Ellicott, the heartless lawyer in *Days to Come*, is the forerunner of the evil brothers Ben and Oscar in *The Little Foxes*. It is not that destructive people do not exist in the real world. The task of the playwright, however, is to explore the complexity of human motives. This requirement is not met by Hellman in *The Little Foxes* because of her unconscious need to split her characters into separate personifications of good and evil, along the lines of a morality play. According to her memoirs, Hellman was unable to fuse her positive and negative images of her mother until late in life.

The persistance of Hellman's archetypal predators and their victims is seen in *Another Part of the Forest* (1946), in which she shows the main characters of *The Little Foxes* at a point twenty years earlier in their lives. The plot is once again mechanical and involves Regina in a scheme to deprive a genteel family of its land, and her brother Ben's successful strategy of blackmailing his father so that he can obtain money to invest in ventures that will make him a rich man. Regina, in her earlier incarnation as a twenty-year-old social climber, is no less aggressive and unscrupulous than as a mature woman in *The Little Foxes*. Her lover, John Bagtry, sixteen years her senior, is a decent man, but unable to find himself since the end of the Civil War, in which he served as a Confederate officer. Like Dashiell Hammett, Bagtry declares that he was happiest when he was in the military (Hammett served in both World Wars). Bagtry is presented as one of life's victims, who can find no purpose to his life other than to go off to Brazil to fight as a mercenary. Bagtry belongs with Hellman's gallery of weak, well-intentioned aristocratic victims. On the manifest level, Hellman's message in this play, as well as in her other plays, is that good people should not abdicate their responsibilities while selfish people run the world. On a deeper level, Hellman conveys her belief that it is almost useless for the weak and well-intentioned to resist the rule of the strong and selfish.

Hellman vacillated between her admiration for masculine power and her fear of its destructive consequences. In *Watch on the Rhine* she tried to resolve this conflict by creating a hero who combined a capacity for violence with commitment to moral virtue. Kurt, the antifascist, murders a Romanian collaborator who threatens to expose his mission of raising money in the U.S. to ransom political prisoners in Nazi Germany. Kurt argues that, until the world is a better place, violent struggle will continue to be necessary. He even considers the possibility that he is becoming bad himself, but is not deflected from his goal. Kurt may be seen as a further elaboration of Leo Whalen, the labor organizer in *Days to Come*. Both men fight against the forces of injustice, but Whalen is fearful of violence and believes that labor's enemies seek a confrontation so that they can exert their superior force. In the end, Whalen is defeated by ruthless men. Kurt, too, hates violence but believes he has no choice; in the end, he too expects to be defeated and to lose his life when he returns to Germany. Nevertheless, the character of Kurt represents a genuine departure for Hellman. An obvious explanation for this shift would be to say that in the interval between the composition of the two plays—1936 to 1941—Hellman had been to Spain and had seen the Spanish Civil War in process. Like everyone else, she had watched the fall of France and the other events associated with the outbreak of the Second World War. A commonsense interpretation of Hillman's shift in characterization would emphasize, in other words, the influence of external events or the atmosphere of crisis in which the world found itself. It should be noted that Hellman's model for Kurt was the Austrian anti-fascist Joe Buttinger, who escaped to the U.S. with his wife Muriel in 1939. Muriel was the model for Kurt's wife Sara, as well as the model for Hellman's "Julia" in *Pentimento*, even though Hellman had never met Muriel.[12]

Another line of reasoning cannot, however, be ignored; namely, that beginning with *Watch on the Rhine*, and becoming more apparent in Hellman's subsequent plays of the middle period, *The Searching Wind* (1944) and *Another Part of the Forest* (1946), Hellman is able to accept her aggressive impulses as ego-syntonic because of the growing ascendancy of the masculine side of her personality. In *The Searching Wind*, for example, the son of an appeasement-minded American diplomat loses a leg in World War II and we learn that his best friend was killed in battle. These good characters are either mutilated or destroyed, while their elders, who made the war possible by their self-deception and moral cowardice, survive, presumably chastened by the consequences of their errors. Like *The Little Foxes*, *The Searching Wind* has a powerful woman at its center, but this time the female protagonist, Cassie Bowman, is an exemplar of moral rectitude, who criticizes her diplomat ex-lover bitterly for temporizing with fascism. Unlike Julie in *Days to Come*, whose industrialist husband is also depicted as weak, Cassie Bowman is a true militant in her own right. In *Another Part of the Forest*, Hellman returns to the theme of violence, revealing that Marcus Hubbard, Regina's wealthy father, had committed a heinous crime before the events in the play unfolded, having caused the massacre of many of his fellow Confederates. In Hellman's first two plays, *The Children's Hour* and *Days to Come*, the victims of violence are female (Martha, accused of lesbianism, dies by her own hand in *The Children's Hour,* and a striker's little girl is killed by strikebreakers in *Days to Come*). In the latter play, an evil strikebreaker is also slain, but his death is at the hands of one of his accomplices. Thus, the pattern of violence changes from the first two plays to the dramas of the middle period, shifting from the death of passive victims, both female, to the death and mutilation of males fighting for what they believe in.

In *The Autumn Garden* violence disappears from Hellman's plays, along with her intense moral indignation. This circumstance is all the more surprising because the writing and production of this play coincided with the height of the McCarthy period and the prosecution of Dashiell Hammett by the federal government. Of this painful period of her life Hellman wrote in *Scoundrel Time* (1976): "My belief in liberalism was mostly gone. I think I have substituted for it something private called, for want of something that should be more accurate, decency."[13] *The Autumn Garden* is, in fact, a play about decent people who are confronted by their self-deceptions and forced to see their lives in a new and less flattering light. As is true of all of Hellman's plays, the characters are wealthy and genteel, an observation I will return to at a later point. Among other things, *The Autumn Garden* is about a young man, Frederick, whose mother, Carrie, objects to his all-absorbing relationship with a young novelist, Payson, who has been described to her as a homosexual. Although the play does not focus on any one character or relationship, the relationship between Frederick and Payson (who never appears onstage) is very similar to that between Martha and Karen in *The Children's Hour,* and carries the same overtones. In *The Autumn Garden* there is no brash, masterful woman, as in *The Little Foxes* or *Another Part of the Forest.* The most attractive of the female characters, Constance, is portrayed as a middle-aged spinster living a drab life in a provincial Southern town. She is a good woman who has wasted her life, dreaming of the man she has loved since girlhood, a libertine who jilted her to marry an heiress whom he did not love. Nor are there any strong male characters. Even the villain, Nick, the object of Constance's misplaced affection, is a failure in life who derives malicious pleasure from wrecking other people's lives by his sneers and innuendoes. It is as if Hellman's fictional Lucifers have shrunk to human proportions and are presented as merely pathetic. There is no one left to fight the good fight in *The Autumn Garden*, which despite its wit and urbanity is a very sad play, the theme of which is disillusionment.

Perhaps the impending McCarthy hearings, Hellman's being blacklisted by the Hollywood studios, and her mounting financial problems combined to weaken Hellman's confidence. Although she acquitted herself well during the McCarthy hearings, her memoirs reveal that she was frightened and confused. Over and above the effects of political repression during the period covered by *Scoundrel Time*, the impression conveyed by *The Autumn Garden* and reinforced by Hellman's revelations in *An Unfinished Woman* and *Pentimento* is one of disillusionment with love relationships and a sense of rejection. Constance's realization, for example, in *The Autumn Garden*, that Nick is a pseudo-artist, a drunkard, and a scoundrel, is the story of a woman betrayed by her romantic ideals. Like Constance, Hellman had strong needs for affection that were repeatedly frustrated, despite her outward brashness and seeming selfsufficiency. Her intermittent relationship with Hammett did not provide her with adequate emotional support, partly because of Hammett's alcoholism and self-absorption, and partly because of Hellman's need for independence. Another female character in *The Autumn Garden*, Nina, who is Nick's wife, resembles Constance in her affect hunger, but Nina is willing to put up with her husband's selfish behavior in exchange for a mimesis of affection. *The Autumn Garden* is not, however, a feminist tract. Hellman's male characters are also victims, defeated by their own weaknesses. Only one female character in *The Autumn Garden* emerges as strong enough to shape her own life. This person is Sophie, Constance's French niece, who, realizing that her fiancee does not love her, decides to return to France. As a parting shot, Sophie, like the mercenary Regina in *The Little Foxes*, compels Nina to pay her $5,000 as compensation for having been compromised by Nick's drunken behavior in her bedroom. This twist of the plot indicates that Hellman's bad protagonist, Regina, in *The Little Foxes*, is interchangeable with a good protagonist in *The Autumn Garden*. Regina and Sophie represent Hellman's ambivalence toward her role as a woman, in which she could not decide whether it was good or bad to insist on her rights and to protect her interests by aggressive behavior.

The Autumn Garden, which Hellman regarded as her best play, was indeed superior to her previous works, although it was not successful commercially. Also, unlike Hellman's other plays, The Autumn Garden was never made into a film, probably because it is, above all, a psychological study. The Autumn Garden is an advance over Hellman's earlier work in the important sense that it deals with inner conflict and self-deception. In addition, Hellman no longer focuses exclusively on the rich and powerful and their exploitative ways. Her political indignation is gone, even though, paradoxically, Hellman at this time was defending herself before Congressional committees. Had the McCarthyites taken the fight out of her? Or does The Autumn Garden signify that Hellman, having looked into herself, had begun to mature as an artist, applying psychological insights that were absent in her earlier plays? Consistent with the theory that stress may serve as a catalyst for artistic growth, it might be argued that The Autumn Garden owes its superiority to its having been written when its author felt herself to be in great danger and summoned up unusual resources of ego strength and imagination. The Autumn Garden, it should be added, is not a total departure from Hellman's familiar theme, which is that people fail because they do not assert their will, whether as citizens who are unwilling to face up to their moral responsibilities, or as private persons who fail to control their lives.

Hellman's last play, Toys in the Attic, was written ten years after The Autumn Garden. As I have noted earlier, Toys in the Attic is also built around the theme of a man who upsets the lives of other people, and whose behavior forces others to face terrible truths about themselves. In addition to the motif of unconscious incestuous wishes, which I have commented upon earlier, the play deals with a young woman's anger toward her mother, who, she believes, regards her as a pathetic, disturbed girl, The young woman, Lily, displaces her anger onto another older woman, Mrs. Warkins, who had been her husband's mistress many years earlier. There are traces of oedipal rivalry in this love triangle, which may be seen as derivatives of Hellman's hostility toward her mother. The issue of feminine attractiveness is addressed also in the dilemma of the play's ingenue, Lily, who discovers that her husband Julian married her only for her money. She herself, though barely twenty-one, had already concluded that no man could possible find her desirable in her own right. Hellman too had felt unattractive as a young woman. The episode mentioned earlier, in which Hellman's first lover told her she had an offensive odor, fit into a pattern of events that intensified Hellman's doubts about herself as a woman. Although she was identified with her two paternal aunts, particularly Jenny, the dominant one, her diffuse emotional relationship with her mother did not provide her with a solid basis for self-acceptance as a woman.

The character of Lily, who appears to be psychotic or borderline, and who swears on her "knife of truth," which she carries about with her, seems to be based on the young Hellman, as well as on her mother. This tendency to identify a certain type of romantic, otherworldly woman as ridiculous and weak-minded reflects Hellman's conflict over strength versus weakness and masculinity versus femininity. Invariably, such pathetic women serve as foils for Hellman's masculinized female protagonists. In *Toys in the Attic,* Julian's two older sisters are the voice of reason and are presented as much stronger figures than is either Lily or Julian. Mrs. Warkins, who represents the bad mother in her capacity as oedipal rival, is victimized by Lily, who deliberately reveals to Mr. Warkins that his wife is of black ancestry. Lily's hostility toward, and her lack of loyalty to her own mother are evidenced by Lily's close ties to a morphine-addicted medium. Her mother says to Lily: "It is not good to know that my child swore fidelity to such a woman and gave her wedding ring as proof."[14] Hellman, too, had given her loyalty to her nanny Sophronia, and not to her mother. The symbolism of the wedding ring suggests a lesbian connection between Lily and the medium. Although *Toys in the Attic* is ostensibly a play about a man who unwittingly injures his beloved sisters by trying to shower them with wealth, the secondary plot centered on Lily consitutes the hidden agenda of the drama and discloses the importance of the mother-daughter relationship in Hellman's life, no less than in her fantasies.

I have mentioned in passing that Hellman's plays usually deal with genteel people who live in a wealthy setting. This characteristic is not a mere stage convention but rather stems from something essential both in Hellman's work as a dramatist and in her unconscious need system. Her concern with the lives of the rich and powerful is Hellman's single concession to fantasy and is as close as she comes to romanticism, lyricism, or flights of fancy—qualities notably lacking in her dramas. Hellman's central conflict, which involves her sense of identity and a related preoccupation with masculine power as contrasted with feminine weakness, is symbolized by her affluent settings. Her fantasy solution to her conflict is a compromise between the masculine and the feminine, strength and weakness, brute power and gentility. This compromise results in a make-believe world in which powerful, evil men and women generally dominate good but ineffectual people against a wealthy, elegant background. The elegant background is important because it speaks of Hellman's feminine identity no less than her concern with power and status. Like Harold Pinter's barren houses and rooms, Hellman's Southern mansions are also mother symbols. But they are symbolic of the wished-for mother, the mother rich in affection and lavish with gifts of the heart. Is it any wonder that Hellman would go on extravagant shopping sprees whenever she felt depressed or unloved, bestowing unneeded gifts on herself? Her fictional winners gain mansions, plantations, and factories, but they are losers in love because, like Hellman, they have suffered narcissistic wounds that cannot be healed. Hence, their consolation is in things, in power, and in status. They are destined to be forever dissatisfied, like Hellman—who had a mother but preferred her father, who had a husband but chose a lover, who needed affection but drove others away with her anger, which she mistook for strength.

Hellman needed to deny the bad-me, as well, and so she created the falsehood that she carried money secretly to Julia, a personification of the good-me. We now know that it was Muriel Buttinger, the heiress-turned-resistance-fighter, the "real" Julia, who gave freely of her own money to help Jews and other victims of the Nazis to excape from Austria.[15] Hellman never went to Germany in the nineteen-thirties, but Muriel, as Julia, Hellman's courageous alter ego, made restitution for her vicariously. Even so, Hellman could not allow virtue to go unpunished, but killed off her fictional Julia after first causing her to lose a leg.

Chapter 4

VLADIMIR NABOKOV

Aestheticism with a Human Face, Half-Averted

The past asserts its increasing hegemony over the present with each passing year of a person's life. It is for this reason, no doubt, that Otto Kernberg[1] observes that identification with one's parents is strengthened as one grows older. In middle age, one revalorizes internalized objects going back to the early years, idealizing the past and overcoming residual oedipal feelings. Kernberg notes that the past is reactivated because it symbolizes a lost stasis, a once-secure world that has vanished. By contrast, the world in which the middle-aged person finds himself often appears to be in a process of imminent dissolution—with the flight of full-grown children, the death of parents, and the loss of old friends. Although Kernberg recognizes the need to consolidate ego identity on a new foundation in middle age, he argues that such consolidation normally involves a "new knowledge about the limitations in one's personality functioning."[2] Kernberg contrasts such self-acceptance with narcissistic rationalization, denial, cynicism, and masochism, on the assumption that the essence of maturity is the recognition that one must no longer expect any "surprises" in the sphere of achievement or emotional fulfillment. Still less, Kernberg implies, should the middle-aged person seek to create new realities by breaking with the repetition-compulsions of the past.

Perhaps Kernberg is right in warning against the dangers of psychic restlessness in middle age. But what if the impulse to be true at last to one's creative birthright makes itself felt with irresistible force? In psychoanalytic terms such an imperative involves trying to recreate the internalized objects of the past on a fully idealized basis, now that one has made his mark in middle age and no longer has to temporize. I will try to show that Vladimir Nabokov is a brilliant but flawed example of a writer who, through shifting the emphasis in his work, sought new achievements in middle age. Nabokov tried to attain two artistic goals: (1) to rediscover and recreate cherished experiences rooted in his childhood and youth, and (2) to put into full practice a theory of aesthetics emphasizing the centrality of concrete sensuous experience. In making the transition to these latter-day objectives, Nabokov attempted to break once and for all with the phobic, dysphoric themes that dominated his writings during his twenties and thirties, and well into his forties. In place of these fatalistic motifs, Nabokov launched a series of ambitious literary experiments in which he displayed a powerful sense of black humor depending on wit and parody. Moreover, in implementing his theory of aestheticism Nabokov drew upon unusually rich resources of language to transform his memories into imaginative images. Nabokov's aestheticism, it should be noted, has important affinities with the art-for-art's-sake orientation championed by Théophile Gautier, Joris-Karl Huysmans, George Moore, Walter Pater, Oscar Wilde, and other nineteenth-century figures. This philosophy, as Nabokov acknowledged, was brought to full fruition in the works of Proust.

Nabokov's aestheticism was clearly formulated in his early writings, long before it became a major if not exclusive concern. The theory is adumbrated, for example, in the short story "Perfection" (1932), in which the protagonist Ivanov, an impoverished Russian émigré supporting himself as a tutor in Berlin, advises his pupil to store up beautiful memories of sensory impressions for solace in future time of adversity:

But the point is that with a bit of imagination—if, God forbid, you were some day to go blind or be imprisoned, or were merely forced to perform, in appalling poverty, some hopeless, distasteful task, you might remember this walk we are taking today in an ordinary forest as if it had been—how shall I say?—fairytale ecstasy."[3]

The function of language for the writer, according to Nabokov, is to capture memories, images, and feelings with precision and elegance. There is a striking parallelism between Nabokov's emphasis on language and the psychoanalytic theory of Jacques Lacan. Summarizing the Lacanian position, Antoine Vergote[4] states that the real efficacy of psychoanalysis depends more on the precise use of language by the analyst than on the therapeutic relationship as such. Vergote refers to the "linguistic structure of consciousness and of the unconscious," which can only be mediated by speech. At the heart of Lacan's effort to put psychoanalysis back on a sound theoretical foundation is the recognition that elucidating the symbolic representation of the unconscious remains the central task of psychoanalysis. Whether one agrees with Lacan or not, it is impossible to ignore the contribution of structuralists like Lacan and, of course, Claude Lévi-Strauss. Structural linguistics views the unconscious as part of an architectonic structure of categories and subsets relating to the elements of consciousness. But Lacan's structuralism insists that consciousness reflects social organization and that most associations are accordingly "universal." By contrast, pathological associations such as occur in psychosis are said to be excessively private and based on "secret motivations."

Nabokov's position is far from identical with that of Lacan. In fact, it cannot be emphasized sufficiently that the principal contribution of modernist writers such as Nabokov—to say nothing of Joyce, Proust, Gertrude Stein, Kafka, Beckett, Alain Robbe-Grillet, and others—consists of expanding the zone of private associations so as to make them public. These private associations differ from psychotic "secret motivations" because they are susceptible to recognizable linguistic representation and not, in my opinion, because they originate in qualitatively different motivational states. Nabokov's gift is not only his ability to perceive fine nuances of light and shadow, to identify all kinds of flora and fauna, or to apprehend any other concrete objects—his gift includes also his ability to share his fine perceptions with his readers through the use of poetic language. In other words, Nabokov is able to raise other people's marginal, even unconscious perceptions to the status of fully conscious data.

Nabokov goes even a step further and communicates normally interdicted, repressed sensations and desires, particularly in such novels as *Laughter in the Dark* (1932), *Lolita* (1955), and *Ada* (1969). I refer, of course, to Nabokov's treatment of the nymphet theme. Nabokov brings the unconscious, in Lacanian terms, into the "circuit of conscious discourse" and calls upon his readers to make themselves at home, however uneasily, in the ambience of forbidden acts and experiences. Nabokov's imaginative reconstruction of evanescent as well as unthinkable events is not to be confused with the crude fantasies of the Marquis de Sade or the hallucinations of William Burroughs. There is a fineness of texture about Nabokov's work that ennobles his effort even when he opens himself to the reproach of decadence.

Nabokov's modernism partakes nevertheless of an outmoded frame of mind. His imagistic writing, particularly as seen in some of his later novels, such as *Pale Fire* (1962) and *Ada* (1969), takes us back in time to a structuralism that is less sophisticated than that of Lacan or Lévi-Strauss. Nabokov's recall of finespun sensations resembles the atomistic structuralism of Wilhelm Wundt and Edward Titchener—a sort of turn-of-the-century *pointillisme*. In recapturing the structure of consciousness through the perceptions of his protagonists, Nabokov sometimes washes out the characters themselves or fails to develop complex relationships between them. Although Nabokov preserves the familiar outlines of character and plot in most of his fiction, he does not always deal successfully with motivation. This failing originates in his self-imposed aesthetic, which makes of his protagonists merely reactive organisms; that is, perceivers who become obsessed with the thing perceived, thereby cutting themselves off from their deepest and most permanent needs. The early short stories and novels, with their original treatment of émigré experience in Berlin between the wars, do not reveal this flaw to the same degree as the later works.

It can also be said of Nabokov's early works that they reveal the writer in the capacity of moralist, although any such role was anathema to Nabokov in light of his thoroughgoing aestheticism. In a detailed analysis of the novel *Invitation to a Beheading* (1938), Robert Alter[5] tries to interpret Nabokov's aestheticism within an ethical framework. Alter points out that Nabokov uses mirrors to reflect false, vulgar, mechanical art, as well as, paradoxically, the magical triumph of the human imagination; that is, of perfected consciousness over the sordid reality of totalitarian society. It is clear from Alter's exegesis that Nabokov conceives of inauthentic art as more than a mere symptom of bad taste; it is an integral part of the process by which all positive human values are degraded and finally destroyed, as in Nazi Germany. If Alter is correct it is clear that Nabokov is truly a moralist in spite of himself. This is to say that his carefully crafted, self-conscious art, with its striking poetic imagery, denotes an aestheticism bent upon upholding the dignity of the human spirit. I believe that Alter is correct but that his observations apply more accurately to Nabokov's Russian works, written before he had developed more complex and convoluted techniques of composition. Even if one were to concede that some of Nabokov's later, English novels, such as *Pnin* (1957), with its vulnerable but very decent protagonist, a Russian émigré professor, are based on fundamental moral judgments, it is necessary to inquire how well Nabokov succeeds in communicating his moral values to his readers by means of his aesthetic affirmations.

There are several reasons for concluding that Nabokov chose an ultimately self-defeating strategy, a weakness shared with other modernists in literature and the visual arts. First, when the reader or viewer is confronted with a work of great cognitive or perceptual complexity or novelty, the danger arises of his being fascinated by the artist's bright surfaces, thereby failing to discern the latter's larger purpose. Second, the writer himself runs the risk of blunting his feelings in the process of trying to express them in a striking, original manner. The result can be mannerism or preciosity rather than powerful, moving art. Nabokov is especially vulnerable on this account in the ambitious latter-day novels *Pale Fire* (1962) and *Ada* (1969). It is as if in Nabokov's case the superego had become a battleground between two sets of seemingly disparate standards, those of art and those of morality. Artistic standards are peculiar in the sense that they derive not only from the conventions of a consensually validated craft but are also subject to modification by the artist's imagination, which, in turn, reflects the operations of the unconscious. Ethical ideals are by contrast normative and nonidiosyncratic and are not the product of primary-process thinking, even though they are acquired unconsciously and continue to operate partly on the unconscious level. Nabokov's argument is that a true artist has the moral right to be different, to be a freak like Nabokov's protagonist Cincinnatus in *Invitation to a Beheading* (1938). Nabokov is less concerned with the social consequences of art than he is with the process by which it is facilitated or deflected from its aim. For Nabokov, then, the artistic ideal of individualism corresponds to the ethical ideal of freedom. Individualism and freedom are seen as ends in themselves and need no validation on grounds of utility.

In effect, Nabokov compels us to take a clear look at superego formation and to ask if psychoanalytic theory can accommodate the artist's private vision within the parameters of the ego ideal. The classical psychoanalytic view of superego formation relates the internalization of superego demands to the abandonment of the selfish and destructive impulses associated with the oedipal stage. Strictly speaking, the child begins to repress, at the end of the phallic period, the very wishes that, properly sublimated and symbolized, can become the raw materials for artistic expression. Access to these raw materials would appear to demand regression in the service of the ego. A question remains, nevertheless, as to how much creative regression can take place without compromising the artist's superego-bound standards of craftsmanship and responsibility to his readers or viewers. Part of the answer is to be found in the observation that the highest forms of art rise above solipsism and tie the artist firmly to human concerns broadly conceived, that is, to an ego ideal, as, say, in the works of Tolstoy.

Nabokov tells us that the highly personalized perceptions and insights of the individual can be transmuted into art only in a social and political climate that respects the truth. The truth, in turn, can be known only by those who dare to see with the mind's eye rather than the communal eye. In this light, Nabokov's aestheticism requires the artist to live up to his ego ideal by respecting the concreteness and particularity of people and things. It would appear that the bond between imagination and conscience consists, in this instance, of the full development of a humanized ego ideal. Hence, to speak of creative regression in the service of the ego is not to ignore the possibility of creative regression in the service of the superego. If the latter can be cruel and unreasonable at times, so too can it guide the artist toward responsibility. As understood by Nabokov, responsibility does not mean that the artist should feel answerable to anyone. Nabokov's aestheticism requires the artist to "answer" the world of external objects by allowing his eye to rest on it lovingly and to communicate his vision to the reader without losing any of its freshness or immediacy. To be able to accomplish this task is to perform a moral deed, with the understanding that beauty itself is goodness and that the artist's record of remembered beauty is a good thing. True beauty, it should be added, is understood by Nabokov to inhere in the singularity of things, and has nothing to do with abstract beauty based on normative values.

Not all things are seen by Nabokov as beautiful, and his view of manmade things is parodic in the extreme. Nabokov reveals in his writings a profound disgust with *poshlust,* an untranslatable Russian word referring to false and meretricious beauty, or more narrowly to the more pretentious excrescences of popular culture. These vulgar manifestations are viewed by Nabokov as not worthy of satirizing. It should be pointed out that Nabokov did not regard himself as a satirist, because he had no wish to instruct his audience as to what is good or bad. Nabokov was content, instead, to rearrange playfully the trivia of the landscape of popular culture so as to dramatize their tastelessness. In fact, the work that belongs to Nabokov's American period

(1940–1960) often resembles the pop art of recent decades, with its collages of familiar, plastic, flashy, and often ridiculous commercial objects. There is a good reason for this development in Nabokov's work and I think it has something to do with what happens when the artist approaches the limits of naturalism. Nabokov appears to have tried to distance himself from the near-sentimentality of his early works, notably *Mary* (1926) and many of his short stories of the 1920s and 1930s. As a consequence, Nabokov turned increasingly to parody and stylistic experimentation. The effect was to render less stark the harsh fictional world that Nabokov had begun to construct during his Berlin years. Nabokov's protagonists, though still under a fatal spell, began to seem less pathetic. In such early novels as *King, Queen, Knave* (1928) and *Laughter in the Dark* (1932), and even such a tour de force as *Invitation to a Beheading* (1938), Nabokov approached the outer limits of naturalism, exploring sadomasochistic relationships that reflected the author's Manichaean view of the universe. The short stories of the Berlin period, for example, "Terror," (1926), "The Return of Chorb," (1925), "Perfection," (1932), "Tyrants Destroyed" (1938), and "Lik" (1939), not only echo the morbid themes of the early novels but also reveal Nabokov's sensitivity and sense of isolation. By later resorting to parody Nabokov sought to denature his fiction and to drain it of its painful emotional content as well as its too-obvious ethical content.

On the surface, parody appears to be an honest and straightforward way of communicating with the reader, telling him not to forget that art is different from life and is not to be understood in the same way. It is not that art is less serious than life but rather than it belongs to the realm of serious play and that its purpose is to show life in a special way. The playful side of art, particularly parody with its emphasis on wit and humor, gives the artist an opportunity to hold his deeper emotions in abeyance, or to express them, at best, as amusing asides. As Nabokov elaborated his aestheticism in his later writings, the emotional intensity of his work became attenuated.

The loss of emotional intensity made it difficult for Nabokov to achieve closure in his later works, except by bringing his protagonist to an abrupt end, as in *Transparent Things* (1972),

Pale Fire (1962), *Lolita* (1955), *Bend Sinister* (1947), and, in a less violent sense, *Pnin* (1957). This tendency toward affective short-circuiting was apparent in some of Nabokov's early novels, notably *Laughter in the Dark* (1932), *The Defense* (1929), and *Despair* (1936), but with the important difference that the author was still able to generate emotional tension, which differs from emotional intensity in the sense that the element of suspense takes precedence over depth of feeling. Martin Amis sums up Nabokov's special brand of detachment by noting that Nabokov looks at his fictional characters from the standpoint of the "sublime directed at our fallen world of squalor, absurdity, and talentlessness. Sublimity replaces the ideas of motivation and plot with those of obsession and destiny. It suspends moral judgments in favor or remorselessness, a helter-skelter intensity. It does not proceed to a conclusion so much as accumulate possibilities of pain and danger."[6]

The obsessional tone becomes pronounced in Nabokov's later works, in which the author tries to return to the unfinished business of his protagonists' lives by tracing the emotional consequences of their childhood and youth. The long and intricate fictional memoir *Ada* (1969) illustrates Nabokov's preoccupation with the past and its associated loss of momentum. *Ada* purports to be the life story of an aristocrat named Van Veen and his interrupted but lifelong romance with Ada, his cousin, who is in reality his sister. *Ada* is a convoluted, parodic novel with some science-fiction features. One of its central concerns is the imaginative exploration of the vicissitudes of memory, and it is written in the best (or worst) Nabokovian tradition of stylistic freedom and experimentation. The tone is lighthearted and filled with mockery as the novel traces the lives of its protagonists into advanced old age. Nabokov's stylistic inventions, linguistic puzzles, and elaborations of the story line represent centrifugal tendencies in his thought processes. It is characteristic of Nabokov that as he approaches material that seems to be personal and important to him he swerves aside, going off in many different directions and leaving behind false leads, as in the chess problems he was fond of inventing.[7]

For Nabokov, writing appears to have been an exercise that starts at the center but moves quickly and disarmingly to the periphery of feeling, where external objects are suddenly perceived with microscopic accuracy, replacing affect with sensation. Nabokov's bent for surrealism and his brilliant gift for describing nature, especially in miniature, are part of his elaborate strategy, forged in childhood, for moving away from involvement with others and escaping into a zone of privacy and daydreaming. The earliest manifestations of this tendency can be seen in his daily disappearance into the forest each morning during his boyhood summers on the family estate near St. Petersburg. These mornings were dedicated to hunting butterflies, and Nabokov remained an enthusiastic collector throughout his life. I suspect there was something defensive about these excursions initially, but it is not clear what the young Nabokov was trying to avoid.

As a writer, the romantic impulse, especially in the escapist sense, underlies Nabokov's evasive strategy. In psychoanalytic terms this impulse is a function of the ego ideal as well as the playful id. The quality of elusiveness identifies Nabokov as one of those "who in the throng of near affections care only for the love which is far."[8] "The love which is far" is the object of Nabokov's artistic quest. The symbolic love object denotes an important dimension of the ego ideal, which, in turn, is normative in a special sense, without being moralistic. Nabokov's standard of perfection is based on the norm of platonic beauty and is therefore presexual but not necessarily asexual. It is a norm that recognizes the sensuous possibilities of nymphets as well as of women, of flowers and trees as well as butterflies. Nabokov's protagonists search for the ephemeral embodiment of this ideal the same way the lepidopterist pursues his fragile prey, net in hand, or the way Humbert plots to possess his forbidden love object in Lolita. The ego ideal furnishes Nabokov with angelic forms in nature and among women (realistic portraits of women are also found in Nabokov's fiction), but they turn out to be angels of dullness, like Lolita, or angels of death, like the young usherette, Margot, in Laughter in the Dark. Like some platonic essence, beauty does not fade in Nabokov's fictional world; it dazzles us by its inhuman brilliance, as Ellen Pifer[9] points out in her analysis of Ada, or it betrays its admirers, as in the short story "An Affair of Honor."

Nabokov's aesthetic ideal combines desire with a self-mocking hunger for the absolute. Good and evil, as Nabokov shows in *Ada,* are irrelevant to those who pursue experience as an end in itself or as an absolute. Nabokov argues that it is possible to uphold this value-free experiential ideal even in hellish surroundings, as in the brothel Villa Venus in *Ada.* Nabokov is correct to the extent that the politics of aesthetics consists of the strategy of distancing, which can be accomplished even under difficult conditions through depersonalization. Distancing involves the paradoxical act of losing oneself in the obsessive contemplation of the object while continuing to think of oneself as the detached observer, even the stage manager of reality. Thus, Humbert knows he is treating Lolita as an object, albeit an idealized object, but he also knows that in her definitive form she is an ordinary, even crass individual. This is to say that Nabokov understands that the object of desire and of minute observation is simultaneously worthy and unworthy of his obsessive concern. The challenge to the artist resembles Humbert's predicament. It is a question of maintaining a double perspective in order not to subordinate the artist to the idealized object through depersonalization, or nullifying the external object by saturating it with the artist's affect.

If, in the name of aesthetics, the artist assimilates the object to his inner world to capture its subjective correletive, he puts the stamp of his personality on the object, casting light or shadow on it, depending on his mood. The artist thereby risks intruding his preoccupations and falsifying reality through objectification. If—again in the name of aesthetics—the artist holds himself at too great a distance from the object in order to "let it speak for itself," he will surely avoid injecting self-pity or any other feeling into his representation. In so doing, the artist will fail with equal sureness to tell the whole truth, which of necessity includes his subjective response to the external object, the very activity that gives it artistic or literary significance. This is one of the faults I find with Nabokov's beautifully written memoir *Speak, Memory* (1966), a weakness that results directly from his aesthetic theory. *Speak, Memory* is a work in which Nabokov achieves a stoical victory over the vicissitudes of his uprooted life by never feeling sorry for himself. But Nabokov pays a price for his effort to distance himself from his experiences. Using selective recall, Nabokov omits almost all references to a number of important relationships, such as those involving his brother Sergei (his junior by one year), his three younger sisters, and his wife. The result is partial truth, a defensive reconstruction of reality that leaves out much that is essential for understanding the author's complex personality or the sources of his literary inspiration.

Nabokov is known, after all, for his strong opinions about art, about contemporary writing, and about other authors. His strategy of distancing himself from his feelings as an artist—critics have described him as cold in his treatment of his fictional characters—seems at first out of keeping with his intensely judgmental personality, until one realizes that Nabokov's aloofness as an artist is the reciprocal of his intensity in the personal sphere. In other words, Nabokov uses aestheticism in the service of affect diffusion, creating a fantasy world in which conflicts are resolved mechanically rather than psychologically. With the possible exception of *Lolita,* Nabokov consistently avoids organic climactic developments in his later works. By omitting psychological closure Nabokov eliminates the need to bring his deepest feelings into sharp focus; by sacrificing emotional commitment to his characters Nabokov frees himself to concentrate on achieving imagistic freshness and linguistic virtuosity.

There is therefore no contradiction between Nabokov the opinionated man of letters, the devoted husband and father, the loving son, or the loyal friend—and the elusive aesthete. The problem remains, however, of trying to understand why Nabokov, whose early Russian stories successfully fused affect with stylistic grace and even moral passion, later replaced intensity with fictionalized reminiscence and literary gamesmanship. Anton Ehrenzweig[10] had provided a distinction that may be useful in this connection. Ehrenzweig notes that perception is governed by two distinct organizing principles. One principle reflects the biological function of adaptation and the other is based on the idea of the "good" gestalt, or aesthetically pleasing form. The latter, according to Ehrenzweig, is repressed but registers on the unconscious level as a response to subtle overtones and elaborations of shapes and sounds. This response is seen by Ehrenzweig as a kind of depth perception that ultimately enriches surface perception and may give rise to artistic symbolization. Nabokov interprets the role of the artist as one who refuses to conform to the principle of vulgar adaptation to the dictates of reality defined as the demand-quality of things, that is, their consensually validated, standardized surface traits. Nabokov's protagonists, even those whom he presents as negative characters with neurotically distorted sensibilities (such as Franz, a coarse, unfeeling farm boy who plots with his mistress to murder her husband in *King, Queen, Knave*, 1928), perceive the world in idiosyncratic terms. The perceptions of Nabokov's fully realized characters, such as Humbert in *Lolita*, or Cincinnatus in *Invitation to a Beheading* (1938), are depth perceptions of a manmade world whose banality is rejected in favor of heightened, intensely focused sensibility.

In keeping with Edward Bullough's[11] distinction between aesthetics and art criticism, Nabokov uses his protagonists to explore the quintessential aesthetic problem of how the artist expresses his ideals through his artistic vision. For this reason Nabokov's fiction is not a direct criticism of life—as would be true of satire—but an attempt to understand certain kinds of subjective experience that he sees as the raw materials for a playful recreation of the world. At the risk of simplification it might be said that Nabokov's main characters usually possess an artistic temperament. Even Dreyer in *King, Queen, Knave* (1928), who might be described as an artist manqué, is fully capable of perceiving the world around him with a sense of immediacy and freshness. Unlike a true artist, Dreyer has no need to take the final step of translating his experience into artistic form. If Nabokov had chosen to use his fictional creations to teach his readers how to appreciate beauty, his work would have fallen short of Nabokov's purist goals. Nabokov is a student of individual consciousness no less than of refined sensibility as such. He tries to rescue consciousness from the brutalizing forces that seek to destroy it. These influences exist, as Nabokov shows, on the interpersonal plane, as well as on the institutional. The dull-witted bully Koldunov in "Lik" (1939) or the homicidal brothers Gustav and Anton in "The Leonardo" (1933) are examples of obtuseness and callousness employed by Nabokov to explore the barriers to the cultivation of human consciousness. These characters are capable only of the most debased sensations and emotions; in turn, they deny others the right to be sensitive human beings.

In his early works, Nabokov has not yet determined to provide his readers with an alternative vision of reality; he does not yet remind us at every turn that we are participating as awakened readers in a highly self-conscious exercise. Hence, the pre-1940 stories and novels are conventional in structure. Only occasionally, as in the novelette *The Eye*, composed in Berlin in 1930, does Nabokov employ illusionary effects. In general, the early work reflects an author who is sensitive to human suffering, despite Nabokov's disclaimers. For example, in his foreword to *The Eye*, Nabokov states that the tale is not "a dreadfully painful love story in which a writhing heart is not only spurned, but humiliated and punished." The fact remains, however, that *The Eye* is truly moving and reminds us, in Nabokov's own words, that "the forces of imagination . . . are the forces of good."[12] Nabokov claims to be repelled by what Ehrenzweig calls the "biological relevance" of things, preferring their less obvious "inarticulate" aspects. To use Ehrenzweig's felicitous phrase, Nabokov savors "interruptions in the stream of consciousness." We must ask ourselves why, in the pursuit of his aesthetic aims, the post-1940 Nabokov begins to show signs of increasing detachment from his characters and their circumstances. Perhaps we should apply Ehrenzweig's judgment (not necessarily intended for Nabokov): "This detached 'thing-free' way of looking at the outside world, as though it were a flat abstract gestalt pattern, presupposes a lessening of the normal libidinous interest in reality."[13] The things that Nabokov has abstracted out of his later fictional works consist of foreground elements that have been replaced by background. Particularly in *Pale Fire* (1962) and *Ada* (1969), Nabokov brings about a reversal of normal figure-ground relationships, dwelling on the sensuous nuances or the grotesqueries of human relationships. The character Smurov in *The Eye* seems to capture the psychological essence of this strategy: "The only happiness in this world is to observe, to spy, to watch, to scrutinize oneself and others, to be nothing but a big, slightly vitreous, somewhat bloodshot, unblinking eye."[14]

By turning his protagonist into part of the background Nabokov fulfills the narcissistic requirements of his failed hero: "I am happy that I can gaze at myself, for any man is absorbing—yes, really absorbing! The world, try as it may, cannot insult me. I am invulnerable."[15] Simultaneously, Nabokov begins to articulate his aesthetic theory of detachment (or distance), which is not without its overtones of self-absorption. Paradoxically, Nabokov produces an art of detachment by drawing the reader's attention to the concreteness of things. By attaching the reader's eye compulsively—but dispassionately—to the surface of things, Nabokov avoids the temptation to promulgate his aesthetic theory by abstract formulations. Nevertheless, he is forever lecturing the reader by indirection, saying, in effect, that the world of sensations is more real and more satisfying than the world of human relationships. In fact, Smurov, in *The Eye,* a character who dies and then becomes a disembodied observer, is an early vehicle for illustrating the artistic possibilities of repression and depersonalization—defenses against acknowledging the tragic side of life. Nabokov tries to conceal his forebodings about human destiny—his thoroughgoing pessimism—by becoming a writer who never takes his eye off his imaginative processes. Accordingly, if Nabokov is parodic he is also self-mocking; if he is mischievous and tantalizes his readers with sudden kaleidoscopic rearrangements, he also plays hide-and-seek with his own deepest feelings, which include compassion, as much for the vulnerable protagonist of "Lik" (1929) as for his tormentor Koldunov, who kills himself in the surprise ending of the story.

Aesthetic theory to one side, one cannot hope to understand Nabokov's fiction without recognizing the centrality of the experience of first love in adolescence or even earlier. This experience lies at the heart of *Mary, The Real Life of Sebastian Knight, Lolita, Ada,* and many short stories, such as "The Admiralty Spire." (1933). Nabokov's habit of evoking the sensuous feelings associated with sexual awakening can almost be called a fixation. I say sensuous because Nabokov's evocation of the preadolescent and adolescent girl as a love object involves only partial idealization. Nabokov idealizes his heroines only on the physical plane insofar as their lovers have few illusions about the true character of these nymphets. Humbert, for example, understands that Lolita is a girl with limited human potential, just as the narrator in "The Admiralty Spire" understands that his beloved Katya is vacuous and potentially vicious. These imperfect, indeed unfinished love objects are perceived as beautiful creatures in the same sense that a butterfly is beautiful. Like a butterfly, Lolita is attractive not only because of her delicate beauty, but also because she is unreachable psychologically. With Lolita, as with a butterfly, there can be no reciprocity: self-sufficient, she does not respond, does not reveal her girlish secrets, even when caught in Humbert's net. Nabokov's nymphets are destined to elude their pursuers and to flee into the commonplace obscurity of adulthood. Thus Nabokov is a naturalist in his depiction of young love, as he is a naturalist in his detailed descriptions of flora and fauna. His approach to his fictional heroines is to depict them as almost pregenital characters who never really become mature women capable of a many-sided relationship with their lovers. Even Ada, whose intermittent love affair with Van Veen lasts a lifetime, is more vivid and more fully realized as a twelve-year-old seductress than as a grown woman.

Nabokov's fictional love objects exercise the same fascination for him as his real-life first love, whom he calls Tamara in *Speak, Memory*. Tamara was fifteen when Nabokov, aged sixteen, met her, and his account of their love affair is the story of an encapsulated episode in the author's life. Like Tamara, who vanished from Nabokov's life when she was still in her teens, Nabokov's young heroines never really age convincingly. They are forever frozen in a tableau, and their image is kept fresh by an act of will. To lose this memory represents for Nabokov the risk of losing a part of his identity.

The link between Tamara and Lolita is obvious, but the nymphet motif did not originate with Lolita and is clearly anticipated in *Laughter in the Dark* (1932) almost two decades earlier. This is a well-crafted, traditional novel about a sensitive art critic, Albinus, betrayed by his vulgar adolescent mistress. The mistress, diminutive Margot, is almost interchangeable with Lolita physically and psychologically, although she is not a product of a middle-class upbringing. Like Lolita, Margot is waiflike and precocious, and, like Lolita, Margot has been seduced and abandoned by a Clare Quilty-like scoundrel named Alex Rex. Nabokov, in effect, has split his male protagonist into a good-me/bad-me in both novels. Although Axel Rex, a commercial artist, is not literally interchangeable with Albinus, he represents—like Quilty—the acting-out side of the respectable middle-aged man's personality. Like Quilty, Rex has possessed his nymphet in the beginning, when he was young, thereby accomplishing what Albinus/Humbert could only attempt when it was already too late. Nabokov's nymphets symbolize lost opportunities, that is, what the protagonist might have enjoyed if he had acted at the right moment. If Tamara was indeed the prototype for Nabokov's nymphets, she represents not only nostalgia for a lost love, but also ambivalence toward accepting the finality of the aging process.

The act of recapturing the past in middle age is defined in Nabokov's fiction as something perverse because it involves regression rather than mere reminiscence. It also entails the abandonment of an ego identity grounded in attachment to the practical demands of living. Nabokov's protagonists in *Laughter in the Dark* or *Lolita* live in present time but are forced to alter their everyday lives radically because of their obsession with their lost youth as symbolized by the childlike love object. This object, in turn, is experienced in an exquisite, sensuous way, but succeeds ultimately in detaching the protagonist from a much wider social world. The outcome is predictable. The self-destructiveness of a Humbert or Albinus is also a defeat for the lover of illusions anchored in the past. But it is a delicious downfall involving the taste of forbidden fruit. This defeat via regression owes its special quality to the unique character of the regression. Albinus or Humbert regress in the service of life-renewal based on imagination and idealization. In so doing they surrender that part of their mature identity that links them with their fading agemates and the urgencies of a life that has no room for fine perceptions, such as asphalt pavement "drying patchily after a recent shower, the damp still showing in the form of grotesque black skeletons as if painted across the width of the road."[16]

Humbert's defeat can also be seen as a punishment for the sadistic act of total domination (mostly by guile) of Lolita. It is significant that the reader learns little of Lolita's frame of mind. Despite her precocity and previous sexual experience, Lolita is after all a frightened and confused child, alone in the world, who finds herself in the power of a grown man who exploits her over an extended period of time. By choosing a childlike victim, Humbert maximizes the distance between himself and the object of his sexual needs. Under these circumstances, Lolita is not even a true love object. What Humbert truly cathects, in the spirit of narcissistic sadism, is the matrix of sensations and memories that is associated with his domination of Lolita.[17] Lolita is merely a means to a narcissistic end. Of course, the act of debasing Lolita, as perceived by the fastidious, guilt-ridden Humbert, is also an act of self-debasement and many times the perpetrator literally writhes with shame and revusion at his own behavior. Humbert's discomfiture has still another source. Although Lolita is in Humbert's power, the relationship between the two also resembles the relationship between an insecure tutor and his privileged pupil, not unlike the relationship described in "Perfection" (1932). In this moving short story, a mischievous pupil pretends that he is drowning, unwittingly causing the death of his sickly, impoverished tutor who wades in to save him. Like the tutor in "Perfection," Humbert finds himself trying to amuse Lolita, to instruct her, and to keep her from slipping away from him. As much as *Lolita* is a novel about a demonic, obsessed man it is also the story of a demonic girl/woman who is licentious and manipulative; and like many of Nabokov's female characters, she is ultimately destructive. Lionel Trilling[18] has likened Lolita, in relation to her would-be lover, to an idealized but unresponsive lady of a medieval court.

The above remarks suggest that there is both a sadistic and masochistic side to Humbert's character. A good example of the theme of sadomasochism is found in what Nabokov regarded as his favorite novel, *Invitation to a Beheading* (1938). This work describes the experiences of a condemned man in his prison cell and the psychological torments visited upon him by his crass jailers in a mythical totalitarian state. *Invitation to a Beheading*, which has often been described as Kafkaesque, represents the culmination of Nabokov's career as a writer in the Russian language. No less important, this novel represents a major treatment of the author's tormentor/victim theme as developed in such early stories as "The Leonardo" (1933), "Tyrants Destroyed" (1938), or "Lik" (1939). On the manifest level, the sadomasochistic motif cannot be viewed apart from the objective facts of Nabokov's banishment and his role as a man who had been ill used by fortune. In addition, Nabokov may have experienced a degree of rejection by his classmates when he was finally sent off to a private school, after having been educated exclusively by private tutors. Nabokov hints at some schoolboy difficulties in *Speak, Memory*, commenting on the reaction of his peers and teachers to the fact that he was driven to school by a chauffeur each day. At Cambridge, Nabokov seems to have kept his distance from his fellow students, and he recalls in *Speak, Memory* that he was regarded as a reactionary in some circles because of his open contempt for the cause of revolution in Russia.

In light of the above circumstances it is not surprising that the tone of *Invitation to a Beheading* and its forerunners is one of victimization. The question is whether to look for a situational or depth-analytical explanation for an apparent preoccupation. Even if one regards Nabokov's characters as merely a means of illustrating his aesthetic theories, that is, as symbols of "a world where brute power seeks to extinguish conscious life"[19] there remains a lingering suspicion that the author's sensibility operates in a concrete, personal way. There is also the assassination of Nabokov's father when the author was still a student at Cambridge. Does Nabokov identify the cruel and oafish police-state characters in *Bend Sinister* (1947) with the Russian fascists who shot his father in Berlin in 1922? A less parsimonious, depth-analytical explanation is that Nabokov's gallery of tormentors, from his earliest short stories to *Lolita*, represent oedipal fathers in pursuit of errant sons. Although this possibility cannot be ruled out, there is no solid evidence to support it on the basis of available biographical materials, which are sketchy to say the least—*Speak, Memory* notwithstanding.

I would like to suggest the hypothesis that Nabokov's sensitive and alienated protagonists stand for a psychological attitude that derives less from a guilt complex than it does from a sense of isolation combined with a need for intense privacy. It is as if Nabokov has divided his fictional world into two sorts of beings, the brutish and the sensitive, and has left no means of escape open to his sensitive protagonists except through fantasy. For example, Adam Krug, the political resister in *Bend Sinister*, is a man who tries to disengage himself from the sordid world in which he lives, but in the end he can escape only through psychosis. The same is true of the obsessed chess player Luzhin, the protagonist in *The Defense* (1929) who kills himself, baffled by the demands of the real world. Even Humbert's love for Lolita has a fuguelike quality, being characterized by flight from everyday life into compulsive sexuality. Although Nabokov's would-be escapees cannot shake off other people, their urge to flee from man and his habitations has the force of a compulsion. As I have mentioned, Nabokov often spoke of his boyhood compulsion to hurriedly leave his family's summer home each morning in solitary search of butterflies. As Nabokov relates in *Speak, Memory*, nothing could deter him from this daily ritual, even the arrival of a friend who had traveled many hours by bicycle to see him.

As an adult, Nabokov continued to find great joy in his pursuit of butterflies, an activity that remained a constant, whether he found himself in Europe or America. Apart from the pleasure that Nabokov obviously took in practicing his hobby and also contributing to scientific knowledge as a lepidopterist, there is also the element of solitary activity. The quasi-playful nature of butterfly collecting, as well as the love of gamesmanship, is seen also in Nabokov's passion for inventing elaborate chess problems, filled with pitfalls even for skilled chess players. Above all, as many critics have pointed out, Nabokov's later novels, notably *Lolita, Pale Fire,* and *Ada* contain much wordplay, coincidence, and mystery clues designed for the perceptive reader. These games are developed with a rich sense of humor and without the slightest trace of didactic or moral intent.

Nabokov goes so far in removing his later fiction from familiar contexts of social significance or human tragedy that the reader is tempted to dismiss him as superficial or deliberately amoral. By contrast, as stated earlier, Nabokov's early stories and novels reveal a deep concern for the fate of his fictional characters. Nabokov's latter-day escapism may be seen as a reaction to his intense empathy, which is evident in almost everything he wrote during his first forty years. Ironically then, Nabokov, a man of compassion, is best known to his readers for his later works, in which the cerebral element—as well as reminiscence—is more salient than the passional. While it is imprudent to identify fictional characters with their author, I believe that the youthful, hard-pressed Nabokov of the Berlin period was still bound to a real world that demanded to be taken seriously. Perhaps the older, successful Nabokov, no longer at the mercy of his environment, could safely revert to the elusive strategy of his childhood. In doing so, Nabokov averted his face from the cruel world to which other writers of the modern period address themselves.

But the need to return to a zone of stillness also led Nabokov along the path of parody and surrealism because the world in its sordid aspect continued to intrude on him and to mock him, as it were. Nabokov is therefore a modernist in the sense that, unlike his idol Leo Tolstoy, he cannot bring himself to gaze unblinkingly at the real world but rather has to transform it magically to make it bearable. Eugène Ionesco is close in spirit to Nabokov because both authors escape from their subjective, hallucinatory worlds by means of humor and self-mockery. Joyce is close in spirit to Nabokov because their love of life transcends anger or despair, enabling them to embellish life playfully. Francois Rabelais, Laurence Sterne, and the Charles Dickens of *Pickwick Papers* also belong to this fraternity whose members see bright sunshine in the midst of dark shadows. But Nabokov is far removed in spirit from modernists such as Kafka or Beckett, who remain half blinded in the shadows, that is, the consciousness that life is inescapably painful. Unlike Nabokov, those writers have forgotten that the world had a paradisical beginning, when innocent love flourished before the birth of tragedy.

Chapter 5

FLANNERY O'CONNOR

The Captive Bird

One of the ways of understanding Flannery O'Connor's work is by tracing the connection between her aesthetic aims and her emotional needs, particularly in relation to her mother, Regina. On one level, O'Connor set herself the goal of symbolically representing man's compelling need for transcendence in a world perceived as radically evil. O'Connor's emotional needs—on the surface unrelated to her metaphysical framework—were those of a would-be independent woman forced into dependency on her mother at age twenty-five by the advent of lupus, a life-threatening disease of the immune system.[1] Although O'Connor was a lifelong model of Catholic piety and a militant defender of the Church, a strong vein of skepticism, accompanied by a satirical turn of mind, are revealed in her work. Her skepticism, however, was never directed to questions of religious dogma. Instead, her doubts found expression in her fictional treatment of religious themes, in which conflict between faith and total disbelief is a central concern. O'Connor was a Catholic who lived almost her entire life in Georgia, in a Protestant fundamentalist setting, and this permitted her to view the special features of fundamentalism with great distance intellectually, but with profound emotional involvement on the unconscious level, as her fiction reveals. O'Connor's treatment of her fundamentalist characters emphasizes the grotesque, gothic elements in their violent, impoverished lives, and enables her to maintain a high degree of cultural aloofness from them. Nevertheless, O'Connor uses the God-intoxicated fervor of her Protestant characters as a counterbalance to society's hypocrisy, smugness, and cheap optimism. In effect, O'Connor appears to be closely identified with the antimodernist, rebellious, and aggressive components of fundamentalism, which she uses as a vehicle for expressing her repressed hostility to authority in general, and to her mother in particular.

A word is necessary about O'Connor's relationship to her father, Edward, who died of lupus, when she was fifteen. In the absence of detailed biographical material it is not possible to characterize O'Connor's relationship to her father, except indirectly, by reference to her fictional portraits of men. It is known that O'Connor's father encouraged her literary interests and that he had tried his hand at writing as an avocation. Prior to the onset of his fatal illness, when his daughter was thirteen, the father had been a successful businessman and had served as an officer in the First World War. That the father's premature death must have had a powerful impact on his only child can hardly be doubted. O'Connor's preoccupation with death and mutilation in much of her fiction may be linked with the trauma of her father's death, although her ambivalence toward her mother appears to be the more important contributing factor. Despite the violence of O'Connor's male protagonists it is incorrect to think of them as predatory or exploitative in their treatment of women. Instead, as will become clear presently, O'Connor uses fictional males and females interchangeably as instruments of retribution against mother figures. O'Connor apparently was asexual, an impression consistent with the fact that romantic love relationships can scarcely be said to exist in her writings, with the dubious exception of the short story "Good Country People." It is not unreasonable to suppose, based on O'Connor's fictional characterizations, that she was as much identified with her lupus-striken father as she was with her mother, if not more so.

O'Connor's fiction was the work of an angry spirit, even though her many letters to literary correspondents reveal her to have been outwardly good-humored and stoical in the face of serious illness and pain. O'Connor's conception of herself as a writer performing the role of angry prophet is consistent with her fierce denunciation of the profane world in her fiction. The anger is intense and pitiless, invariably culminating in the violent destruction of her protagonists, or, at the very least, in outbursts of almost gratuitous fury. This affinity for violent endings cannot be explained exclusively by reference to her fear of death due to lupus, because it appears in her earliest writings, dating back to 1947 when at the age of twenty-two she submitted six stories in fulfillment of her master's thesis at the State University of Iowa. These stories were later incorporated into her first novel, *Wise Blood* (1952), and their tone is no less violent in the novel. Her first story "The Geranium" (1946), for example—her favorite story—is about an ailing, pathetic old man, a traditional Southern white, who lives with his married daughter in her small apartment in New York City. He feels humiliated when he discovers that his next-door neighbor is a black man. In addition, her suffers another blow to his self-esteem when his black neighbor overhears him talking to himself and reliving his old possum-hunting days while struggling up the stairs of his apartment house. To add to the old man's discomfiture, his confused, feeble condition makes it necessary for the black man to escort him up the stairs. The story ends on an ominous note when another neighbor across the rear courtyard threatens the old man, accusing him of peeking into his apartment through the window: " 'I only tell people once,' the man said and left the window."

The six thesis stories are linked in important ways with O'Connor's next three stories: "The Peeler" (1949), "The Heart of the Park" (1949), and "A Strike of Good Fortune" (1949), also titled "The Woman on the Stairs." These three stories, like their predecessors, belong to the brief period of O'Connor's growing independence as a young woman living away from home for the first time. The pre-lupus stories begin to provide a focus for the author's diffuse anger, whose object continues to be deeply repressed. In these three postthesis stories, O'Connor appears to have realized the symbolic possibilities, especially the theological implications, of the intense affects she was experiencing. Despite this realization, bitterness and anger pervade the pre-illness stories, including the three postthesis stories, two of which were incorporated, along with "The Train," into *Wise Blood*, albeit with a number of changes.

Seen in his light, O'Connor's brand of fictional asceticism, as exemplified by the self-mutilation of Hazel in *Wise Blood* (he blinds himself with lye), turns out to be a consequence of the thwarted pleasure principle, or, more precisely, of Eros denied, and is in accordance with Freud's insight into the connection between frustration and destructiveness. O'Connor's mature work, in fact, is remarkable for its sustained attempt to provide the death instinct with a religious meaning, which can be expressed in the formula: sin-equals-death, but violence-equals-life. The ultimate sin for O'Connor is hypocrisy; the saving grace is a moment of revelation, an epiphany that can be produced only by an act of violence. Thus, O'Connor's precondition for the salvation of her characters is an act of sacrifice, or the traditional religious requirement that spiritual rebirth must be based on antecedent death. Here, too, it can be seen that violent impulse release, that is, acting out by the bad me, is justified by O'Connor in the name of a greater good, namely, the destruction of hypocrisy. In her stories, self-righteous hypocrites frustrate the protagonist and bring on their own destruction, which is also their moment of spiritual truth or rebirth. Invariably, the murderous acts committed by these protagonists are directed at sanctimonious parent figures and are designed to punish them, producing an epiphanic experience in the victim as a side effect. O'Connor's fictional aggressors are portrayed as having a more honest vision of man's depravity than do her respectable characters. In effect, the superego of O'Connor's destroyers is subverted by their devastating id impulses. Hence, they are permitted to act as the avenging hand of God, and the author permits them to dance on the graves of their victims in a triumphant satanism masquerading as authenticity or God-intoxication.

We see evidence of Hazel's ambivalent identification with his dead mother in *Wise Blood* in the scene in which he tries on his mother's little silver-rimmed glasses and studies his face in the mirror: "He saw his mother's face in his, looking at the face in the mirror." It is at this moment that Sabbath Hawks, the adolescent girl who has attached herself to him, enters the room, cradling Enoch's stolen little mummy in her arms, and saying, "Call me Momma now." Hazel's reaction is to smack the effigy against the wall and to throw it out into the rain. Moments later, he pulls off the glasses and throws them out the door. Symbolically, Hazel has repudiated his mother in casting out her glasses, also rejecting the effigy in its capacity as a mother's child. In so doing, Hazel communicates self-hatred, which is the result of his conflicted incorporation of the bad mother. Hazel's fear of death, then, seems to reflect not only O'Connor's association of sexuality with death, but her equation of the maternal role, as well, with death and destruction.

Enoch Emery in *Wise Blood* is no less a victim of parental rejection and loss than is Hazel. Motherless, and turned out by his irresponsible father, Enoch looks for a "new Jesus," a source of nurturance, as avidly as Hazel does. Enoch finds his false god in the form of Gonga, the fake gorilla, ultimately merging with his idol in mock mystical union. In this way, Enoch identifies himself with his totem, symbolically affirming his links with his animalistic father. Hazel is not fated to find a way out of his isolation because his "Church Without Christ" contains neither Father nor Son, and its would-be prophet—Hazel—is completely alienated from himself. In the end, he destroys himself twice over; first, symbolically, by running over his double, Solace Layfield, and later, by blinding himself. Solace's dying confession, made as he lies bleeding to death on the road, is Hazel's confession, too, of filial disloyalty—a final revelation of the bad me and its inevitable punishment: "Give my mother a lot of trouble. . . . Never giver no rest. Stole theter car. Never told the truth to my daddy. . . ." Hazel will not allow the dying Solace to find "solace" when Solace wheezes, "Jesus, help me," but strikes him hard on the back, extinguishing his life. Strikingly, there is no solace anywhere in O'Connor's fictional world, where violent death is everywhere, awaiting a multitude of miscreants, whose sin is that they cannot return the love they never received from their unfeeling parents. These parents, like

Hazel's "adjusted" elderly landlady, are would-be hedonists who are afraid of death, and insist on looking at life with wide-open but unreflective eyes.

A symbiotic, conflicted relationship between the ambivalently responsive mother figure and the injured child is portrayed in the final chapter of *Wise Blood*. Hazel, having blinded himself after losing his car and his illusion of independence, is forced to live with his landlady as a helpless dependent. The composition of the last portions of *Wise Blood* coincided with the advent of O'Connor's lupus and her return to her mother as a permanent invalid. If O'Connor was trying to come to terms with her need for independence, she reveals indirectly in *Wise Blood* why this was a doomed effort. Hazel and Sabbath Hawks are two sides of the same fictional entity: a rebellious child face-to-face with an unloving mother figure in the form of Hazel's landlady. The latter, wishing to be rid of Sabbath, callously arranges for the fatherless girl to be sent to a detention home. The landlady is also heartless toward the blinded Hazel, extorting money from him, and envying his presumed ability to see "something that he couldn't get without being blind to everything else." When Hazel's cough deepens and he begins to limp (like O'Connor after steroids had weakened her pelvis), the landlady feels little compassion for him, but only wonders maliciously what might be in his head. She is an ambivalent mother figure, however, vainly trying to encourage her boarder/son to take up guitar playing, and even to preach again. She also considers the possibility of marrying him, not only to obtain his veteran's pension, but also out of concern for his failing health, and as well out of a mysterious attraction to him and the mystery he represents for her. Hazel, in turn, is rude and stand-offish, but he is also self-punishing, filling his shoes with broken glass and pebbles, and wrapping barbed wire around his chest. Is Hazel punishing himself for the murder of Solace Layfield, or is he grappling with a more basic guilt, rooted in his hatred of the bad mother as personified by the calculating landlady? As if to atone for *her* past sins, the landlady indulges his passive-aggressive dependency, preparing tasty dishes for him and hovering over him, while he eats them, making a wry face, to express his resistance.

O'Connor has created a prototypical mother-infant feeding situation in which the ambivalent mother feeds her child, half out of self-interest, and half out of exaggerated solicitude, until Hazel, the resentful child, tells her that he will henceforth eat at a diner around the corner. The landlady's eventual offer of marriage reflects her ambivalence because she had planned originally to marry Hazel and confine him to an institution, but changed her mind and decided to marry him and "keep" him. She echoes the philosophy of most of O'Connor's protagonists when she says to Hazel: "If we don't help each other, Mr. Motes, there's nobody to help us. . . . Nobody. The world is a empty place." This formulation is the opposite of O'Connor's personal philosophy, of course, and constitutes her indictment of atheistic existentialism, which she equates with ordinary nominal religiosity no less than with outright Godlessness. There is another reason, however, for O'Connor's rejection of humanism and her failure to create fictional characters who love each other or are capable of being merciful toward their fellows; it is the same reason that explains her failure to create a character who loves God—a surprising omission considering that her protagonists are often obsessed with God. I have already referred to the absence of the ego ideal, a weakness that is especially evident in the anticlimactic final chapter of *Wise Blood* following Hazel's self-mutilation, and one that points to a more terrible tragedy than his blinding. The last chapter deals with Hazel's unbearable fate as a helpless, dependent child who is in danger of losing his last shred of autonomy vis-a-vis his all-powerful landlady/mother. His response is to try to flee, ending up close to death in a ditch, and finally being killed by a policeman's gratuitous blow to the head with his billy club. Hazel's lifeless body is brought back to the landlady, who, not realizing Hazel is dead, momentarily has the satisfaction of thinking that she has him all to herself. The rebellious child has had the last word, however, because the bad mother has gained an empty victory, a suitable punishment for failing to embody the ego ideal.

After the publication of *Wise Blood*, O'Connor produced two collections of short stories, *A Good Man Is Hard to Find* (1955) and *Everything That Rises Must Converge*, which appeared posthumously in 1965. In between, she wrote her other novel, *The*

Violent Bear It Away (1960). The stories in *A Good Man Is Hard to Find* invariably depict people as cruel, insensitive, and godless. The psychopathic Misfit in the title story, for example, and the scarcely less reprehensible grandmother, both exist in an existential universe, but the Misfit, like Hazel Motes, wants "to know why it is." Dressed in a black preacher's hat like Hazel, the Misfit is driven to satanism by his inability to believe in divine transcendence, despite his yearning for some kind of absolute. The grandmother is a copy of Hazel's grandmother, a hypocrite who is concerned only with her own well-being. There is an important difference, however, between the Misfit and Hazel. The Misfit has concluded that his punishment does not fit his crime, even though he apparently has murdered his father. By contrast, Hazel punishes himself for being "unclean," and, later, for murdering his double, Solace Layfield. O'Connor has deprived the Misfit of the last vestige of a superego, whereas Hazel, a character conceived at least six years earlier, and prior to the onset of the author's illness, still retains the capacity for judging himself. This is a significant transformation and sets the tone for O'Connor's later work, Hazel and the Misfit are interchangeable, however, in their hatred of the mother figure. In fact, the Misfit shoots the manipulative grandmother at the exact moment when she reaches out to touch him. "Don't touch me!" is a recurring note in O'Connor's fiction, and points indirectly to O'Connor's self-concept as an independent "tough gal" who does not wish to accept tokens of "insincere" affection, perhaps on the assumption that people in general, like the fictional bad mother, are incapable of loving her.

In "The Life You Save May Be Your Own" (1953), O'Connor provides her readers with another encounter between a misfit, the tramp Shiftlet, and an old woman with the same unreflective but calculating mind as the grandmother in "A Good Man Is Hard to Find." Like the Misfit or Hazel Motes, Shiftlet is a man who looks for some transcendent meaning to life and, not finding it, is drawn into an anomic existence. O'Connor again makes the mother figure the object of her protagonist's wrath. "The Life You Save May Be Your Own" is another illustration of the vital connection between the fictional search for transcendence and hatred/longing for the mother, which I mentioned in my analysis of *Wise Blood*. In the ending to "The Life You Save May be Your Own," Shiftlet, having swindled the old woman out of some money, stolen her car, and abandoned her retarded daughter, tells a young hitchhiker how much he loved his angelic mother, and how sorry he feels that he left her. The hitchhiker, a young boy, answers: "You go the devil? My old woman is a flea bag and yours is a stinking pole cat!" Here O'Connor has treated the theme of ambivalence and guilt in relation to the good/bad mother in a way that suggests not only her hatred of sentimentality, but also her intense antipathy toward the bad mother.

"Good Country People" (1955) is not only a satirical portrait of a secularized, atheistic young woman, but a tract on the dangers of sex, which is equated with betrayal. The protagonist, Joy/Hulga, has a wooden leg emblematic of her deformed conscience, and this implicates her in her own betrayal. The author depicts her as no less culpable than her cynical lover, a rustic lecher who sells Bibles from door to door. Like the tramp Shiftlet in "The Life You Save May Be Your Own," Manley Pointer (did O'Connor consciously phallicize his name?), the young bible salesman, personifies the male in the role of sexual intruder. Pointer insinuates himself into a female household, impelled by ulterior motives, by masquerading as a wholesome, God-fearing country boy. Like Mrs. Trollope writing about the erotic overtones of frontier revival meetings, O'Connor has a built-in hypocrisy detector. But more important than her satirical intent is her insight into the psychology of a bitter woman. Joy/Hulga is on the surface a fiercely independent, skeptical woman who is not reconciled to her physical handicap, even though she is devoid of self-pity and does not allow herself to be slowed down by a wooden leg. O'Connor punishes Joy/Hulga for not making a private peace with God, like the reconciled hermaphrodite in "A Temple of the Holy Ghost." In stealing Joy/Hulga's wooden leg, her would-be seducer reveals to her the shattering knowledge that she is truly helpless and dependent. It is not even necessary to speak of her wooden leg as a symbolic phallus; it is a literal crutch without which all her pretensions to self-sufficiency come to naught.

Is the fictional humiliation of Joy/Hulga O'Connor's way of

reminding herself, crippled and dying, not to surrender to despair? I raise this question because Joy/Hulga, with her keen, self-critical intelligence, is similar to O'Connor, forever poised on the edge of radical doubt. Unlike her creator, Joy/Hulga cannot find refuge in religious orthodoxy, stating: "I don't have illusions. I'm one of those people who see *through* to nothing." Here is Hazel Motes all over again, without an ego ideal, and therefore incapable of faith, hope, charity, love, or heroism. Critics like Brainard Cheney[2] who declare that O'Connor's fictional victims of violence and cruelty find grace moments before death (e.g., the crass grandmother in "A Good Man Is Hard to Find"), or at the height of their humiliation, like Joy/Hulga, confound the author's impersonal eschatology with her strategy as a writer. O'Connor clearly accepts the traditional religious belief that human suffering points in an impenetrable and not-to-be-questioned divine plan—God can "write straight with crooked lines." But this is not to say that she has succeeded in creating an objective correlative for testing this belief in her fiction. On the contrary, insofar as her characters have no saving graces of their own in life, it is difficult to accept the premise that by affirming with their dying breath their belief in God's saving grace they will magically achieve salvation. It is not a question of whether one agrees or disagrees with O'Connor's theology; the issue is rather whether she has created her characters in the round, so that we can believe in the possibility of their redemption in human terms, no less than the probability of their damnation. O'Connor fails to communicate, in Tolstoy's words, "That sense of infection with another's feeling, compelling us to joy in another's gladness, to sorrow at another's grief, and to mingle souls with another—which is the very essence of art."[3] O'Connor is by no means lacking in empathy for her protagonists, including Joy/Hulga, or when she portrays children, but her strengths and weaknesses as a writer are traceable to a punitive superego. Her cruel conscience enables her to draw brilliant, scathing portraits of sinners and hypocrites, but she is devoid of love; that is, of an ego ideal based on identification with another person.

The absolute failure of a parental love object is depicted in "The Artificial Nigger" (1955). A vain boastful grandfather who is a country bumpkin, appears to momentarily abandon his equally arrogant ten-year-old grandson in the middle of a strange city they are visiting. The symbolic act of rejection takes place after the little boy has accidentally knocked a woman to the ground, causing a crowd to gather in response to her shouts. She cries out that her ankle has been broken, that she intends to make the boy's father—whoever he is—pay for her injuries, and that she wants a policeman. At this point, the frightened grandfather pulls himself away from his grandson, who has been clinging to him in desperation, declares to the hostile crowd that "I never seen him before," and walks away from the terrified child. Although grandfather and grandson are united moments later, when they are out of sight of the crowd, the child's bitter resentment is evident. Moreover, the foolish grandfather, who had tried to impress the boy with his worldliness and knowledge of city ways, is forced to admit that he is lost and cannot find the train station. That the act of abandonment was intrinsic to the grandfather's flawed character is indicated by the fact that, moments before the boy had bumped into the woman, the grandfather had hidden himself from the child's view, intending to frighten him into thinking that he was alone in the fearful city. The climax of the story consists of the grandfather and grandson's discovery of a broken lawn statue of a black, a discovery that has the effect of a mystical relevation on both of them, especially the old man: "They could both feel it dissolving their differences like an action of mercy. . . . He [the grandfather] stood appalled, judging himself with the thoroughness of God, while the action of mercy covered his pride like a flame and consumed it." O'Connor makes it clear that the grandfather's humiliation or agony has prepared him to acknowledge to himself the full extent of his sinful nature. The half-toppled, disfigured statue of the black is obviously intended as an image of the suffering Christ, an icon that has the power to evoke contrition and to heal the rift between self-centered mortals.

What is the author's intention in introducing an icon as a healing symbol in relation to a rejecting parent figure and a resentful child? O'Connor seems to be saying, perhaps unconsciously, that the only real tie between her fictional "parent" and child is a common love of God and a sense of their own helplessness: "They stood gazing at the artificial Negro as if they were faced with some great mystery, some monument to another's victory that brought them together in their common defeat." In light of the bitter adversarial relationships between young and old that are a feature of O'Connor's fiction, it can be concluded that nothing short of a miraculous gift of divine grace can breach the generation gap. Parenthetically, there is another factor at work in the author's choice of a Christ symbol; namely, her sacrificial psychology, which requires a victim as a precondition for vicarious atonement and salvation, as mentioned earlier. After all, it is not only through the humbling of the grandfather, but also through the degradation of the black, as symbolized by the crumbling statue of a black eating a watermelon, that O'Connor's whites effect a reconciliation.

We see further evidence of this mode of thinking in the ambitious story "The Displaced Person" (1954), the last story in *A Good Man Is Hard to Find* and one that is widely anthologized. This is a story that is rich in religious meanings, employing the peacock as a traditional symbol of the bread of the Holy Eucharist[4] and of divinity. The story counterposes the practical, essentially Godless self-sufficiency of Mrs. McIntyre, a portly woman who owns a large farm, with the altruism of a Catholic priest, Father Flynn. When Father Flynn arranges for Mrs. McIntyre to hire a Polish displaced person, Mr. Guizac, as her farm manager, he inavertently sets in motion a train of events that leads to the Pole's "accidental" death. The Pole had "displaced" Mrs. McIntyre's former manager, Mr. Shortley, and the latter had worked on her guilt feelings until she was ready to fire Mr. Guizac. Just as Mrs. McIntyre was about to dismiss Mr. Guizac, the refugee was accidentally run over by a tractor parked on an incline by Mr. Shortley. Although Mrs. McIntyre, Shortley, and a black farm worker had seen the tractor slide toward Mr. Guizac, no one had called out to warn him, as if they were in silent collusion to destroy him. Soon thereafter, each of the surviving characters is displaced, abandoning the farm, and Mrs. McIntyre, formerly a robust earth mother, is reduced to the status of a helpless invalid.

Critics have not failed to note that O'Connor's message is that we are all displaced persons, or sojourners, and that we do not welcome the stranger in our midst with a spirit of love. Mr. Guizac is obviously an innocent sacrificial victim, but his death does not atone for the sins of those who have injured him. In this sense, it is incorrect to speak of Mr. Guizac as a Christ figure, even though the old priest says, "He came to redeem us." If it was O'Connor's intention to portray Mr. Guizac as representative of suffering humanity, she has succeeded in her artistic aim; if her intention was to suggest that Mr. Guizac's death was redemptive, she has failed to achieve her end. Insofar as O'Connor punishes Mrs. McIntyre for her callousness by practically killing her off, it is obvious that the Pole's death is followed by divine retribution rather than redemption. More to the point, O'Connor's sacrificial psychology, with its sadistic aim, has prevented her from exploring the redemptive possibilities of her fictional situation. She has demonstrated the destructive power of those who cannot empathize with their fellows, a fine achievement in its own right, but artistically and psychologically flawed.

This one-sidedness, resulting from the weakness of the ego ideal, is given its proper demonic expression in the remaining story of *A Good Man Is Hard to Find,* namely, "A Circle in the Fire," in which three malicious boys proceed to burn down the woods belonging to a smug, Pollyanna farm woman, Mrs. Cope. Like Mrs. McIntyre, Mrs. Cope deserves to be punished for her philistinism and self-sufficiency, and, more significantly, because both women are bad mothers who have sinned against the innocent by their obduracy.

The publication of *The Violent Bear It Away* (1960), which O'Connor dedicated to her father (*Wise Blood* had been dedicated to her mother), marked a return to the central theme of *Wise Blood,* and contains echoes of "The Displaced Person." Briefly stated, *The Violent Bear It Away* chronicles a struggle of wills between a secular-minded, humanistic uncle and his rustic nephew, an orphan raised by a God-intoxicated fundamentalist great-uncle. The atheistic uncle, a widower with a retarded son of his own, tries briefly to educate his fourteen-year-old backwoods nephew after the death of the great-uncle, but the nephew rejects his help, along with his rationalist worldview. In the end, Tarwater, the fourteen-year-old boy, who earlier had burned down his great-uncle's house, drowns the retarded child, baptizing him at the same time, thereby reluctantly fulfilling his late great-uncle's fondest wish. In the final pages of the novel, following the drowning, Tarwater decides to return to his great-uncle's abandoned farm to take possession of it. He is picked up by a homosexual motorist, and after being encouraged to drink himself into unconsciousness is sexually abused. Upon regaining consciousness, the boy, realizing what has happened, makes his way to the burnt-out farm and his great-uncle's graveside. There, overcoming his religious doubts, he has a dramatic conversion experience, renews his covenant with the old man, and resolves to preach God's word in the city and to "warn the children of God of the terrible speed of mercy."

Like Hazel in *Wise Blood,* Tarwater escapes from the control of a would-be parent figure, commits an act of murder, is punished (by being raped—rather than blinding himself), and, presumably humbled, experiences a moment of grace at the very end. O'Connor even speaks of Tarwater's "singed eyes, black in their deep sockets," as if he had been seared, like Hazel. Tarwater's uncle resembles Hazel's landlady in his godlessness and egotism, masquerading as charity. He is also similar to Mrs. McIntyre in "The Displaced Person" for the same reason. Moreover, the Pole who is victimized in "The Displaced Person" is the counterpart of the retarded child who is sacrificed in *The Violent Bear It Away,* though without redemptive consequences for Mrs. McIntyre. The sequence of sin-guilt-punishment-redemption, which is the thematic substructure of most of O'Connor's fiction, corresponds to a special kind of parent-child relationship. It is a symbiotic relationship in which a self-willed but dependent child, imbued with a hunger for transcendence, acts out a scenario of would-be independence and defiance in relation to a controlling, materialistic parent, with destructive consequences.

As the years went by and O'Connor's physical condition grew worse, her fiction took an increasingly satirical form. This trend is apparent in her posthumously published collection of short stories, *Everything That Rises Must Converge.* The earliest story in this collection, "Greenleaf," was published in *Kenyon Review* in 1956. Like O'Connor's earlier stories, "Greenleaf" describes parent-child conflict, this time between an elderly woman and her two grown sons. Mrs. May, the protagonist, is a widow who manages a farm with the help of a hired man, Mr. Greenleaf, while her two bachelor sons refuse to take an interest in the farm and poke not-so-gentle fun at their mother. Her hostility toward Mr. Greenleaf and his family—poor, but ambitious Southern whites—leads her to insist that he shoot a stray bull that has wandered onto her property, even though it belongs to his sons. The result is that she is gored to death by the bull, which is then shot by Mr. Greenleaf. Although Mrs. Greenleaf's sons are not presented as admirable, O'Connor's portrait of the mother is far more damaging because, "she was a good Christian woman with a large respect for religion, though she did not, of course, believe any of it was true." The ending is unnecessarily cruel and violent and conveys the author's intense rage against the fictional mother.

To determine whether a real change had occurred in O'Connor's outlook, it is necessary to look at her story "The Comforts of Home" (1960). Unfortunately, O'Connor has reverted to her usual formula, in which a dependent, failed "child" brings disaster upon himself and death to his mother. "The Comforts of Home" describes the protracted rage of an aging bachelor who lives with his do-gooder mother and has to contend with the sudden intrusion of a promiscuous, acting-out young woman whom the mother has taken under her wing. The girl is lower-class, irresponsible, and bent on flirting with the self-righteous, panic-stricken man—a flirtation that is half-consciously promoted by the self-deceived mother. Like most of O'Connor's stories, this one ends violently when the son tries to plant his gun in the girl's handbag so that she will be arrested by the local sheriff, whom he has summoned in advance. In the resulting confrontation with the girl and his mother, the son accidentally shoots and kills his mother.

There is an obvious sexual motif in the business of putting the gun in the girl's handbag, particularly after she had taken the gun from the man's desk drawer, ostensibly as an unvoiced suicide threat. But O'Connor's main emphasis is, as usual, on the incongruity between the crass mother and her pretentious son, as well as on the ambiguous position of the dependent, threatened son. The son is threatened not only by the girl's sexual advances, but also by the challenge to his comfortable, regressive relationship to his mother. In this context, the intrusive nymphomaniac, as she is described, personifies anarchic impulse release, and is as much a projection of the man's repressed drive for independence as she is a projection of his sexuality. The man and the girl are the two sides of the author's personality, in which moral absolutism is the reciprocal of repressed rage, destructiveness, and sexuality. The man's conviction of his moral superiority reflects the author's uncompromising moral stance vis-a-vis her fictional creations. But he also embodies her ambivalence, and her partial insight into her need for dependency and emotional response. Critics have pointed to O'Connor's use of the wayward girl in this story as a symbol of absolute evil and corruption; the mother is seen for the same reason as a futile person because she attempts to redeem the girl by means of secular do-goodism. This interpretation is correct on one level, but is not sufficient because it does not account for the act of matricide. The mother is slain because she is perceived by her son—like all of O'Connor's parent figures—as a failed parent. The son, in turn, exemplifies "the terrible radical human pride that causes death."[5]

In 1961 O'Connor published "Everything That Rises Must Converge" in *New World Writing*. Again, an intellectual son, Julian —a liberal on the race issue—confronts his traditional Southern mother, who has a patronizing attitude toward blacks and clings to her frayed gentility despite her reduced circumstances. O'Connor describes the son's reaction to his mother as follows: "He felt completely detached from her: At that moment he could with pleasure have slapped her as he could have slapped a particularly obnoxious child in his charge." In a passage that brings to mind Enoch's false god, the shrunken mummy in *Wise Blood*, O'Connor says of the son: "He saw his mother across the aisle, purple-faced, shrunken to the dwarflike proportions of her moral nature, sitting like a mummy beneath the ridiculous banner of her hat." In this story, as in "The Comforts of Home," the mother dies at the end, brought low by a stroke after being assaulted by an angry black woman whom she has insulted by her patronizing behavior. At this moment, the son realizes the enormity of his guilt, based on his lack of compassion for his mother. "Everything That Rises Must Converge" concisely expresses the central drama of O'Connor's writing, which is the tension between rebellion and guilt. Hazel Motes in *Wise Blood* is Julian's prototype, a rebel against all parents who inspire resistance because of their narrowness and their wish to control, but whose shortcomings do not excuse cruelty and insensitivity on the part of their children.

"Parker's Back" (published posthumously in 1965) recounts the futile efforts of a simple man, Parker, to impress his rejecting, fundamentalist bride with his elaborate tattoos, acquired during his years in the Navy. Unable to modify her seemingly contemptuous attitude toward him, Parker resorts to a strategy of appealing to her strong religious feelings by having his back tattooed with a Byzantine image of Christ. His wife's reaction, however, is one of overwhelming anger and rejection: " 'Idolatry!' Sarah Ruth screamed. 'Idolatry! Enflaming yourself with idols under every green tree! I can put up with lies and vanity but I don't want no idolator in this house!' and she grabbed up the broom and began to thrash him across the shoulders with it." On the surface, "Parker's Back" is about a conflict-ridden husband-wife relationship involving two poor, uneducated Southern whites. A closer look reveals the asymmetry of the relationship, in which the wife is a dominant, ungiving, judgmental parent figure in relation to her infantile, emotionally dependent husband, whose tattoos are like a child's drawings designed to please a severe parent. The wife is depicted as homely and sexless, but she is pregnant, indicating her role as a mother figure. Thus, this story is a thinly disguised account of a child's pathetic effort to win over an unyielding parent, a harsh mother whose moralistic stance is the antithesis of the child's innate longing for spirituality. Parker's spiritual destiny is revealed by his first and middle names, Obadiah Elihue, or Servant of God, which had attracted his wife to him initially. She, in turn, is characterized by her witchlike association with her broom. The parent figure is simultaneously adamant on the level of religious dogma and inaccessible as a love object. "Parker's Back" confirms the meaning of transcendence in O'Connor's fiction: the child's search for revelation or for a transcending experience is a cry for love. The spiritual quest is also marked by destructive rage at the rejecting and spiritually dead parent, usually the mother.

The struggle for liberation from a dominant mother figure by a dependent and objectively helpless child figure is an important key to O'Connor's fiction and explains the symbolic meaning of the peacock for O'Connor, a meaning that is as much idiosyncratic as it is universal and religious, as is revealed by the following passage from the autobiographical essay "King of the Birds" in *Mystery and Manners:* "From the beginning relations between these birds and my mother were strained."[6] O'Connor then goes on to relate how her peacocks ate her mother's flowers, her uncle's figs, her dairyman's peanuts, and his wife's garden vegetables. The peacocks were apparently a perpetual nuisance to everyone on the O'Connor farm, shedding their feathers everywhere, and bending the fence posts and gates by sitting on them. O'Connor's attitude is summed up as follows: "I intend to stand firm and let the peacocks multiply, for I am sure that, in the end, the last word will be theirs."[7]

Evidently, the peacock was O'Connor's symbol and vehicle of rebellion and retribution. The stubbornness and splendid pride of these arrogant birds, described as not budging an inch in the face of an oncoming truck, undoubtedly appealed to O'Connor. The independent peacock, like O'Connor's stories of destructive but divinely inspired rebel "children," were her weapons against her long night of physical suffering and dependency. Like her gothic tales of Southern grotesques, O'Connor's peacocks stand as symbols of a spiritual quest for beauty and transcendence, but like the stories, they also symbolize the condition of isolation and the absence of human love. Would O'Connor have written about love and intimacy if she had not become chronically ill? I do not think so, but she would have had less reason to turn her fictional protagonists loose in search of vengeance against a cruel world. And she would not have lived in fear that her mother would die before her, thereby jeopardizing her dependency, and perhaps threatening to bring to the surface her dreaded ambivalence.

Chapter 6

TENNESSEE WILLIAMS

The Incest Motif and Fictional Love Relationships

The dramatic works of Tennessee Williams provide a number of insights into the interplay of oedipal and preoedipal motifs in life and art. Williams created a memorable gallery of doomed, rebellious oedipal sons, and sons attached symbiotically to their destructive mothers.[1] His female protagonists combine the roles of mother and mistress, as well as the roles of earth mother and vestal virgin. Williams' treatment of homosexuality reveals many fictional disguises as well as the playwright's strategy of raising homosexuality to the level of a metaphor for ideal love. The sources of Williams' oedipal themes are to be found in his relationship with his father and mother and in his partial identification with his schizophrenic sister, as I will try to demonstrate. Another important influence is seen in the writings of D. H. Lawrence, whose misogynous views reinforced Williams' perception of women as dangerous and destructive. Unlike Lawrence, who equated the female principle with false spirituality and antisex, Williams vacillated between viewing the female principle as destructive or as the last remaining expression of innocence and romantic idealism in an unfeeling world.

Williams' ambivalence toward women is one of the powerful

motivating forces behind his drama. His acceptance of his own femininity from an early age provides some understanding of Williams' ability to empathize with female vulnerability in a male-dominated world. This is not to say that Williams had a profound grasp of the problems faced by women, but rather that his identification with women enabled him, at times, to defend simultaneously the dignity of women and the nobility of the spiritual ideal. Williams' affinity for idealism is all the more paradoxical in light of his sensational use of sex and violence in his plays, and is consistent with the concept of splitting, based on the assumption that the good-mother imago may become split off from the bad-mother imago during early ego development.[2] Williams' melodramatic devices reflect the intensity of his inner conflicts, in which sex is equated either with violence against the oedipal mother of with fatal risk for the guilty oedipal son. In addition, preoedipal derivatives shape the characterizations and actions in Williams' plays and are expressive of the protagonists' frustrated infantile dependency needs. Thus Williams can give us only weak, affect-hungry antiheroes in search of the good mother/mistress. The mother, in turn, fails her son/lover either because she is too weak to protect him from the powerful father or because she cannot fulfill his regressive needs.

Williams' own family constellation consisted, as we will see, of an overprotective mother and a threatening, rejecting father. Williams' development took the form of alternation between symbolic acting out of infantile dependency needs through alcohol and drug dependency, and more direct acting out of homosexual needs. Incestuous wishes and fear-ridden attempts to avoid their punitive consequences were deflected into "safe" homosexual channels. Like Williams, because of their dependency needs, his fictional characters are unable to tolerate the idea of psychological separaton from love objects.[3] They project incestuous and sadistic fantasies onto love objects and act out regressive, pansexual needs in which incorporation of the object is obsessively linked with fantasies of castration and death. Williams' protagonists are usually self-destructive for the same reasons as Williams: They are under pressure from a primitive, retaliatory superego formed under the condition of oedipal rivalry and deformed by excessive guilt. I will try to show that

Williams' protagonists function neurotically for the same reasons as Williams, namely because their unresolved oedipal and preoedipal attachments, intensified by punitive superego demands, create guilt-induced inhibitions and conflicts.

Unlike his fictional characters, Williams was able to transmute his pathology into art. He was able to communicate with his audiences using symbols that were based on his fixations and obsessions, and he was usually able to avoid being swamped by the regressive or destructive contents of his fantasies. Moreover, Williams came to his artistic task well prepared, having devoted his seclusive childhood to eager but selective reading, followed by years of apprenticeship in the craft of theater as a writer, actor, stagehand, and so forth. His gift of eloquence and poetic lyricism may or may not have been linked with his emotional difficulties; its source remains uncertain. It is noteworthy that Williams underwent psychoanalysis and came to be familiar with Freudian concepts, a circumstance that added poignancy to his artistic handling of his overdetermined needs. In effect Williams—a dramatist of great eloquence and evocative power—succeeded in educating a worldwide audience concerning some of the truths of depth psychology. His way of treating normally repressed materials anticipated the theater of the absurd and much of the experimental theater of the 1960s and 1970s in which sexual and aggressive themes are treated openly. Yet Williams stands in marked contrast to some of the more recent trends in theater or films because of his almost old-fashioned attempts to deal with the symbolic disguises for sex and aggression. These disguises conceal fictional defense mechanisms of a classical type, in which oedipal guilt feelings give rise variously to self-destructive behavior, doomed love relationships, and flight into homosexuality.

In Williams' case, oedipal fears are best understood within the context of a generalized phobic attitude toward the world. For example, as a sickly child who was often kept out of school for long periods, Williams came to regard himself as a frail and vulnerable individual. He was constantly abused by other children and called a "sissy" from his first days in school. When Williams was eight, his father, a noisy, hard-drinking, card-playing traveling salesman, finally moved in with the family on a full-time basis. This move was the result of the father's promotion to the rank of sales manager for the shoe company that he had represented on the road. The father rejected his son, calling him "Miss Nancy" because of his obvious effeminacy, the result of many years of overprotection by Williams' anxious mother, the puritanical daughter of a liberal Episcopal minister. The affectionate and intellectually stimulating maternal grandfather provided a measure of security and family pride for the young Williams during his childhood years in small-town Mississippi. After the age of eight, Williams, now removed with his family to a working-class neighborhood in St. Louis, lived in an unfamiliar and frightening urban environment.

In St. Louis, Williams was the constant butt of ridicule by other boys, whom he learned to avoid whenever possible. Williams' sister Rose, one year his senior, shared the boy's phobic existence. The two children spent long hours daily in Rose's room, the shades drawn to shut out an ugly dead-end alley filled with noisy cats and a vicious dog that periodically would tear one of the cats to pieces directly under their window. To blot out the harse reality of the outside world, Williams became a voracious reader and began to write stories—often filled with violence and death—at an early age; Rose, who was less resourceful, became schizophrenic in her teens. Williams remained very close to his sister during the years that she was gradually becoming increasingly detached from reality and empathized with her mounting terror. A younger brother, Dakin, did not figure prominently in Williams' childhood and was to remain a remote presence in Williams' life, trying vainly in later years to help a resentful Williams overcome his alcoholism through treatment.

Although Williams' father eventually came to accept his son's writing activities half-grudgingly, especially when the young Williams began to sell his stories to magazines, the elder Williams did not conceal his distaste for his son's literary interests. As Williams relates in his *Memoirs*,[4] the breach between the crude, dominating father and his frightened, inadequate son was never healed, but Williams came to "understand" his father long after the latter's death. Unable to identify himself with his father and to draw upon his strength Williams settled into a withdrawn, phobic style of life. Even in high school Williams found it difficult to talk to people or to make friends, except for a girl named Hazel Kramer who apparently appreciated his qualities of sensitivity and intelligence. Williams found an outlet for expressing his feelings of loneliness and inward rebellion by writing poetry, modeling his efforts on the works of Edna St. Vincent Millay. The fusion of almost unbearable self-consciousness with fear and hatred of his father (freely avowed in later years) culminated in an obsessive, lifelong fear of death expressed through hypochondriacal concerns centering on his heart, which Williams was afraid would stop at any moment. Possibly these symptoms, beginning in adolescence, represented a guilty turning inward of Williams' death wish toward his father.

Later, as a college student at the University of Missouri, Williams began to come out of his shell and even became a fraternity member, but drank heavily to overcome his shyness. He also began to be attracted to homosexual relationships, as he relates in his *Memoirs*. Williams' high school girlfriend Hazel had been prepared to join him at the University of Missouri, but instead was sent by her family to a distant university at the instigation of Williams' father, thereby terminating the relationship. The most likely explanation for the father's interference is that he feared his son would marry Hazel, who came from a humble background. Unconsciously, perhaps the father wished to punish his disappointing son. There can be little doubt that Williams' father continued to be angry at him, withdrawing him from the university in Williams' third year after he failed ROTC.

The young Williams was to spend three years working as a clerk at the shoe factory where his father was a sales executive. During these years of monotonous and depressing work Williams continued to write short stories and poems but met with little literary success. He eventually completed college at the University of Iowa, assisted financially by his maternal grandmother. Williams was now twenty-seven years old and had gained considerable experience writing for an amateur theatrical group, the Mummers, in St. Louis, and through his activities as a drama major. Williams' goal was to become a professional writer; he had already developed the scenario for his future lifestyle, which was to consist of a blend of bohemianism and intense commitment to serious writing. The oedipal themes that were to dominate Williams' later works were evident in his early plays, which also reflected the social protest movement of the 1930s. An early example of this trend is provided by the one-act play *Twenty-Seven Wagons Full of Cotton*, which was to become the basis of the movie *Baby Doll*. "Twenty-Seven Wagons Full of Cotton" deals with the seduction of a large woman by a small man who is intent upon obtaining revenge against her sadistic, plantation-owning husband, the arsonist responsible for the destruction of his cotton gin.

With the notable exception of the semiautobiographical *The Glass Menagerie*, Williams' first successful full-length play (1945), almost all of Williams' dramatic output deals with the romantic, Lawrencean theme of rebellion against a destructive, puritanical social order. The outlines of this theme—the philosophical analogue of the more personal oedipal motif—are strikingly revealed in the earlier play *Battle of Angels*, later produced as *Orpheus Descending*. When *Battle of Angels* was shown in Boston in 1941 it lasted only one night, the audience walking out en masse, infuriated by the play's glorification of illicit sex and its sacrilegious tone. This play, which Williams considered better than *The Glass Menagerie* (generally regarded as his masterpiece), contains the essentials of Williams' thematic content. Williams presents a love triangle involving a cruel, dying old man, his beautiful young wife, and her handsome young lover. In the end the lovers are slain by the old man. In addition to being a parable of unsuccessful oedipal rebellion, *Battle of Angels* casts the oedipal "son" as a life-affirming, idealistic figure, but one who loses his life in the service of the pleasure principle. The character of the old man, impotently thumping his cane on the floor while his young wife and her lover embrace in the room below, is presented as that of a wrathful father figure who is antilife and antisex. Characters such as these, unabashedly archetypal, were to people almost all of Williams' plays and stories.

Although *Battle of Angels* is typical of Williams' work (even though it is less polished than are his later works), *The Glass Menagerie* provides important insights into a side of Williams' creative self that is often obscured by his penchant for melodrama, violence, and futile rebellion. This play is dominated by affect hunger but pits the need for human closeness against the impulse to cut oneself loose from emotional commitments of any sort, and particularly commitments that threaten to destroy the hope of freedom and escape from a sordid existence. *The Glass Menagerie* is clearly based on Williams' relationships with his mother and with his sister Rose. Like the young Williams, Tom, the protagonist (Thomas was Williams' real name) feels trapped in a no-exit life situation that consists of working in a shoe factory and supporting his erstwhile Southern belle mother and his sister, Laura, who wears a steel brace on one leg due to a childhood illness. The play ends on a tragic note, with Laura resigned to a loveless existence and Tom ready to run off like his footloose father.

The Glass Menagerie reveals an author who is capable of dealing with object relations without allowing his narcissistic needs to dull his sensibilities. Even though this play is presented as a remembrance of his youth by Tom and therefore has a dreamlike, static quality, Williams develops his characters with great insight and compassion, so that their anguish seems real. Williams is also able to control his weakness for using symbols needlessly, with the result that his characters are truly concrete individuals. The author's usual preoccupations are not in evidence, permitting *The Glass Menagerie* to unfold without the elaborate machinery of acting-out-and-retribution that turns *Battle of Angels* and other Williams plays into melodrama. In depicting Laura, Williams also provides one of his many sympathetic portraits of life's victims. Even the mother, despite her hysterical behavior and self-dramatization, emerges as a woman who has the strength and courage to face the truth about her blighted life. By creating these characters from life, Williams avoided the pitfall of self-absorption. In later plays Williams often succeeded in depicting lost souls, wounded by circumstances and above all by self-inflicted injuries. But these later characters are shown as grotesques—prostitutes, mutilated men, pyromaniacs, psychotics—and pariahs. Even though these gothic characters are based on real people Williams knew during his many years of poverty and obscurity in New Orleans and other cities, they are best understood as personifications of the author's fears. Like Laura's glass unicorn, their symbolic horn has been broken off; this is how we know they stand for Williams himself rather than his fellow suffers.

If *The Glass Menagerie* possesses psychological validity it is because Williams has told the story of his family with candor, entering the inner lives of his unhappy mother and terrified sister not as a bold explorer of the psyche but as a son and brother. Such plays as *A Streetcar Named Desire, Cat on a Hot Tin Roof,* or *Night of the Iguana* also convey important psychological truths, but the raw materials employed by the playwright are more difficult to manage. The forces that Williams releases on the stage in these and other powerful dramas are personifications of maternal and other introjections, but do not correspond to real people. The decadent Blanche of *A Streetcar Named Desire,* for example, is Williams himself in the capacity of mother-identified temptress, victim of sexual trauma, and fantasy-ridden escape artist. Like Williams, Blanche is drawn toward degradation and simultaneously revolted by the sordidness of life. Her love relationships are exercises in self-debasement. It is true that the brutal Stanley symbolizes barbarism, but he is also the frightening father figure who completes the humiliation of the pretentious, self-centered mother by raping her. Blanche, in turn, is an incestuous mother figure who seduces the newsboy who comes to her door. Her sister Stella, who has turned her back on her patrician past, surrendering voluntarily to the overpowering Stanley, is the other half of the introjected mother figure, the mother who betrays her oedipal son by giving herself completely to the dreaded father.

The oedipal son in *A Streetcar Named Desire* has two personas. He is the homosexual youth Blanche had once been married to, and for whose suicide she feels in part to blame; he is also Mitch, the mama's boy who adores Blanche because, in his eyes, she stands for spiritual beauty and everything genteel. Mitch represents the author's conscious, sublimated attitude toward his own mother, but the homosexual youth who could not satisfy Blanche sexually embodies Williams' unconscious attitude. In this way the incest motif is raised to the level of art by the imaginative act of personifying its dangers no less than its repression-based ideal of feminine purity.

Maternal introjects are handled in an analogous manner in several other plays. In *Cat on a Hot Tin Roof,* a rich, powerful father, Big Daddy, confronts his alcoholic son, Brick, with the implications of his destructive style of life. Brick's problems are traceable to his fear of homosexuality. Also contributing to his difficulties are his wife, Maggie, who drove his best friend Skipper to suicide, and his devious, materialistic brother, Gooper, whom the father rejects along with Gooper's grasping wife Mae.

Skipper, Brick, and the rejected brother Gooper may be seen as facets of the same syncretic son. Brick and Skipper represent maternal introjects because of their repressed homosexuality, which provides the principal theme of the play. Gooper denotes the son who cannot hope to please his father even though he has demonstrated his virility by siring many children. By contrast, Brick, the hard-drinking, outwardly macho football star, closely approximates the father's ideal of a real man. The composite of Brick, Skipper, and Gooper signifies for Williams the-son-that-might-have-been—ahtletic, at home in the world of men, and sexually active—no less than it also signifies the son that Williams actually became—homosexual and devoted to effete interests such as drama and poetry.

Maternal introjects are projected onto the good mother Big Mama, who loves her husband and children; the more ambivalent attitudes are personified by the adulterous but loving Maggie and the mercenary Mae. In this play Williams characteristically separates the good mother from the bad in a way that denotes pathological splitting, but also reveals that he is capable of internalization[5] in his positive treatment of Big Daddy. *Cat on a Hot Tin Roof,* seen as a realistic drama, owes much of its warmth and vitality to Williams' temporary intrapsychic reorganization on a relatively mature level. The word *temporary* seems appropriate because Williams' subsequent plays indicate a disintegrative process in which an infantile introjective organization is reinstated. The ambivalent portrait of Maggie points to a nuclear conflict that remains unresolved. This conflict centers around a mother figure who, like Maggie, seduces an oedipal son, Skipper, in order to unman him.

Williams was aware that he suffered from inner conflicts

and possessed partial insight into his difficulties. His symptoms included increasingly severe hypochondriacal and phobic reactions, as well as alcohol and drug abuse. By now—the late 1950s—Williams' style of life as a homosexual had been well established for many years. This lifestyle was based not only on a few long-standing relationships but also on a compulsion to pick up male prostitutes, including young street boys. Against this background, Williams' next major play *Suddenly Last Summer* (1960) became the vehicle for expressing mounting superego pressures. The play was written at about the time Williams entered into analysis with Dr. Lawrence Kubie.

Suddenly Last Summer is about an idle, pleasure-seeking homosexual of forty, Sebastian, who has long used his attractive, widowed mother to unwittingly lure beachboys whom he has then exploited sexually. When the mother suffers a stroke, Sebastian uses his cousin Catherine for the same purpose. In the end, Sebastian meets a grisly death when he is pursued by a band of street children and partially devoured by them. Once more we see a protagonist whose sense of self is based on identification with his mother. But Sebastian's narcissism has suffered an unexpected fatal wound with the collapse of his mother, his alter ego. The threat to the integrity of the infantile, dependent self drives Sebastian to use a young woman as his alter ego. The need for this substitution, and its failure, point up Sebastian's difficulties insofar as neither Catherine nor anyone else can serve as an object for internalization. Sebastian is brought face-to-face with his regressed, vulnerable self without the ego support once provided by his mother. This sudden, terrifying self-experience, in some ways resembling depersonalization, leads to paranoid flight occasioned by the involuntary release of defensive projections. Although Williams saw this drama as a morality play in which Sebastian suffers retribution at the hands of his erstwhile victims, *Suddenly Last Summer* is also an unconscious drama of maternal abandonment or ego loss and its feared consequences in the form of annihilation. The play provides insight into the intensity of Williams' guilt-induced aggressive feelings. Williams had always though of himself as an idealist and a compassionate man. Nevertheless, he lacked the ego strength to resist giving in to his sexual compulsions, often at the expense of homeless street children, as he candidly reports in his *Memoirs*.

Tennessee Williams was beginning to break off his one-year analysis when he wrote *Sweet Bird of Youth*, a play that is at least as violent as *Suddenly Last Summer*, and which, in a manner reminiscent of the early *Battle of Angels*, deals with oedipal rivalry. *Sweet Bird of Youth* is about an oedipal loser, Wayne Chance, who has infected his girl, Heavenly, with venereal disease, while sponging money off his aging, dissipated, and sexually demanding mistress/employer, Alexandra. The unforgivable sin of the male protagonist in *Sweet Bird of Youth* is not having infected Heavenly, but is rather his incestuous relationship with a mother substitute, Alexandra. For this offense, the parasitical son is castrated by the dangerous and powerful "father," Boss Finley. Chance's love affair with Heavenly is an impossible hetersexual relationship, given Williams difficulty in creating characters capable of true object involvement. The figure of Alexandra is that of a bad mother who threatens to abandon her son to the castrating father if the son refuses to become her slave. But Chance, the exhibitionist and would-be extortionist, has introjected not only the bad mother but also the grandiose, omnipotent mother. Williams has remarked about himself that he often experienced feelings of "infantile omnipotence," and it is such feelings that produce the pathogenic narcissism of Chance Wayne and other Williams protagonists, not unlike some of the borderline patients described by Kernberg.[6]

These unrealistic and inadequate protagonists relate to other people by alternating between rhetorical, fantasy-ridden self-dramatization and demanding, infantile attitudes. When they are cast as males they are destroyed when they are abandoned by their magically powerful incestuous mothers; cast as women they are undone when their magical powers of illusion are taken away from them by the force of circumstance. Thus Williams' male characters live off the borrowed narcissism of their seductive mothers, whereas his females must draw on their own psychic resources, which are quickly exhausted when tested by reality.

It is because Williams' protagonists fear maternal abandonment or the loss of magical omnipotence in their love relationships that they are terrified of the future. In this respect they resemble Williams, who was unable to build an enduring love relationship with anyone, and who was fearful of the future in a more general sense, continuing to write compulsively to earn enough to provide for his old age even when he had become a multimillionaire. Having forfeited the future, Williams' protagonists are obliged to imagine a glorious past to sustain themselves. This tendency is shown even in early short stories by Mrs. Hardwicke-Moore, the genteel prostitute of "The Lady of Larkspur," or old Charlie Colton of "The Last of My Solid Gold Watches." The impulse toward regression is especially strong in Williams' characters because the future holds only the promise of psychosis, as in the case of Blanche in *Streetcar Named Desire,* or annihilation, as in the case of Chance in *Sweet Bird of Youth.* Such individuals have a choice between the infantile omnipotence of their past or the victimization of the present. As a consequence they are in no position to shape their future, which they face in complete helplessness.

As if the present moment were not disastrous enough for Williams' characters, he drives them toward an apocalyptic future presided over by the ghosts of the evil past. The result can take the form of guilty hallucinations, as in the case of Miss Collins in the story "Portrait of a Madonna," or guilt-based sexual inhibitions, as in the case of George, the reluctant bridegroom in *Period of Adjustment.* When Williams' characters try to revive the past as a hedge against the future they stir up forgotten memories and desires. These instinctual derivatives produce depression even as they revive old ghosts and give them one last chance to be exorcised. By attempting to relive the past, Williams' characters only make matters worse for themselves, reviving feelings of inferiority that break through into consciousness despite attempts at grandiosity and retrospective falsification. These feelings can only be put to rest in Williams' canon by the intervention of death. Unlike the tragic heroes of traditional dramas who must die because they are vulnerable, despite their indifference to pain, Williams' protagonists must die from the burden of reliving too much pain, still reaching for love relationships that have evaded them in the past.

In general, Williams is not concerned with finding a psychological resolution to the problems raised by unsatisfactory love relationships. Instead, he allows his characters to act out their regressive, deadly impulses, and then presents them to us on the eve of their execution. In *The Purification,* a short play reminiscent of Federico Garcia Lorca's *The House of Bernarda Alba,* Williams recounts an incestuous relationship between a brother and a sister, and clears the air by means of a retributive ax-murder and a double suicide. In this way, Williams' characters gratify their id impulses and are punished automatically, but the punishment is no more rational than the offense because it is mandated by a primitive superego. A similar pattern of acting out followed by punishment is seen in several other early one-act plays. In *Auto-Da-Fé,* a sexually frustrated bachelor immolates himself as a punishment for allowing his sexual curiosity to overflow into action. In *Hellow from Bertha* and *This Property is Condemned,* Williams gives us a brief retrospective account of a woman's life as a prostitute and focuses the dramatic action on the destructive consequences of dissolute living.

It is important, however, not to be misled by the motif of punishment. Although Williams' characters usually come to a bad end or come close to it as a result of acting out their libidinous impulses, Williams is invariably on their side. His cry is, "Let them be what their nature leads them to be!" In this sense, *Twenty-Seven Wagons Full of Cotton,* the prototype of the full-length play *Battle of Angels,* sets the tone for the bulk of Williams' work, though appearing to stand out as an isolated example of unpunished impulse release (in contrast to *Battle of Angels,* where the protagonist is lynched). Williams usually punishes his fictional sinners but he is never a moralist. Instead, he is a confessor with great compassion for human weakness, which he freely admits to finding in extraordinary measure in himself. If Williams appears to be in favor of sinners, it is because he regards them as tragic culture heroes of a sort who have the courage of D. H. Lawrence's convictions. Williams shows us that though they are too weak to gratify their desires guiltlessly they are too strong to surrender to convention shamelessly. He shows us sinners who are rarely cruel or selfish and whose only crime is the choice of an inappropriate narcissistic love object, which in turn leads to their degradation.

Although Williams sides with sinners he is also puritanical—and his ambivalence leads him to create characters who equate sex with degradation. Even such a phallic hero as John in *Summer and Smoke* has a tendency to regard sex as unworthy of a decent woman. Despite Williams' effort to make the spinsterish protagonist Alma the advocate of spiritual love, it is John's view of sex as lust that is built into most of Williams' plays. In part, this equation has oedipal, incestuous roots, for example, since John "matures" and prepares to settle down only after the violent death of his cane-wielding father. In another sense, the identification of sex with lust is a natural product of Williams' exploration of the mores of a particular social stratum in an identifiable social and cultural context. Williams sings the swan song of once-repressed, genteel middle-class people who are in the process of being vulgarized/liberated by the leveling influences of our time. They are being told by Williams that romantic, sublimated love is an impossibility and that sex is sex, just as greed is greed and cruelty is cruelty. The old repression-based euphemisms and idealizations have become inoperative, leaving Williams' protagonists, as well as his audiences, with no choice but to face the inescapable and to accept it without falsifying its essential content.

Apart from his treatment of sexual acting out and its fearful outcome, Williams explores a fear that is akin to the fear of punishment. I refer to the fear of failure in love relationships. Williams' characters are always glimpsed in the aftermath of ruined relationships. They are through with life and life is through with them. They are failures by necessity; they have willed their failure in love, in their careers, or in their lofty aspirations. And yet they are afraid of the regressive choice they have made. Shannon, the defrocked Episcopal priest in the play version of *The Night of the Iguana,* has long been under the domination of the death wish, and has edged steadily closer to his doom, but with fear and trembling, and much sweating. He is not afraid of death as much as he dreads the destruction of his remaining illusions about himself, which would lead to the complete loss of his human dignity. What Williams speaks of as human pride and dignity may also be viewed on another level as wholeness or identity. Williams' failing protagonists fear the disintegration of ego functions and the diminution of a sense of selfhood already weakened by too many past humiliations. Williams' strategy as a dramatist is to give his narcissistic characters permission to regress until they lose ego control and are overtaken by powerful drive derivatives that produce traumatic anxiety. In this process their love relationships disintegrate with the fragmentation of their identity as would-be adults.

Williams' drama is, par excellence, a drama of extreme situations, and his characters are driven by inner need to confront the crises of life with extreme reactions. Their behavior corresponds to the workings of id impulses that have broken away from the restraints of the ego and have been reinforced by the promptings of a cruel superego. Seen on the stage, Williams' characters personify normally unconscious fears and desires rather than fully realized, many-sided human beings capable of joy and sadness, work and responsibility, nurturance and altruism. Does this make them any less real? If Williams' characters do not behave like people who are in realistic contact with the external world it is because they exist outside the universe defined by social norms. They value their world of inner experience even though it prevents them from testing reality and leads them toward destruction. If Williams' desperate characters, their eyes turned inward, express themselves melodramatically, perhaps it is because life itself, beneath the surface, is melodramatic and we have only succeeded in repressing the chaos of existence.

Chapter 7

JOHN CHEEVER

Situation Normal—Desperate

Heinz Kohut[1] has argued that the artist succeeds through his craft in transforming archaic and essentially asocial narcissistic conflicts into consensually validated works. The symbolic representation of such conflicts through artistic activity is seen as an alternative to acting out (including addictive behavior). For John Cheever, as I will try to show, narcissism—based on the early withdrawal of parental empathy—served as a stimulus to wish fulfillment as well as phobic fantasies, which he crafted into fiction of great poignancy and beauty. When Cheever's powers of transformation failed him, however, he sought the soothing effects of alcohol and drugs, all but destroying himself in an effort to apply balm to his narcissistic wounds.

Narcissistic motifs highlight Cheever's strengths, as well as his weaknesses as a writer. The sources of these motifs are recognizable in the special features of Cheever's life, as described in Susan Cheever's[2] biography of her father John. Evidently, the emotional distance that Cheever's parents established from him, and to a lesser extent, his older brother Fred, left Cheever with an enduring preoccupation with the impermanence of supportive parent figures, a theme that is prominent in his fiction. On a more abstract level, one of Cheever's important themes is the fragility of the home and the community in the face of destructive forces released by the individual. These forces—essentially uncontrolled, projected id impulses—alienate the individual and produce a maleveolent transformation of the community.

A second circumstance of Cheever's life was the sudden and permanent psychological collapse of his father as a result of financial failure when Cheever was in his teens. Cheever's father had been the affluent part-owner of a New England shoe factory, but had sold out his interest in the mill to speculate on the stock market in the 1920s. When the father was ruined, he became alcoholic, the family lost its large, impressive home, and Cheever's mother was obliged to open a gift shop to support the family. Cheever never got over this reversal of the family fortunes. His fiction reveals an unusual preoccupation with grandiose lifestyles and palatial settings. The special meaning of this concern is found in Cheever's inability to invest his luxurious settings with permanence, or even dignity. In Cheever's fiction, everything is shabby around the edges and every seemingly solid structure rests on a precarious foundation. Insofar as Cheever's protagonists define their identity contextually, their destiny is linked to the impermanence of their stage settings.

In a very real sense, then, the search for self against an illusory, insubstantial background is the heart of Cheever's effort as a writer of fiction. This search presupposes a poorly structured self, resulting from early narcissistic injury. The vicissitudes of the self in Cheever's fiction, as we will see, are profoundly affected by the persistence of narcissistic self-objects, with the result that intimate human relationships are never fully achieved in Cheever's fiction, a defect that I will return to at a later point. Much of Cheever's creative energy is directed toward an attempt to reconstruct the process by which relationships either failed to crystallize or fell apart after a tentative beginning.

Another feature of Cheever's life that is intimately linked with his fantasy themes is his addictive behavior involving alcohol, drugs, and sex, including bisexuality. Outwardly a much-respected, conventional family man and the father of three children, Cheever was also an alcoholic and sometime drug addict. His marriage of over forty years was marred by numerous infidelities, including homosexual realtionships, particularly in his later years. These circumstances are reflected in Cheever's exploration of the secret lives of proper suburbanites and upper-middle-class urbanites, whose outward existence provides few clues to their obsessions and guilt-laden compulsions.

This contrast between appearance and underlying reality is one of Cheever's basic concerns as a writer. Cheever is a master of lyrical prose when describing the tranquil but unreal surface of life, with only a hint of his satirical purpose. The inner life of Cheever's driven characters provides a counterpoint to his celebration of life and his depiction of peaceful communities menaced by the fears and insecurities of their inhabitants. As I will try to demonstrate, Cheever undertakes to resolve the contradiction between his wish for a secure world and his profound lack of trust by plunging his fictional characters into impulse release, the effect of which is to test the durability of the social fabric. Acting out by Cheever's characters also tests the limits of endurance of fictional husbands, wives, lovers, and children. When Cheever's erring protagonists cross a certain line, they either destroy their love objects or provoke retribution by their victims or by malevolent fate. In real life, too, Cheever repeatedly exceeded the limits of toleration by his family, eliciting scorn and rejection from his wife and children.

Of Cheever's early life, his daughter reports an inauspicious beginning, stating that his parents had not wanted another child: "His conception was a drunken accident between two people who no longer cared about each other. When his mother found out that she was pregnant, his father had tried to force her to have an abortion."[3] Little is known about Cheever's childhood and adolescence. In his junior year of high school Cheever was expelled from Thayer Academy for reasons that are not clear. He had evidently made up his mind to become a writer by this time and published his first short story "Expelled" in *The New Republic* about a year later, in 1930, when he was eighteen. Cheever moved to New York and became a protege of Malcolm Cowley at *The New Republic*. Cheever subsequently

became a member of the Yaddo writer's group at Saratoga
Springs, serving as an unofficial assistant to its director,
Elizabeth Ames. During the 1930s he was admitted to the inner
circle of writers for the *New Yorker*, publishing many short stories
and establishing a modest reputation as an up-and-coming
writer. Cheever married in 1941, but the marriage was a
troubled one almost from the start, interrupted by Cheever's
military service and marred by his heavy drinking. Frequently
on the verge of divorce, Cheever and his wife nevertheless
stayed together nominally until his death in 1982. Cheever
attained literary fame with the publication of *The Wapshot
Chronicle*, for which he was granted the National Book Award in
1958. Following this success, Cheever purchased an estate in
Ossining, New York. His daughter observes that Cheever was
never comfortable among his suburban friends and neighbors
and felt like an outsider. After Cheever acquired his house,
Susan Cheever reports that "his anxiety equalled his euphoria.
For years he roamed the house at night, convinced that it was
about to burn down, or break down somehow, or just vanish into
thin air."[4]

Cheever's subsequent literary career was uneven. Following
the appearance of *The Wapshot Chronicle*[5] in 1957, Cheever
published a collection of suburban stories titled *The Housebreaker
of Shady Hill* in 1959 and a second collection, *Some People, Places,
and Things That Will Not Appear in My Next Novel* in 1961.
Although these stories were well received, they did not add
appreciably to Cheever's reputation. In 1964, Cheever's second
novel *The Wapshot Scandal*[6] was published and helped establish
him as a major literary figure, earning the William Dean Howells
Medal among other honors. Cheever's reputation suffered a
major setback when critics attacked his third novel *Bullet Park*,[7]
published in 1969. Cheever's heavy drinking, smoking, and use
of drugs increased and he resorted to travel and extramarital
affairs. In 1971 Cheever taught writing for a year to inmates at
the Ossining Correctional Facility, apparently identifying himself closely with the prisoners. With the publication of *The World
of Apples*, another collection of stories, Cheever was once again
praised by critics. He suffered a heart attack in 1973, accompanied by delusions that he was in a Russian prison camp

and was being made to sign a confession. Cheever recovered quickly and continued to live a rather dissolute, wandering existence as a guest instructor at the University of Iowa and at Boston University. By 1974, Cheever's alcoholism had reached a critical point and he was hospitalized for several months. Cheever quit drinking the following year, began to attend religious services at his Episcopalian church, and in 1977 published *Falconer*,[8] a novel of prison life. In 1978 Cheever achieved his greatest success with the appearance of *The Stories of John Cheever*,[9] which won the Pulitzer Prize and the National Book Critics Circle Award. Cheever's last work, a novelette titled *Oh What A Paradise It Seems* (1982)[10] was respectfully reviewed on the front page of the New York Times Book Section. Cheever died in 1982, rich, famous, and widely admired.

A chronological approach to Cheever's fiction reveals surprisingly little progression, either in his characterizations or choice of themes. Cheever the writer is very much like his fictional characters who move around randomly on a chessboard, checkmated in the end because they have been forced to act out self-defeating scenarios or because they are trapped by obsessions rooted in their past. These characters reflect Cheever's passivity and feelings of vulnerability in the face of a world that is beyond control. Only the past, falsified beyond recognition, is safe because it is manageable and its images can be evoked selectively in the interest of the pleasure principle. In *The Wapshot Chronicle*, Cheever's first major work, the old family mansion, West Farm, serves as an emblem of a once-secure past, before Cheever's family became improverished. On a deeper level, West Farm is a symbol of a lost stasis in relation to an inaccessible mother, a misfortune that antedated the loss of the Cheever home. Such symbols of a lost Eden were filled with anxiety for Cheever, for whom every attempt to create new realities or to reshape old ones is filled with menace and the threat of disaster. This is why so many of Cheever's protagonists suffer sudden reversal of their fortunes, ending as destitute and even shorn of their erstwhile identity—like the protagonist of "Metamorphoses," a wealthy investment banker who comes to be mistaken for a delivery man. The banker falls from grace after witnessing a kind of primal scene involving his boss and a female partner in his firm. In this way Cheever sets up a connection between the banker's malevolent transformation and sexual discovery.

Cheever's characters are not punished for their sexual behavior; nor do they suffer from sexual guilt. When Cheever's protagonists are traumatized and set on a downward course, it is because they stumble upon others engaged in sex. This is the case with the eccentric matriarch, Cousin Honora in *The Wapshot Chronicle,* who inadvertently is a witness to a sexual act involving her young relative Moses Wapshot and his girlfriend, Rosalie. Honora, who was once briefly and disastrously married to a fake Italian nobleman, is infuriated by hearing the sounds associated with the sexual act. She proceeds to blackmail Moses' father Leander into sending his errant son away to a distant city. Honora's blackmail finds expression in two hostile acts toward Leander. First, she threatens to deprive Leander of his ferryboat, with which he earns a meagre living. Later, Honora threatens to turn the family farm into a boarding house, thereby displacing Leander and his family, who live on the homestead at Honora's discretion. Cheever does not portray Honora as entirely bad by any means. She is one of Cheever's good/bad mothers, who has the power to give love with one hand and to take it away with the other. In this regard Honora is similar to old Mrs. Brownlee in "The Children." Mrs. Brownlee is a dowager who generously shares her palatial estate with the middle-aged protagonist Victor and his wife, but only as long as they serve her as dutiful surrogate children. However, she sends the couple packing when Victor offends her daughter Hester. Only rarely are Cheever's fictional women totally destructive, as is the case with Joan in "Torch Song." Joan is a hearty, seemingly indestructible woman who becomes the mistress of a series of men, each of whom is destined to die. Thus Joan is portrayed as a kind of Angel of Death. Even Joan, however, is free of conscious malevolence, and is nurturant toward each of her dying, often abusive lovers.

Evidently, Cheever cannot bring himself to deal with his hostility toward the good/bad mother. His daughter Susan, in her biography of Cheever, points out that he rejected the interpretation by his psychiatrist that he hated his mother.

Although Cheever blamed his mother for hastening his father's destruction by her self-sufficiency and success as a business-woman, he could not bring himself to recognize her effect on himself. Cheever's repressed hostility toward his mother is the source of his anxiety, his dread of failure, and his fear of exposure as a moral leper. This hostility is related, however, to the mother's relationship with the father in his capacity as oedipal rival, and is produced by the mechanism of dis-placement.

Cheever's concern with oedipal themes is illustrated by his treatment of an episode of Leander's youth in *The Wapshot Chronicle*. As a young man, Leander had been blackmailed by his paternalistic boss, Whittier, into marrying a girl that Whittier had gotten pregnant. Although Leander and the girl had come to love each other, the child that Whittier had sired was taken away from them at Whittier's instigation. Immediately thereaf-ter, the young wife Clarissa drowned herself out of grief. The meaning of Clarissa's death may be interpreted as follows: The young Leander had fulfilled a prototypical oedipal wish, pos-sessing the woman who had originally belonged to his fatherly employer. Cheever does not, however, punish Leander for gratifying a forbidden wish. Indeed, it was at the insistence of the employer that Leander had married Clarissa in the first place. Clarissa's death, then, is a punishment that has been displaced from the culpable father figure to the wife-mother.

Reference to the mechanism of displacement is helpful in explaining why Cheever's fictional women, like Anne in "A Woman Without a Country," are often shown as victims of life. Anne, a suburbanite wife married to a man of great wealth, lost her husband and her only child after being caught in adultery, and was condemned to spend the rest of her life as a rootless expatriate. In actuality, Anne had been seduced or possibly raped by the town rake in the hallway of her house after he gave her a lift after her car had run out of gas. Anne chose exile to escape a humiliating song that was composed about her and became famous throughout the country following a highly publicized custody trial. Of course, Cheever's male protagonists are usually victims, too, but they are betrayed by their own impulsivity, whereas the females are made to suffer through no fault of their own. On rare occasions, these fictional women obtain revenge against the men who have wronged them, as is the case in "The Five-Forty-Eight," in which an armed woman forces a man to make an abject apology on his knees for having seduced her earlier. This scenario can be interpreted as a fantasy of oedipal retribution against the father, in which the mother serves as a vehicle for expressing hostility vicariously on behalf of the son. In general, Cheever punishes his fictional males by making them the agents of their own undoing, as I have suggested; but the background for their failure implicates the women in their lives, as if the oedipal mother is still being blamed for her complicity in relation to the father.

Although Cheever's protagonists, men and women alike, are generally depicted as victims, there are grounds for concluding that the females possess greater resources. This conclusion is consistent with Cheever's early identification with his mother. It is also supported by the assumption that in narcissistic disorders the traumatizing parent has been internalized as a powerful but hated self-object that can be neutralized only by the satisfaction of archaic wishes or selfish demands. These demands are linked with the grandiose self, which in Cheever's case resulted from overidealization of his controlling mother combined with scornful neglect by the father. The assumption is that Cheever invested his mother with narcissistic cathexis and came to experience her narcissistically as a self-object. The mechanism involved is expressed by Kohut as follows: "I am perfect. You are perfect, but I am a part of you."[11] Such introjection eventually leads to the integration of the archaic grandiose self into the adult personality, contributing to self-esteem and superego formation. In the face of narcissistic injuries, however, the grandiose self resists integration into the adult personality, pursuing its narcissistic and exhibitionistic aims. Simultaneously, as Kohut notes, the idealized parent imago remains an archaic self-object or pathogenic part of the narcissistic personality.

Cheever's youthful decision to become a professional writer and his corresponding disinclination to attend college attest to his early compensatory grandiosity. His homosexual tendencies are traceable to an idealized image of his mother and a sexualization of his rejecting father, who had tried to persuade the mother to have an abortion when she was pregnant with Cheever. Cheever's rejection by his father, or at least his conviction that his father did not esteem him, prevented him from developing a firmly idealized superego. This deficiency helps to explain Cheever's vacillation in his fiction between moral righteousness and lapses into an easy tolerance of amorality. The gap between Cheever's often-frustrated aspirations and his consciousness of his shortcomings, particularly in the moral sphere but also as a literary figure, created serious intrapsychic tensions. Cheever's alcoholism and his drug addiction later in life may be seen as a response to his compulsive promiscuity on the one hand, and his failure to establish a literary reputation of unambiguous superiority on the other. The use of alcohol was a defense against the depression and guilt caused by his sense of failure as a husband and as a writer. The use of alcohol may also have enabled Cheever to satisfy his need for grandiosity and to restore his impaired narcissistic balance. In this context, Honora, the grande dame of the Wapshot family, represents Cheever's idealized mother imago. Her narcissism is expressed through her willfulness and self-justifying dishonesty, which takes the form of never paying her taxes on the grounds that she is a superior person. In short, Honora symbolizes the pathogenic component in Cheever's structure of the self.

Cheever's *The Wapshot Scandal* deals with the same family constellation as *The Wapshot Chronicle* and follows the development of the two sons, Moses and Coverly, into young adulthood. The father, Leander, rejects Coverly (modeled after Cheever) in favor of his brother Moses. Coverly's mother Sarah, we learn, had once beaten him mercilessly with a buggy whip after she caught him watching women undress in the bathhouse. Coverly is a prototypical Cheever character who lives forever in uneasy expectation of losing his place beside the bright family hearth. Nevertheless, he longs for a falsified past and even pays a visit to West Farm long after it has been abandoned, searching for something to reassure himself.

The futility of longing for the past is illustrated in *The Wapshot Scandal*, which is dominated by the refrain: "Oh, Father, Father, why have you come back?" Coverly Wapshot repeats this sentence throughout the book, commencing with a futile attempt to spend a night in the family's abandoned home. Coverly had concluded that the house was haunted by his father, and had fled to his wife and children in another city, unable to understand why his father's spectral presence should have driven him from his boyhood home. The meaning of Coverly's lament becomes apparent when we identify the psychological problem that he shares with his brother Moses. The central motif of the novel is the helpless predicament of the two brothers (both married by now and with careers of their own) following the discovery that the family's matriarch, Cousin Honora, has never paid income taxes and has thereby endangered the family fortune, now that the government has caught up with her. Honora, the quintessential good/bad mother, causes her dependent "child" to feel suddenly abandoned. Cheever's male protagonists are helpless infants, and Coverly's cry, addressed to the ghost of his father Leander, is not so much a query as a wish fulfillment. The hapless sons do not strive actively to make their way in life but remain at the mercy of an ambivalent mother figure. Honora resembles Cheever's other fictional women insofar as the men in her life remain tied to her despite her inability to satisfy their need for security. Coverly's relationship with his wife Betsy follows a similar pattern. Betsy, whose father used to discipline her with a strap (Cheever's father-in-law had beaten his sons with a belt and had traumatized Cheever's wife, as well, Cheever was convinced), confuses Coverly with her cruel father and refuses to allow him to approach her. Coverly, whom Cheever has portrayed as repressive in all matters, denies the seriousness of his wife's condition, and is sustained by the few crumbs of affection that Betsy bestows on him when she is not acutely disturbed. The affect hunger and insecurity of Cheever's male protagonists is matched only by the lack of nurturance of his females, a failure that is due to inadequacy and preoccupation—like Cheever's mother—rather than to malice.

In *The Wapshot Scandal* Cheever explores the themes of affect hunger and emotional dependency not only through the lives of his male protagonists, but also by examining a married woman's hopeless infatuation with a young delivery boy. The woman is Melissa, Moses Wapshot's neglected wife, and nothing comes of her involvement with the puzzled youth except a momentary reactivation of her maternal impulses. A parallel relationship involves Cousin Honora and a youngish gigolo whom she meets onboard an ocean liner. When Honora discovers the gigolo in the act of trying to steal money from her cabin, she strikes him with a lamp and is convinced for a time that she has killed him. When the gigolo shows up later, walking arm in arm with another older woman, Honora is so incensed that she deliberately shorts out the ship's generator with her old electrical curling iron, plunging the ship into darkness and setting it adrift in the bay, powerless and without direction. In the relationship between Melissa and the delivery boy, sexual fulfillment is followed by the stirrings of protective impulses in the woman and a loss of autonomy by the young male, who is corrupted by Melissa. In the encounter between Honora and the gigolo, there is no sexual consummation, but rather a rejection by the man of the woman's motherly concern shown by his trying to steal her money.

These two sets of fictional relationships express Cheever's conflict in relation to women. To accept a woman's love, as in the case of Emile the delivery boy, carries with it the danger that the self will be destroyed. To try to emancipate oneself from a woman involves an act of betrayal. Cheever's gigolo feels no guilt, however, over his criminal behavior. In fact, Cheever's errant protagonists are rarely described as conscience stricken. The amorality of the gigolo, like the amorality of Cheever's bored housewives and lecherous householders, signifies their incapacity for remorse. His male protagonists, like the gigolo, are faced with the alternative of either being used by women in the name of maternal love, or using women in a ruthless way, thereby insuring their freedom. These fictional conflicts may be seen as projections resulting from Cheever's failure to internalize empathic self-objects in an integrated self-structure.

The absence of a well-integrated self-structure is also revealed in the novel *Bullet Park* (1969). In this novel, Cheever's third, a happily married suburbanite named Nailles represents the voice of moderation and sanity, and bourgeois acceptance of a comfortable world with a comely landscape and a sense of community. Nailles' opposite, Hammer, has been scarred by childhood emotional deprivation, is unhappily married, and is alienated from his suburban surroundings. He is obsessed with a thought inspired by his psychotic mother, namely, to kill someone—in this case, Nailles—as a sort of mystical, sacrificial act, and as an expression of his quiet desperation, as revealed by his journals. In the course of *Bullet Park*, Nailles becomes a drug addict while trying to overcome a fear of trains by using medication. It is not clear whether Nailles' addiction is a response to his son's illness or whether it comes about as a result of his gradual loss of innocence and trust. Nailles is not so much Hammer's opposite as his double, because he too is driven by murderous impulses and nearly kills his son with a golf club during a fit of rage, thereby precipitating his son's mysterious illness. The son is ultimately cured by a black swami. Hammer decides to kill Nailles' son instead of Nailles, but Nailles rescues his son at the last moment, removing him from the church where Hammer was about to sacrifice him on the altar.

In this scenario, Hammer and Nailles are largely interchangeable, except that Hammer is depicted as psychotic. Nailles' death wish against his son is merely transferred to Hammer, who attempts to act it out, only to be stopped by his alter ego Nailles. *Bullet Park,* then, is a story about a man divided against himself. On the manifest level, it is also a story about a father's rage against his beloved son for doing poorly in school and being taken off the football team as a result, for watching too much television (Nailles had thrown the set out of the house in anger), and generally for not living up to his father's expectations. In many ways, Cheever's characters represent (a) a precarious balance between the author's id impulses and his controls, and (b) a recapitulation of Cheever's relationship with his father, in which Cheever, through his characters, is alternately the failed son and the disillusioned father. On the level of latent content, *Bullet Park* is also a treatment of marriage as endless alternation between sexual fulfillment and sexual rebuff. Nailles, for example, has a loving, acquiescent wife, whereas Hammer has an unpredictable, sexually withholding wife who can make love only during storms or after learning about calamities. Cheever's fictional wives, like his fictional mothers, are as ambivalent toward their sons/lovers/husbands as his fathers are ambivalent toward their sons. The relationships between Cheever's fictional parents and their sons are undoubtedly based on Cheever's perception of his own parents, as described by Susan Cheever in her memoir of her father.

Several dynamic factors that point to Cheever's salient problems can be seen operating in *Bullet Park*. First, Hammer conceives of his plan to murder Nailles (and later, Nailles' son) after being approached by a homosexual whom he manages to evade.[12] Second, the decision to sacrifice Nailles, the good me, is also made shortly after Hammer's recovery from a prolonged depression, which Cheever speaks of as a "panic" and also as a "cafarde."[13] This depression disappears after Hammer impulsively joins a funeral procession for a slain communist official in Rome. Hammer weeps uncontrollably as he marches in the silent parade, but observes:, "as soon as I began to march I felt the cafarde take off."[14] The murdered communist delegate was someone entirely unknown to Hammer, but shedding tears over his death brought Hammer relief. Why? The answer is understandable only in the light of Hammer's decision to murder Nailles, reported a few lines further on in the novel. There exists a close connection between Hammer's depression, his recovery after a cathartic experience involving a murdered communist, and his decision to commit murder. In addition, an important part of the mosaic is the fact that Nailles' wife becomes sexually excited by "convulsions of nature and history": "Her passion was boundless when they shot the King of Parthia. (He was saying his prayers in the basilica)."[15]

Cheever is telling a story about a man who decides to extinguish his good side after mourning the death of a communist (i.e., bad) rebel and recovering from a depression. At the same time, we learn that for Nailles good sex is possible only in the context of the slain "father" ("they shot the King of Parthia"). The equation is: Recovery from depression results from acceptance of the bad me, and sexual fulfillment is made possible by the overthrow of the sanctimonious father/king. But Cheever is not talking about heterosexual love or oedipal rivalry, in which the son, in fantasy, possesses the mother in the wake of the father's destruction. The key to Hammer's recovery from his depression is given in the passage that describes his evasion of a homosexual who had approached him on a beach. Hammer's response was to turn away from the homosexual and to impulsively join a middle-aged father who was trying unsuccessfully to fly a kite with the aid of his wife and two children. Hammer helps the father get the kite into the air: "At this the faggot sighed, hitched up his trunks and wandered off as I had intended that he should, but the filament of kite line in my fingers, both tough and fine, that had quite succinctly declared my intentions to the faggot seemed for a moment to possess some extraordinary moral force as if the world I had declared to live in was bound together by just such a length of string—cheap, durable and colorless. . . . The faggot had vanished but I longed then for a moral creation whose mandates were heftier than the delight of children, the trusting smiles of strangers and a length of kite string."[16]

Now we are in a position to understand Hammer's cafarde and its resolution. His recovery is linked with the acceptance of the bad me, defined as the homosexual side of his nature. At the same time, Hammer understands that his pose as a respectable member of suburban society is a defense against the open acknowledgment of homosexuality. This interpretation is consistent with Cheever's life history, in which he tried simultaneously to be a good husband and father, a respectable church-going member of suburban society, and a secret homosexual. The homosexuality was an affront to everything his father had stood for. It represented Cheever's oedipal rebellion in the special sense of wishing to possess the mother, not as a sex object but as an internalized object. Hammer, the would-be murderer is therefore also the would-be homosexual, the bad son. Such a son can find sexual gratification only when the king is dead and the son has become a queen out of retribution because the father, his mortal foe, had sought to have him aborted, as in Cheever's case. Hammer's mother is made to resemble Cheever's mother, complete with her English accent and a pretension to culture. Hammer's father, who never married his mother (his parents turned him over to his maternal grandmother at an early age) resembles Cheever's father in his neglect of his son. *Bullet Park* was the last novel Cheever was to write from the standpoint of the conflicted oedipal son; *Falconer*, which followed *Bullet Park,* reveals Cheever's acceptance of his homosexuality and the impossibility of oedipal rebellion. The abandonment of the motif of rebellion also signals the start of a phase of expiation and a coming to terms with inner demands and the demands of conventional society.

Cheever's commitment to social stability is the key to understanding his highly successful next-to-last novel *Falconer* (1977), published when Cheever was sixty-five. *Falconer* is about a genteel fratricide named Farragut, who is imprisoned for his crime and finally escapes. Farragut's real crime was not the slaying of his brother, however. After all, Cheever devotes only a few lines to the crime and says nothing at all about Farragut's feelings about his violent act, leaving the impression that he feels neither guilt or depression. Farragut's offense, in essence, is that he showed a regrettable departure from good form when he lost his temper and struck his aging brother with a poker. Oh! The shame of it! One can imagine the headlines in the vulgar tabloids: PROF LOSES COOL, ICES BROTHER. No wonder Farragut's punishment consists of having to associate with the assorted lowlifes in his cell block. But Cheever will not abandon his scapegrace protagonist even in his sordid prison surroundings, conferring upon him the boon of a young, handsome homosexual partner. And even though Farragut has been sentenced to life imprisonment, Cheever arranges for him to escape magically at the end of the novel. Impulsivity is bad form, but it can be forgiven ultimately, even if it has led to fratricide.

It is true that Cheever wrote *Falconer* when his drinking was entirely out of hand, but his value system remained unaffected. He knew that his alcoholism was a transgression, but not because he felt he had failed those who depended on him. His own children, according to his daughter, believed he had abandoned them, and abandoned him, in turn, during this protracted crisis. Cheever finally stopped drinking to save his life. He realized too that his drunken behavior in public during this period, particularly on the streets of Boston, was disgraceful. *Falconer* emerged out of this context as a morality play. Its message, which Cheever did not necessarily intend on the conscious level, is: If you make a spectacle of yourself, instead of sinning with circumspection, you will be punished. Fratricide is a side issue in *Falconer,* although it is not unreasonable to speculate that Cheever had considerable hostility, repressed or otherwise, toward his brother Fred, to have written such a story. This supposition is supported by the fact that Fred, who was sick and close to death, being advanced in years, traveled to Boston to nurse his younger brother back to health. Fred's solicitude may have earned him as much resentment as gratitude, in light of Cheever's need to act out his self-dramatizing, self-destructive needs.

For all the critical acclaim it received, *Falconer* is in some ways the least accomplished of Cheever's works, because he was unable or unwilling to use his descriptive gifts, and, above all, his fine sensibility to depict prison life. Whether as a result of diminished creative power, or for the sake of sounding tough and modern, Cheever replaced his customary tact and sensitivity with crassness. Cheever was, after all, a writer of great subtlety—if not on the interpersonal plane, then on the phenomenological level. The phenomenology of prison life did not escape him entirely, but the characters whom he invented, including his protagonist, are not finely textured enough in conception or execution to provide Cheever with adequate scope for his special talents. As I have noted, *Falconer* was written when Cheever, separated from his family and living alone in Boston, was virtually killing himself with alcohol and drugs. He was unable to fulfill his duties as a visiting lecturer at Boston University. Feeling more helpless and abandoned with every passing day, Cheever appears to have undergone a coarsening of his sensibilities. In a sense, the incarceration of his protagonist, which provides the entire subject matter of *Falconer,* was Cheever's effort to describe his feelings of confinement and alienation at this junction of his life, which he is said to have regarded as its lowest point. Ironically, his brother Fred died soon after rescuing Cheever from his desperate situation, while Cheever was still at work on *Falconer,* a novel about the sudden, unpremeditated slaying of an older brother by a college professor.

For a variety of reasons, Cheever's satirical eye and ear are useless within the walls of his fictional prison. Cheever finds little to satirize in a world in which men are stripped bare of all pretensions. For a writer who can take the measure of shallow

Philistines, such as the Reverand Bascom in *The Wapshot Scandal*, Cheever can ridicule neither his fictional guards nor the pathetic, one-dimensional prisoners of *Falconer*. From the reader's standpoint, Cheever's characters in *Falconer* do not invite an emotional response any more then they challenge the intellect; they are merely caricatures of impoverished souls. The quality and intensity of human relationships in *Falconer* are not communicated in a way that captures the imagination or engages the reader's sympathies. A comparison with Nabokov's treatment of the prisoner-jailer relationship in the surrealistic *Invitation to a Beheading* reveals the most essential ingredient that is missing in *Falconer*, namely the sadomasochistic dimension of prison life. Nabokov understands the elemental importance of power in human relationships in which there is no escape from the presence of others. Nabokov captures the phenomenal content of life in confinement by demonstrating that its essence is the violation of human dignity. Cheever mistakes the vulgarity of prison life for its underlying terror and fails to grasp, in Sartre's words, that hell is other people[17]—above all, the other prisoners, and the guards, as well. Cheever is content to portray his prisoners as grotesques or as merely picturesque; their menace escapes his protagonist who seems to repress his deepest feelings in favor of surface emotions. Unable to distance himself from his protagonist, Cheever portrays him with the utmost sympathy, even though he is self-indulgent and self-pitying. The greatest disappointment in Farragut's life is the loss of his homosexual partner after the latter escapes. Although Cheever speculates about the symbolic meaning of the young lover to the aging Farragut, he does not provide any insight into Farragut's need system.

One of Farragut's dreams in *Falconer* provides some clues to his emotional needs. Farragut dreams that he has debarked from a large cruise ship, which then runs aground and bursts into flame: "She is a very big old-fashioned cruiser, named for a queen, white as a bride. . . . She goes crazily off course." This fantasy restates Cheever's prototypical conflict, which, like Farragut's conflict, involves his resentment at having been abandoned by his ambitious mother. Like the ship named for a queen, Cheever's mother was named Mary and she was English.

Upon awakening from his dream, Farragut listens to the rain falling outside his prison cell: "The noise of the rain seemed to be a gentleness—something his bellicose mother, pumping gas in her opera cloak, had missed."[18] Farragut's dream, and his thoughts following it, occur at a time when he has vainly built up his hopes that a prison riot would erupt, breaking the monotony of his existence. The riot does not occur because the prisoners are bought off with marijuana supplied to them by their guards and free photographs of themselves to send to their families. *Falconer* can be seen as a story of would-be oedipal rebels who are easily distracted and pacified by substitute father figures. Farragut and his fellow prisoners, especially the pathetic Cuckold, are all powerless, onanistic men who have never grown up and who accept their dependency and degradation with resignation.

Like many of Cheever's protagonists, Farragut is a man who does not change, and who does not grow or progress, but who is limited by inertia. This limitation may explain the static quality of *Falconer,* in which almost nothing happens until Farragut escapes from prison by changing places with a corpse. Cheever provides a series of vignettes of life in Farragut's cell block, but otherwise there is no movement. In the final pages of the novel, Cheever reconstructs the act of murder that came about when Farragut's brother angrily said that their father had wanted Farragut aborted: " 'He wanted you to be killed,' screamed Eben. 'I bet you didn't know that. He loved me, but he wanted you to be killed. Mother told me. He had an abortionist come to the house. Your own father wanted you to be killed.' Then Farragut struck his brother with a fire iron." In the end, Farragut is safely out of the prison, and a stranger gives him a raincoat and a free ride on a bus. Farragut has miraculously obtained his freedom, but, like Tennessee Williams' Blanche DuBois, he depends on the kindness of strangers. Thus passivity and dependency on fortuitous salvation are the hallmark of Cheever's characters. These fictional traits are compatible with the structure of Cheever's fine short stories, but do not sit well on characters in a novel, in which forward movement and self-direction, in the mind if not in action, are essential even if the protagonist is otherwise confused or harassed. This is to say that *Falconer* and Cheever's other novels are less successful than his short stories because Cheever's poorly integrated self does not permit him to develop his characters in depth or in time. By contrast, Cheever's short stories are effective because they achieve their results by the evocation of novel and ingenious situations rather than by the exploration of character. Cheever's gift for the keen observation of the surface of life, along with his lyricism, contribute to the unity and poignancy of his short stories. The same gifts, supplied to the writing of a novel, result only in loosely connected scenes in which some characters appear more often than others.

Cheever's last novel, *Oh What A Paradise It Seems*, confirms the impression that Cheever was basically conservative in outlook, despite his history of deviant behavior. In this novella, the protagonist, an aging, wealthy widower, has a love affair with an attractive middle-aged woman who mysteriously leaves him in the lurch one day. His response is immediately to begin a homosexual relationship with a middle-aged elevator operator in the woman's former apartment house. That the elevator operator, like the protagonist, is an outwardly conventional family man, is intended to convey the meaning that homosexuality, like the heterosexual liaison between the protagonist and his mistress, can be a natural, emotionally gratifying relationship between two good friends. On a deeper level, the experience of being abandoned by a female love object carries the threat to the male that his homosexual inclinations will be activated. Unlike the deserted husband in the strange short story "The Cure," the protagonist of *Oh What A Paradise It Seems* does not have a homosexual panic, indicating that Cheever had come to terms with his bisexuality toward the end of his life. "The Cure," it might be added, which combines paranoia with the threat of possible suicide, is one of the few stories written by Cheever in the first person.

Two related wish-fulfillments are dramatized in *Oh What A Paradise It Seems*. First is the wish to make love to a completely satisfying, undemanding woman who is nevertheless beautiful and clever. The gratification of this wish regenerates the declining protagonist Sears, even though his mistress ultimately leaves him without warning. The second wish that is granted to Sears is the preservation of his favorite skating pond in the country. Sears is thereby regenerated in another sense, restoring his ties to Mother Earth after having experienced a revival of his dormant sexual powers. It would be wide of the mark, however, to regard *Oh What A Paradise It Seems* as Cheever's last hurrah, a paean of praise for the redemptive power of physical love and the love of nature. On the manifest level, this last work appears to fulfill its author's aim, and with a greater economy of means than any of his preceding novels. But as much as *Oh What A Paradise It Seems* is a novella of life affirmation, it relies on magical solutions to real problems, namely, the threat of loss of a love object and the menace of ecological disaster (developers had been planning to turn Sears' beloved pond into a toxic waste dump). Sears loses a maternal, all-giving love object and instantly replaces her with a fatherly love object. What was Sears looking for and what did he find? Apparently, Sears sought to be united with a magical father, having lost his maternal love object. Insofar as the sought-after father is found in a homosexual relationship, the parallel with Cheever's life is not hard to find.

Sears resembles Cheever's other protagonists who strengthen their hold on life by the power of physical love and by their response to the beauty of nature. In this way, paradoxically, Cheever's characters renew their commitment to the outward forms of the social contract, which, in their hearts, they have pledged to uphold by fornicating only in secret places for the sake of good form. There is a connection between civic virtue and private vice in Cheever's fiction, and it is no less essential than Adam Smith's linkage of the common good with the pursuit of private gain. Although Cheever's most sympathetic characters believe in traditional values, they do not believe in substantive values. Cheever's protagonists have faith only in the efficacy of instrumental values, of which the foremost is the usefulness of an orderly society to provide a secure framework for the discreet expression of unruly and potentially dangerous impulses. For example, the members of the Wapshot clan, who are not "bad" people in any egregious sense, are kept from destroying themselves because they are sustained by the divine gift of trust funds. When caught in the act, Cheever's protagonists don golden parachutes and bail out from their high-flying beds. They descend gently to earth and take their place quietly among the other choir members, radiant and shameless. This is the world as it is and as it should be, according to Cheever, who is a gentle satirist about human foibles, but not about the structure of society. Imperfect as this world is, Cheever tells us, this world provides a setting in which good taste and decorum, with the assistance of quarterly dividends, serve the purpose of hedonism, the only substantive value in Cheever's fiction. All other values are judged according to whether they promote hedonism or frustrate it. Altruism, courage, truthfulness and honesty are useless or irrelevant in Cheever's fiction because they lead to frustration and the denial of the pleasure principle. Above all, unmodulated passion is dangerous and tends to defeat the pleasure principle by shocking people's sensibilities and disturbing society's equilibrium. Fundamentally, Cheever's protagonists, though they are often anxious and preoccupied, live only for happiness. They are relieved, like Sears in *Oh What A Paradise It Seems*, when "the loveliness of the landscape had been restored,"[19] but it is a landscape that is not intended for the eyes of the vulgar or for disturbers of the peace.

What, then, is the secret of Cheever's immense gifts as a writer of fiction? His strengths represent the triumph of realism over narcissism, without the sacrifice of his grandiosity, including his high standards as an artist. This victory was made possible despite incomplete ego development and a pattern of self-destructive behavior. Cheever's great strength is the strain of bitter humor that runs through his work, reflecting a unique sense of perspective about human frailty. He has achieved a blend of the ridiculous with an appreciation of the pathos of life, as in his classic "The Enormous Radio," in which a radio begins to broadcast the terrifying and pitiful ordinary conversations of all the tenants in an apartment house, destroying his protagonists' illusions about the human condition and their own relationship. By fusing the disparate elements of intellectual detachment with a sense of pity, Cheever has entered into the frame of reference of his obsessed antiheroes, humanizing them while exposing their nakedness and cruelty. The self-deceiving housewife Irene in "The Enormous Radio" addresses her husband, summing up the tragicomedy that Cheever has identified as the core of human experience: " 'Life is too terrible, too sordid and awful. But we've never been like that, have we, darling? Have we? I mean, we've always been good and decent and loving to one another, haven't we? . . . We're happy, aren't we, darling? We are happy, aren't we?' "

" 'Of course we're happy,' he said tiredly."[20]

Chapter 8

JORGE LUIS BORGES

Blindness and the Art of Seeing

Gene H. Bell-Villada,[1] Borges' friend and critic, is convinced that Borges' period of greatest creativity coincided with a series of devastating crises in his life. These profoundly unsettling events occurred between the ages of thirty-eight and fifty-three in Borges' native city Buenos Aires. Borges, who had hitherto led a sheltered life as a gentleman scholar and poet, found himself thrust into a threatening world. A decline in the family's economic situation forced Borges to take a frustrating, ill-paid job as a library assistant for nine years. A year later, in 1938, his father died. The same year, Borges came close to death from blood poisoning due to an accident. In the ensuing years, Borges was persecuted by the Peronist regime and eventually fired from his miserable job. During this period, his mother, sister, and nephew were imprisoned by the fascist regime. These depressing circumstances appear to have jolted Borges out of his calm existence and resulted in the composition of Borges' most important works, *Ficciones, El Aleph,* and *Dreamtigers.* Bell-Villada argues that Borges' literary productions before 1937 were minor contributions and that Borges was stimulated to do his best work because his entire world was endangered.

Bell-Villada notes that Borges' personal crisis coincided with a turbulent period in the history of Argentina and that Borgas responded with a burst of extraordinary originality—but without arriving at any new sociopolitical or psychological insights. This qualification is important because it underscores the reactive character of Borges' behavior as an artist, behavior in which, despite appearances, conative and affective influences overshadow the conceptual component. Throughout his period of greatest innovation, Borges remained a traditionalist who showed no understanding of the major intellectual currents of his time, and was dismissive of Freud. Characteristically, in 1945, Borges listed psychoanalysis, Nazism, communism, and surrealism as examples of a "basely romantic age."[2] By the 1960s and 1970s Borges had become an admirer of Richard Nixon and an apologist for Augusto Pinochet, the Chilean dictator.

These affinities have little connection with ideology, but result rather from Borges' admiration for leaders whom he sees as holding the line against social change. His psychology is not unlike that of a dependent son who is pleased that the good father—masterful but benign—is once more seated at the head of the table, and that the bad father—M. Juan Peron—has vanished. Peron was bad, however, because of his vulgar, populist manner and his rude criticism of the old monied aristocracy to which Borges' family belonged, despite its financial difficulties. Peron was bad, in other words, because he was unsettling, rather than because of his links with fascism, or even his persecution of members of the Borges family. As a projection of Borges' destructive rage, the bad father, as we will see in Borges' fictional characterizations, is also intolerable because he stirs up id impulses in the repressed author that are best left quiescent. The bad father in Borges' fiction is the powerful, knife-wielding adversary, a gangster or a gaucho, who destroys the protagonist. As a representative of the author's repressed id impulses, the adversary is the protagonist's double, or as Freud put it, a "compromise formation" reflecting the fact that affects experienced as frightening and ego-alien have been turned into something ominous and "uncanny."[3]

Otto Rank[4] saw the double as resulting from projection of guiltridden destructive impulses, and attributed the sinister character of the double to the ego's rejection of these impulses. Viewed in this light, the double is as much a symbol of aggression as an objectless flight response aimed at tension reduction. In their essay, "On the Concept of Aggression," Joseph H. Smith et al.[5] characterize such a flight reaction as seeking an object that will satisfy dependency needs, with the implication that such unfocused aggression contains a libidinal element. This formulation is useful for understanding the creative strategy used by Borges, who combines in his fiction scenes of violent aggression with a flight into intellectualization, in which ideas are libidinized to the point where they take precedence over characterization, concrete description, and sometimes even narrative, as in "The Library of Babel." His fictional protagonists, who stab or shoot each other, are not motivated by aggression as it is usually understood. Their violence is objectless, but constitutes an integral part of a self-imposed scenario of intellectual problem solving in which Borges attempts, in Smith's terms, a "reasoned repudiation" of a source of internal threat.

The wish to repudiate disruptive, tension-producing impulses is seen by Michael Eigen[6] as one of the sources of creativity. Commenting on the duality of human experience, Eigen sees creative behavior as resulting from the effort to reduce the conflict within the ego between the threat and urgency of immediate experience and the need for symbolic, problem-solving activity. The reduction of such tension produces inner harmony, according to Eigen. Insofar as the mind can create transcendent, or ideal images leading to inner harmony, it is faced, however, with still another challenge. I have in mind the often unrealistic requirements of the ego ideal, which are not necessarily in harmony with even the most idealized representations of material reality. This is because the ego ideal, despite its inflexible and unrealistic character, provides a standard for judging the objectivity of all transcendent solutions to problems. The ego ideal, which consists of a set of criteria by which to distinguish between self-seeking solutions and a disinterested search for the truth, is threatened by defensive intellectualizations. Unlike the ego, which allows itself to be deceived by retreating upward into intellectuality when it is menaced by hostile thoughts and feelings, the ego ideal insists upon attaining inner harmony by allowing full expression to the person's needs. Intellectualizations that are largely defensive not only take on an obsessive quality, but also make use of disguise and repudiation in place of direct expression of aggression. Borges will not allow himself such duplicity. He is remarkable in that he creates a plurality of fictional worlds in which transcendant ideas are developed side-by-side with themes of violence, thereby accommodating the ego ideal and the id, and barring the ego from playing its usual tricks.

Borges' imaginary settings, each of which, as Ronald J. Christ[7] observes, is the embodiment of a metaphysical idea, are totally unlike the experiments in time and space that are the subject of science fiction. Each of these fantastic, albeit prosaic environments represents both a hell in which murderous acting out takes place, and a heaven, as well. In this hell-heaven, guardian angels, camouflaged as magical ideas, attempt to preserve the individual from destruction, often without success. Unlike science fiction, which creates new realities merely by the alteration of material circumstances, Borges creates alternative worlds by the bolder expedient of asking his readers to shift their perspective and to try out a logically compelling but impossible idea. Borges is aware that his metaphysical experiments are not designed to produce perfect solutions, but rather to test the limits of logical deduction in an exploratory manner. Thus, Borges' intellectualizations are not defensive in the sense that applies to neurosis. As Pinchas Noy[8] suggests, neurotic problem solving may appear to be successful "in solving a problem in one of its mental spheres while repressing, isolating, or dissociating the problem in other spheres." Referring to the creation of new forms in art, Noy emphasizes the artist's search for new means of adaptation that will permit full communication; that is, expression that is not distorted by denial, repression, or compartmentalization, and does not endanger inner unity.

Borges achieves his greatest success when he combines his intellectual adventures or metaphysical conceits with narrative movement, including the element of violence. In those instances in which Borges is unable to go beyond metaphysical exploration, as in the static "The Library of Babel," the reader is aware that Borges' ingenious structure of improbable facts remains isolated from life and from human destiny. An act of compartmentalization has indeed taken places. By contrast, in "Death and the Compass," or "The South," Borges creates an artistic unity, in which an idea is successfully fused with feeling and imagination. K. R. Eissler's[9] analysis of *Hamlet* throws some light on Borges' varying success in fusing metaphysics with creative activity. Eissler introduces a construct that he calls the *doxaletheic function* which he identifies with the ego's ability to continue testing reality in "states of high drive arousal accompanying creative activity." Reality testing in the case of a creative writer involves awareness of the need to be able to communicate with the public. The doxaletheic function permits reality testing to reassert itself following a temporary blurring of the line between internal stimulation by wishes and needs, and the external world, which demands that the artist share his vision with other people. In this process, according to Eissler, the creative process provides a temporary solution to an inner conflict in the form of primary gain, and secondary gain as well, in the form of external rewards and fame. Eissler rejects the hypothesis that works of art produced primarily for secondary gain will be of inferior quality. Where there is only primary gain, it is obvious that the artist will fail in his social function, having lost sight of the need to build a bridge between his preoccupations and his readers' need for structure. A puzzling question that surrounds Borges' fiction is whether his philosophical constructions or his violent themes represent the working out of inner conflicts, or whether both preoccupations reflect the struggle to achieve inner harmony. Each of Borges' stories is an intellectual game, and this provides some clues to the respective roles of primary and secondary gain in his creative activities.

In his article, "Passive Mastery of Helplessness in Games," Martin D. Capell[10] distinguishes between active reality-based attempts at conflict resolution and passive mastery, which, following Otto Fenichel's lead, he defines as the effort to remove obstacles with the help of powerful, often magical external objects. Fenichel had described games as involving the expression of libidinous needs combined with procedures designed to obtain reassurance against threatening forces. It is noteworthy that Borges' intellectual games, which are guided by the rules of strict logic but are based on improbable assumptions, ultimately fail to provide reassurance and even result in the death of the protagonist. Thus, Borges' games are not pleasurable in their outcomes even though they hold out the promise of intellectual adventure and escape through fantasy. If we assume, for the sake of argument, that the knife fights in Borges' fiction are a symbolic acting out of castration fears, why does the worst always come to pass, and the protagonist is killed, even in fantasy? This outcome contradicts the pleasure principle and directs us to interpret play as embodying features of a traumatic neurosis. But what of the philosophical framework that is the basis for Borges' stories, with its emphasis on the subjective construction of reality inspired by Borges' favorite, George Berkeley? Why does Borges stop short of carrying his philosophical idealism to a triumphant conclusion? The answer to this question should contain within itself the answer to the problem of the respective contributions of primary and secondary gain to Borges' writing.

Following through on the assumption that Borges' fictional knife fights are linked with castration fears, let us make still another assumption consistent with psychoanalytic theory. In line with Freud's analysis of the legends surrounding Oedipus, let us assume that blindness is symbolically equated with castration—an unconscious equation in which blindness would seem to imply helplessness. But this formula is open to question, according to Ernest A. Rappaport,[11] who relates blindness to omniscience, as in the case of the blind seer Tiresius in Sophocles' *Oedipus Rex*. Rappaport's point is that blindness, instead of leading to helplessness, can result in impaired ability to test reality, accompanied by a false sense of omniscience. The assumption of prophetic powers thus becomes a safeguard against undesirable reality. If Rappaport is right, then an essential connection exists between Borges' construction of hypothetical worlds and his penchant for violence and tragic outcomes. I do not want to make too much of Borges's lifelong struggle against blindness. It is true, after all, as can be seen in Borges' early essays in *Inquisiciones*, published in 1925, that

Borges had formulated his aesthetics long before he became blind, but not before he began to suffer from failing eyesight. But blindness is the starting point for Borges' literary strategy of solipsism, of preferring the abstract to the concrete, of insisting upon conciseness—in short, of placing the operations of the mind on a higher plane than that of consensually defined reality. If blindness poses the threat of helplessness, then Borges' imagination is the antidote—not because the author believes himself to be omniscient—but because his mind liberates him to examine the limits of logical possibility.

I speak of limits advisedly. Borges is both a skeptic and a believer in dreams. As a dreamer he dares to summon up from his unconscious no less than from his idealist philosophy (and who can say that his choice of a philosophy to guide his writing is not overdetermined) a degree of optimism about man's fate. As a skeptic who is well aware that Berkeley's philosophy is not a guide to the real world, however useful it may be for literary purposes, Borges does not believe in happy endings. However, he was compelled by his incipient blindness to use his imagination to reinvent a world of objects and possibilities that were slipping away from him. Following up Kris'[12] emphasis on early traumatization as a common factor in the psychic makeup of creative people, William G. Niederland[13] suggests that tragic events in childhood may heighten the individual's sensitivity to certain kinds of stimuli. Niederland lists a number of variables, such as loneliness (Borges was kept out of school by his father until he was nine), narcissistic injury to the body image, and early object loss, which may have the effect of stimulating a creative search for reparation and wholeness.

Borges' sequestered childhood was not marked by any sudden deprivation, but the gradual onset of his hereditary blindness undoubtedly represented a threat to the integrity of the ego. For someone as bookish as the young Borges, the potential loss of his eyesight must have meant an end to his greatest joy in life, which was reading. Borges prepared himself, in effect, for the eventuality of object loss by cultivating a highly idiosyncratic Neoplatonism, in which ideas and other object representations were cathected with unusual intensity. The idea of the thing, rather than the thing itself, assumed an importance for Borges that cannot be overestimated. This psychologically determined idealism is at the root of his stubborn conservatism. It is as if, as a near-blind person, Borges had to hold on to what he had patiently observed and reflected upon along the way—if not to every remembered signpost, then hold on to the significance of signposts in general. The world of multifarious possibilities that Borges has created in his fiction is designed to replace the perdurable world that he once knew intimately through his own eyes. Borges protects himself against loss in this way by reinventing the lost object, not as it was before, but as it could be in a universe of infinite potentialities.

Borges' lifelong self-subordination to his work as a writer— he freely admitted that he had practically no life apart from his writing—is partly a consequence of his blindness, but it also illustrates the central role of the ego in creativity. It is incorrect to think of the ego as exclusively an instrument for adaptation; it is a tool for renewal, as well. As K. R. Eissler[14] observes about Shakespeare, his plays represent "creations of a new world." This newly created world, Eissler argues, is not a mere improvement over nature, but something entirely new and even antinature. Borges' creations, especially his intellectual games, demonstrate the deliberate artificiality of his fiction, and his ability to formulate and solve problems that are not rooted in reality. Borges challenges reality, rather than affirms it. This challenge is different from the involuntary and purely defensive distortions of neurosis because it is unforced, and because its purpose is to solve problems that, far from being merely intellectual exercises, are psychologically real and compelling. By addressing these problems Borges also addresses the issues of emotional growth and artistic development: "I went from myths of the outlying slums of the city to games with time and infinity, but those games are now part of Borges and I will have to turn to other things."[15] It is not that Borges expects to arrive at an illumination, because he has understood all along that he is moving toward darkness. His idea of creativity does not involve a breakthrough, but it involves the positive application of skepticism, particularly to cast doubt on reassuring certainties and to confront the unknown with all its terrifying possibilities, especially for one who is about to lose his sight. Consequently, disbelief is the basis for Borges' writing; it is the weapon with which he has armed himself to confront the unexpected, just as his conservative ideology is the means of holding fast to the familiar.

Perhaps Borges' obsessive doubting minimizes not only the threat of external dangers, but minimizes also the threat of his own aggressive impulses, which are translated into fictional scenarios. By trying to imagine the shape of future disasters, Borges brings into question the reality of familiar tragedies, including the tragedy of his sightless life, and the anger associated with the knowledge of his loss. This strategy still leaves the unknown unaccounted for, but provides the opportunity to try to solve the riddle of all future catastrophes by imagining the defenses that can be mobilized against them. Accordingly, even the menace of a dark future can be made to wear a familiar face, so that it can be addressed as "thou" rather than "it." Also, Borges' fictional worlds enable him to operate according to his own rules, and to overcome the sense of helplessness and its associated rage. One has only to read "The Library of Babel" to see how Borges dealt with the futility of his life as an assistant librarian by constructing an imaginary library that is a paradigm of an infinitely boring universe, but a universe which, unlike the real world, can be abolished by an act of the mind. "The Library of Babel" also illustrates Borges' conservative philosophy because it describes a place where only superficial change can take place, without progress or hope. The history of this fictional library, Borges suggests, corresponds to human history, leading only from one feverish quest to another, but without making any true discovery. The sense of helplessness conveyed by "The Library of Babel" originates in Borges' fatalism about his future as a blind man and his immediate predicament as an impoverished clerk. His barely suppressed rage and helplessness are expressed as follows: "Like all men of the Library, I have traveled in my youth. I have journeyed in search of a book, perhaps of the catalogue of catalogues; now that my eyes can scarcely decipher what I write, I am preparing to die a few leagues from the hexagon in which I was born. Once dead, there will not lack pious hands to hurl me over the banister; my sepulchre shall be the unfathomable air: my body will sink lengthily and will corrupt and dissolve in the wind engendered by the fall, which is infinite."[16]

The violence that appears in certain of Borges' stories attests to the pressures exerted on the superego by rage. But Borges' superego is not a punitive one, as we see from his compassion for the victims of life's cruelty, such as Hladik in "The Secret Miracle." If reaction formation enters into Borges' compassionate portraits of victims, it is overshadowed by his vigilance, which causes Borges' to avoid creating fictional relationships based on love, or even on mutual concern. He seems to draw away from such relationships to neutralize the danger from his anger, which, as an artist, he perceives as a barrier to objectivity. This is another reason for Borges' abstractness and convoluted plots, namely, that they erect a wall between his feelings and the symbolic people who make up his fictional world. Nevertheless, he does not succeed in depersonalizing his protagonists. Although Borges systematically subordinates his characters to his plots (which, in turn, are ancillary to his philosophical speculations), he allows them to experience intense emotions. For example, in "Emma Zunz" a young woman resolves to avenge her father, who was driven to suicide by his unscrupulous business partner. Her plan is to have sexual intercourse with the first sailor she meets on the waterfront, and then to shoot the business partner, explaining moments later to the police that he had raped her and that she had killed him in self-defense. The girl's plan succeeds, but we gain an insight into her character that Borges may not have fully intended, and which is not intrinsic to the story. What is revealed is that Emma's rage is as much self-directed as it is focused on the business partner. The motif of masochism occurs frequently in Borges' fiction, even though it plays no essential role in his grand design of creating a literature of ideas, timeless and expressed with classical restraint, a strategy broadly hinted at in his essay "The Postulation of Reality."

Sadomasochism is perhaps the dominant strain, for example, in "Deutsches Requiem," in which a Nazi official of a concentration camp torments a Jewish poet, and drives him to suicide. For Borges, of course, the point of this story is quite different. It consists of a fictional interpretation of Arthur

Schopenhauer's thesis concerning a universal will. Borges illustrates his theme by causing the Nazi—finally captured and condemned—to attempt to convince himself that the Germans willed their own defeat for the sake of a higher purpose. Is Borges repressive about the cruel fictional relationship (less cruel, admittedly, than the real relationship between the Nazis and their victims) he has constructed in the interest of exploring an impersonal idea? I believe the answer must be in the affirmative because Borges' essays—"Our Inadequacies" is as good an example as any—no less than his short stories, reveal a capacity for anger and a fascination with violence, yet these elements are treated merely as means to an abstract goal. In "Our Inadequacies," for example, Borges is unremitting as he describes the inhabitants of Buenos Aires as ignorant and cruel, and filled with petty envy. There is nothing repressive about Borges' sense of patrician disdain for the unwashed masses of his native city, but it is a disdain tinged with fear and secret admiration for the tough guy. This ambivalence becomes clear when one reads his stories about gauchos, urban hoodlums, and soldiers, particularly "The South," "The Other Death," "Streetcorner Man," "The Meeting," and "The Challenge."

"Streetcorner Man" in particular reveals Borges' ambivalence toward his violent protagonists, who are as boastful and cowardly as they are vicious. Borges' special fascination with knife fights is not a fictional conceit, because his biographer and close associate, Alicia Jurado, remarks on his strong attraction to daggers.[17] In light of Borges' early frailty and incipient blindness, which led his parents to be extremely overprotective, it is understandable that the unknown world of street violence might have represented a threat to the sheltered child, growing up on the edge of the city's slums. There is also the implied threat to the masculinity of Borges' protagonists, who are compelled to prove their manhood by their physical courage. Borges comments on the tendency of Buenos Aires men to taunt each other with being sodomists: "In all countries, an indivisible reprobation falls upon the two practitioners of this unimaginable contact. . . . Not so with Buenos Aires' tough guys, who virtually venerate the active partner, because he took advantage of his companion. I hand over this fecal dialectic to the apologists for the wise guy, to those staunch supporters of backbiting and leg-pulling, all of which conceal so much hell."[18] The tone of these remarks reflects the feeling of vulnerability of one who cannot distance himself completely from the crudities of his fellow countrymen, and who, as a young poet and aesthete, might easily have become the victim of their cruel insults. The fact that Borges did not marry until he was sixty-eight (he separated from his wife three years later), and appears to have had no deep emotional involvement with a woman, adds to the impression that Borges must have felt uncomfortable, to say the least, in a society based on the cult of machismo.

Borges' preference for the world of ideas also appears to be a reflection of his aversion to his concrete surroundings. Like Nabokov, whose later fiction is characterized by exercises in logical ingenuity, fantasy, and black humor, Borges creates a world of the imagination that permits him to cathect non-threatening object representations. These representations are not entirely free of a residue of dread and loathing, but they nevertheless constitute a fictional world of their own that Borges can control. This control is maintained by creating literary fantasies that are safely anchored in the historical past or in the context of a science-fiction universe in which Borges can shape the future by the power of reason. Borges' ambivalence toward his fictional objects, however, results in a splitting process. For example, some of his fictional victims, such as the murdered cabalist Yarmolinsky in the detective story, "Death and the Compass," are identified as clearly blameless, but are destroyed nevertheless on a purely chance basis. Other victims, such as the determined rationalist, the detective Lönnrot in the same story, are not without culpability, but are destroyed because they stubbornly persist in searching for structure and meaning in an absurd universe. Parenthetically, Borges stated in his essay on Hawthorne[19] that Hawthorne detracted from the dreamlike and truly creative aspects of his fiction by trying to inject a large meaning, often in the form of a moral lesson. It is as if a part of Hawthorne, the rational ego and the Puritanical superego that abhorred naked statues, was split off from the fantasist, and stood off to one side, cruelly mocking the futility of all dreams. The splitting process in Borges' case takes a somewhat different form, insofar as it affirms the superiority of dreams over reality, or, in literary terms, a preference for romanticism over realism.

To return to "Death and the Compass," it would appear that the splitting process also involves the familiar dichotomy between the victim and his assailant, the malevolent Red Scharlach. But an important superego function has been omitted, permitting the murderer to go unpunished. The hunted malefactor kills his pursuer, the detective, with impunity. I believe Borges has arranged matters in this way to demonstrate the power of unreason over reason, both of which are attributes that reside in each person and cannot be integrated because of their essential incompatibility. Scharlach the criminal and Lönnrot the detective may be seen as each other's double, each one striving to be a creature of reason in a world of chance. The single identity of the pursuer and the pursued implies that there is no way out of our dreams or nightmares because reason is an illusion and a trap. In depth-analytical terms—how Borges hated such formulations—the trap also involves the inability of the superego, acting in the name of abstract justice, to overcome repressed rage and its consequences. The ego, too, is caught in a snare, Borges insisting that human reason cannot impose order on the mindless flow of events. On this basis, Borges is clearly not a moralist but an elegist, writing a requiem for man's hope of redemption through sublimation. To the extent that the mechanism of splitting characterizes Borges' fiction, it prevents him from exploring the healing power that other writers, like Tolstoy or Faulkner, profess to find in human tragedy. Who is to say that they are right and Borges is wrong?

Critics have made much of Borges' use of the labyrinth as a metaphor for the hopelessness of man's search for a way out of ignorance and fatality. It is useful to think of the labyrinth also in relation to Borges' themes of flight and pursuit. His very first story, "King of the Jungle," written when Borges was thirteen, is an account of a tiger who is being stalked by a huntsman. A jungle is as good a labyrinth as any, and in some of Borges' best stories his protagonists wander about in mazes that may take the form of a logically structured cosmic library, as in "The Library of Babel," or the itinerary of the spy Yu Tsun in "The Garden of the Forking Paths," or the trackless Arabian desert in "The Two

Kings and Their Labyrinths." The labyrinth is a place where men perish, whether it be an artificial maze or the work of nature. Its significance for Borges consists of its confounding mystery and its fatality. The maze may be thought of as Borges' symbol of the unconscious, that labyrinth of dark emotions that can lead the light-seeking ego to destruction. Borges is attracted to the unconscious, but fears it as well for the same reason, according to his testimony, that he has always feared and hated mirrors. The mirror, like the endless maze, permits of no escape from self-confrontation. It leaves the viewer alone with himself, or as Borges prefers to put it, alone with the image of himself, and no matter which way he turns he finds that his reflection, which is also his character and his fate, has followed him.

The labyrinth is more dangerous than the mirror, which, after all, is regarded by Borges as merely an image of an image. For example, in the story "Ibn Hakkan al-Bokhari, Dead in His Labyrinth" the reader learns that an exiled Sudanese tyrant once built a labyrinthine house on the coast of England so that the ghost of his cousin, whom he had murdered, would not be able to find him, along with his stolen treasure, and exact vengeance. The king was killed, nevertheless, along with his slave and his pet lion, all of whom were found with their faces smashed in. Although Borges causes the narrators of the anecdote to speculate that the cousin may have killed the king initially, stolen the treasure, and taken on his identity, the violence that occupies such an important place in the narrative cannot be ignored. The maze, after all, is the place where one is hounded by a Minotaur of one sort or another, and is therefore a symbol of doom. And what if one imagines himself not only lost in a labyrinth, but also handicapped by failing eyesight? This, of course, was the predicament of Borges, condemned to a narrow, affectless existence by his timidity, and by the influence of his powerful mother, who lived to be ninety-nine, dying when Borges was seventy-six years old. Hemmed in on all sides, Borges carried a heavy burden of impulse control not to strike out in obscure anger.

The metaphor of the spider's web, which Borges develops in the story of Ibn Hakkan, is the perfect symbol for Borges' predicament. He was caught in the invisible web of his mother's solicitude, and only in his convoluted fantasies could his repressed rage surface. If one were to ask who the king really is, who his murdered cousin is, and what the true significance is of the treasure, the slave, and the lion, the answer might best be as follows: The treasure is the literary gift that the son, (i.e., the "cousin") obtained from the father (i.e., the "king"), just as Borges as a child was led into precocious literary activity by his intellectual father. The slave represents Borges' self-concept in relation to his mother; the captive lion denotes his repressed emotions and the life of impulse that was in general stifled from childhood onward. The faces of the lion, the slave, and another person have been crushed beyond recognition. Why? Perhaps it was to prevent even the author from recognizing the configuration of his unconscious self-hatred, because *he* is the other person.

Borges' literary treatment of the double provides strong evidence of his ambivalence toward himself. Borges made it no secret that he was deliberately nonpsychological in his fiction, preferring to concentrate on aesthetic and philosophical problems. It is therefore safe to assume that his use of the double in "Biography of Tadeo Isidoro Cruz (1829–1874)," "The Duel," and "The End of the Duel," is not intended to describe inner conflict or the mechanisms of self-deception or self-defeat. Borges' intentions as an artist are not the same, however, as the effects of his art on the reader. These effects consist of showing a self that is forever destroying itself or being destroyed through violence. An obvious example of this predilection is seen in "The End of the Duel," in which two prisoners of war are made to run a race with their throats slit. Their cruel captors know that the two men, longtime rivals, will compete fiercely even though they are already dead men. The key to the meaning of such stories can be found in "Theme of the Traitor and Hero," in which Borges is explicit in telling the reader that his two protagonists are really the same man. In this instance, a man thought to be a great patriot turns out to be a turncoat and is subsequently executed, but in such a way as to make it look as if he had been assassinated. This subterfuge leaves his heroic image untarnished. Borges, too, is his own enemy, and his remarkably static existence—his feverish travels and lectures after he became famous in his sixties remain impersonal acts—attests to his inability to overcome his dependency needs, which immobilized him psychologically. Borges' fictional double, then, is an unconscious metaphor for one who tries feebly to rise above his self-imposed limitations and is extinguished as a result of his immaturity.

It is instructive to seek out the apparent instrument of destruction. We notice at once that Borges has given us an extensive gallery of antiheroes who are vanquished either by their doubles or, of equal importance, by an omnipotent godlike figure who toys with them, giving them the illusion of autonomy, only to stamp them out in the end. Many examples of such executioners can be found in Borges' stories. These conquering figures include James Alexander Nolan in "Theme of the Traitor and Hero," Suárez in "The Challenge," Juan Patricio Nolan in "The End of the Duel," Scharlach in "Death and the Compass," Bandeira, the gaucho chief in "The Dead Man," and the Nilsen brothers in "The Intruder." These powerful figures may be thought of as oedipal fathers who triumph over their rebellious sons. In "The Intruder," however, Borges seems to deviate from his usual formula because the victim is a young woman. "The Intruder" is a story about two brothers who share their mistress, a prostitute, over a period of time. Finally, one of the brothers murders her in cold blood to prevent her from spoiling their relationship of perfect loyalty and trust, and the two men embrace. In addition to being one of Borges' most brutal stories, it is also in Borges' opinion one of his best stories. There is also the curious circumstance that the murdered woman is named *Burgos,* a name that is almost identical with Borges. This story, which Borges' mother detested, represents a wish fulfillment in relation to Borges' mother, I suspect, and the Nilsen brothers can be reduced to Borges and his violent, repressed double. At the very least, "The Intruder" tells us more than Borges would have cared to communicate about his attitude toward women. For even if we accept the manifest story as Borges' interpretation of the cult of machismo and male bonding as a deadly conspiracy against the dignity of women, the manner in which the story is told carries overtones of misogyny. In general, however, Borges' male protagonists are depicted as helpless in the face of more powerful adversaries, and an oedipal drama of frustrated rebellion is acted out. A reasonable interpretation is that Borges was dominated by his father and mother alike, but that the relationship with his father provided more material for fantasy, perhaps because it produced a stronger fear reaction.

The fear of death, in particular, seems to be bound up with Borges' use of the double. This connection is illustrated in "The Theologian," in which a theologian who is jealous of the success of a rival is responsible for having the rival burned at the stake as an exponent of heresy—the very same heresy that once was orthodox belief. In reality, the identities of the two rivals are interchangeable; only their beliefs change with changing theological fashions. Borges' tale is satirical, but it is also an indictment of the divided individual in his capacity of self-destroyer. In Borges' defense, it must be admitted that he has also argued in "The Approach to Al-Mu'tasim" that the individual can find truth and divinity only in himself, rather than in an external object. But what a difficult and circuitous route the student protagonist must take in this tale! By contrast, the confrontation with the double, as in "The Challenge," requires few preliminaries. This story describes a knife fight between a brave and honest rope-maker, Suárez, and a stranger who challenges him to a contest, having heard of his reputation for skill and bravery. Suárez kills his rival, but only after losing his left hand, which had been half-severed in the fight. This is how Borges describes the climactic scene: "The knife enters his wrist, his hand hangs there deadened. Suárez, with a great leap, falls back, lays his bloodied hand on the ground, steps on it with his boot, tears it off, fakes a blow to the stranger's chest, and with a thrust opens his belly."[20] Significantly, Suarez is a man without a wife or children. He lives with his aged mother on his ranch and is described as middle-aged, whereas his antagonist is a younger man. Like "The Dead Man," in which an aging gaucho chief kills a young upstart in his band, "The Challenge" bespeaks the victory of the bad father over the oedipal son. In "The Dead Man," the younger man even dares to sleep with the chief's mistress, underscoring the theme of oedipal rivalry. Evidently, a close connection exists between the motif of the double and

Borges' tendency to inflict defeat on his young protagonists who challenge their older rivals.

Insofar as the double is an unconscious metaphor for the divided self, Borges, in defeating the rebel, also stifles impulse release. Oedipal defeat in Borges' stories signifies that acting out is dangerous. Paradoxically, in "The Challenge," it is the older man Suárez who is symbolically castrated by the loss of his left hand. He is still formidable enough, nevertheless, to kill his young rival. "The Challenge" and "The Dead Man," like most of Borges' stories, were written when he was past forty and may reflect his self-concept as an aging man. His early career as a bold, innovative poet and political liberal suggests that in his youth Borges was not closely identified with the authority of the elders, and was somewhat rebellious, at least on the plane of ideas. Borges' basic identification has always been with the past, however. The past, for him, was enshrined in his family's long military history and its aristocratic background. It is also the starting point for his lifelong autodidacticism, which consists above all of delving into ancient and half-forgotten legends, beliefs, heroes, historical events, and literary works.

The conservative bent of Borges' political attitudes throughout most of his life is consistent with his nostalgia for the past—his own past as well as that of frontier Argentina or periods of remote antiquity. Borges' early years were the time, after all, when he was not yet blind, and when the streets of Buenos Aires beckoned to him with the promise of the unseen. But the real basis for his attachment to the elders, and his penchant for defending them in the guise of fictional characters, is to be found in his ties to his parents. His father, also blind, died when Borges was thirty-nine, and his mother lived, as I have noted, until Borges himself was a very old man. It is clear that Borges loved his parents. Can we really speak with confidence of oedipal struggles between fictional youths and their powerful adversaries, if Borges loved his parents and never had any resentments to repress? And what is the meaning of violence and Borges' obsession with knives in his writings? We know little about Borges' early childhood, but we can guess that he did indeed undergo an oedipal crisis of great severity. Further, it is apparent that in the face of castration fears, Borges abandoned not only the mother as incestuous love object, but women in general. The knives, and the repetition-compulsion centering on knife fights, with the older man always the winner, tell us through the medium of fantasy that Borges never overcame his fear of his father. The father was a lawyer, an essayist, and a poet—in short, anything but an untamed gaucho with a knife in his hand. But as seen through the eyes of a child, the image of the father can be threatening in proportion to the child's emotional dependency on the mother. And what kind of mother did Borges have? We can learn nothing directly about her from his female protagonists, who are mute and docile, mere sex objects for their arrogant males. These fictional women are fantasy figures, because everything we know about Borges' mother suggests that she was intelligent, forceful, and deeply involved in her son's personal life and literary career. The fictional women are also wish fulfillments in the same sense that Hemingway's fictional women are the antithesis of his dominant mother (with the exception of Mrs. Macomber, modeled after the Countess Blixen, Isaak Dineson). Real women were off-limits to the young Borges because of his castration fears and his guilt-laden reliance on his mother.

Borges' inability to make a life for himself apart from his parents meant that he lived in a world of limited choices or possibilities on the plane of action. As Carter Wheelock[21] notes, Borges is pessimistic about identifying the truth because he regards the world as ambiguous and even illusionary. Hence, his art is highly subjective and seeks to infer an unnamed reality by means of symbols that can be elaborated in ways that open up new possibilities. Thus, Borges' fiction is the answer to his sense of stasis or paralysis that dominates his consciousness, and which is reflected in his cyclical view of history. By embracing a mythic view of the world, in which the imagination is free to create new worlds, Borges escapes from his father's house into Plato's lofty mansion of infinite possibilities. The theoretical formulations of Albert Rothenberg[22] are helpful for understanding the mechanisms used by Borges for creating a fictional universe of limitless possibilities. I refer to Rothenberg's concept of "janusian thinking," which he defines as "actively conceiving two or more opposite or antithetical ideas, images, or concepts simultaneously." Rothenberg adds that such opposites are conceived as "equally operative and equally true." He insists that janusian thought should not be confused with ambivalence or with pathological cognitive processes. It belongs, instead, to the domain of clear, goal-directed, fully conscious cognition (i.e., secondary-process thinking). As such, the mirror images of janusian thought are different from the spontaneous images that occur in dreams, which they resemble superficially.

As applied to Borges, the function of mirror images undoubtedly reflects his deliberate aesthetic strategies and goals— up to a point. Borges' ambiguities and multiple choice-points, for which he has supplied the metaphor of "forking paths," also express conflicts that exist below the level of full consciousness. Rothenberg's analysis of the creative process takes into account the existence of parallel conflicts, those aroused by contradictory emotions and those the writer is able to express in intellectual terms. It is Rothenberg's contention that the creative act merges conflicts that exist at the conscious and unconscious levels simultaneously. This fusion is accomplished by means of the defense of negation, the concept of which was originally introduced by Freud. As applied by Rothenberg to the creative process, negation involves the entry of preconscious or unconscious fantasies in conscious thought, but without the removal of repression or evoking anxiety. Borges' stories illustrate this process with particular clarity because of his love of paradox. An example is provided by "Pierre Menard, Author of Don Quixote," Borges' first mature attempt at writing fiction, a decision that followed his recovery from the head injury and blood poisoning that nearly cost him his life in 1938. This is a highly representative story about a twentieth-century Frenchman who sets himself the impossible task of writing Cervantes' *Don Quixote* anew because "every man should be capable of all ideas." Like many of Borges' tales, "Pierre Menard" contains Borges' trademarks: anachronisms, false literary attributions, and Freudian negations. For example, the narrator of the story reports that Menard published an attack on the French poet, Paul Valéry, in the *Journal for the Suppression of Reality*, and adds, "This invective . . . is the exact reverse of his true opinion of Valéry."

Such contradictions are basic to Borges' art, in which he sets impossible intellectual tasks for his protagonists, shares this information with his readers, and then allows his protagonists to explore the limits of their impossible situation. The mechanism of negation as employed in "Pierre Menard" illuminates Borges' repudiation of Freud and surrealism, because Borges typically brings to the surface his characters'—and his own—unconscious wishes, but does so humorously and while seeming to protest the logical absurdity of those very wishes. That Borges recognizes the unconscious truth embedded in his absurdist fantasies is suggested by the narrator's tongue-in-cheek observation in "Pierre Menard" that the few fragments of *Don Quixote* written by Menard long after Cervantes' original was composed, were, in fact, more subtle than Cervantes' work.

Rothenberg maintains that creativity does not involve direct access to the unconscious, but is rather the product of defensive negation, which permits the author to draw upon unconscious materials while reassuring himself that "this is not about me, it is about imaginary people." Borges, of course, gives us imaginary and implausible situations, rather than articulated characters, but the effect is the same, revealing Borges' deepest concerns under a veneer of subtle humor and logical brain teasing. Typically, Borges denies the centrality of the affective component in his work. In "An Examination of the Work of Herbert Quain," the narrator says of Quain, a kind of fictional counterpart of Borges, that Quain had valued his own writings less for their emotional intensity than for their novelty. Borges disclosed his ambivalence toward his own technique of composition and his way of coping with the real world in "Death and the Compass." As mentioned earlier, this tale advances the thesis that to try to solve the dilemmas posed by the real world in a strictly rational way is inherently mistaken. The protagonist of "Death and the Compass," the overly cerebral detective Lönnrot, is destroyed precisely because he allows his need for logical symmetry to lead him into a trap. His adversary, Red Scharlach, had sworn to kill Lönnrot in revenge for the detective's capture of Scharlach's brother, but Lönnrot "had never allowed himself to be intimidated. Lönnrot thought of himself as a pure thinker." If Borges is fully aware of the futility of trusting reason and ignoring passion as a motivating force, why does he assign a higher place to logical exploration than to the fictional treatment of human emotions? Why, in other words, is his literary career a monument to the omnipotence of the imagination and to the idea that everything that the human mind can conceive is true? This is to say, *everything* outside the affective realm.

Perhaps Borges understood that his sheltered childhood did not equip him to create a convincing fictional world that would mirror the emotional complexity of the real world. Such a supposition might explain why Borges confined himself to the composition of highly sophisticated, self-consistent literary puzzles. He was not prepared to do otherwise, and so chose, more or less consciously, to write about what he knew best, namely, books, ideas, and odd, antiquarian facts. Another interpretation is that Borges' stories became the vehicle for symbolically resolving intrapsychic conflicts of which Borges may have been partly conscious. These conflicts center on Borges' ambivalent identification with the bad me. A story that illustrates this interpretation even more tellingly than does "Death and the Compass" (in which, after all, the criminal kills the detective) is "Three Versions of Judas." The protagonist of the story, Nils Runeberg, a Swedish theologian, becomes obsessed with the idea that Judas' betrayal of Jesus was in accordance with the divine will, and that, most startling of all, it was Judas, rather than Jesus, who took it upon himself to expiate the sins of mankind by deliberately becoming the universal symbol of betrayal. By stating explicitly that God assumed the form of Judas, rather than that of Christ, Runeberg of course brings down upon himself the wrath of his colleagues and ends his life in obscurity and historical ignominy. What Borges is saying, in effect, is that unsettling possibilities exist and can bring about a radical shift in one's perspective.

Borges intrudes the possibility of the sinister in "Three Versions of Judas" in a manner that resembles his intrusion of a make-believe world in "Tlön, Uqbar, Orbis Tertius." In Tlön, evidence accumilates that another, nonmaterial world exists somewhere in space. In this world, actions take place in time, but not in space, and objects exist only in the form of mental processes. This well-ordered universe, with its own system of ideas, is described by Borges in the most menacing terms: "Contact with Tlön and the ways of Tlön have disintegrated this world. Captivated by its discipline, humanity forgets and goes on forgetting that it is the discipline of chess players, not of angels." Borges uses the sophistries of the world of Tlön to make an important point about man's susceptibility to evil influence: "Ten years ago, any symmetrical system whatsoever which gave the appearance of order—dialectical materialism, anti-Semitism, Nazism—was enough to fascinate men. Why not fall under the spell of Tlön and submit to the minute and vast evidence of an ordered planet?" Whether Borges is using the symbolism of Judas or Tlön's arbitrary distortions of the real world by means of false ideas, he is talking about dangerous id impulses that threaten to overwhelm the ego and to upset its hard-won security system. Borges is nevertheless drawn to the world of Tlön—his partiality to philosophical idealism is well known—and his modus operandi as a writer is to displace the objects of the real world with his own highly idiosyncratic object representations, in which good and bad are intermixed. The good me and the bad me are never far apart, even though Borges recognizes that lofty ideas can provide a place of concealment for destructive impulses.

The interchangeability of the good me and the bad me is seen not only in "The Theme of the Traitor and the Hero," in which a traitor is allowed to remain a hero in the eyes of his admirers so as not to demoralize them, but also in "The Form of the Sword." In the latter story it is revealed that John Vincent Moon, in narrating an incident from the Irish struggle for independence, had presented himself as a patriot, rather than the traitor he actually was. In the end, Moon confesses to his listener that he was indeed a traitor, and that the scar on his face was inflicted by the brave man whom he had betrayed. These tales attest to Borges' conviction of the ambiguity of all appearances, just as the story "Funes, the Memorious" testifies to the oppressive weight of the world of concrete appearances. Unlike Borges, condemned by blindness to dwell in the subdued light of abstractions, the youth Ireneo Funes is fated to dwell obsessively on the vivid images of all concrete objects that come before his eyes. His retentive memory is like a "garbage disposal." Ideas betray, appearances betray, concrete objects and a superfluity of details betray the mind into mindlessness, making it impossible to think and to form generalizations. The good me of Borges fears entrapment by the appeal of false ideals, and the bad me shrinks back from the temptation to express pent-up hostility. Out of this tension, Borges creates unprecedented fictional situations, ideal worlds no different from our own, but filled with undreamed-of possibilities. His blindness permits him to see the essential, and not to be misled by the merely circumstantial. Yet he does not proclaim the ultimate triumph of philosophical idealism as a guide to truth because Borges is a realist and a true artist, whose passion is to communicate his private vision to his readers. The fictional world that Borges has invented is self-sufficient and its place in our memory and affections unassailable because it cannot be confused with any lesser vision.

Chapter 9

SAMUEL BECKETT

On the Borderline

Too much has been written about Samuel Beckett's works without reference to the man. With the publication of Deirdre Bair's[1] excellent biography it is possible to study Beckett's literary output in its human context and without attributing false intentions to the author. Ms. Bair's insightful study leaves no doubt that Beckett's writings can be understood in all their richness only by reference to his complex and difficult personality. There is no boundary between art and inner life in Beckett's highly original, idiosyncratic writings. These are the cathartic outpourings of a truly tormented man who has vast literary gifts. As I will try to show, Beckett's work, with its morbid obsessions, its pessimism, its stylistic innovations, and its universal implications, is partly by design and partly a byproduct of severe pathology. I do not mean to diminish Beckett in any way. My intention is to demonstrate that, in Beckett's case, at least, artistic creation of the highest order is inconceivable without the impetus of intense anxiety, rage, and despair. I also wish to show that willfulness and its reciprocal, obsessive doubt—two important characteristics of Beckett's work—are symptoms of a character disorder marked by extreme rigidity and self-centeredness.

It is difficult to determine if Beckett experienced psychotic episodes at various points in his life. Bair's biography makes it clear that for the first forty years of his life, if not longer, Beckett showed serious ego defects. As a result, he was unable to cope effectively with even the minimal demands of life. Until the unexpected success of *Waiting for Godot* in 1952 when Beckett was forty-six, transformed his life overnight, Beckett had been unable to support himself, had remained tied to his mother in an ambivalent relationship, and had been unable to interact with others in a socialized way due to his hostility and egocentricity. Moreover, Beckett had suffered from recurring illnesses diagnosed as psychosomatic reactions. To complicate the picture, Beckett's heavy drinking can be classified as alcoholism by any reasonable definition of that term. If Beckett was not manifestly schizophrenic during the first half of his life, at least on an episodic basis, his condition was surely borderline. In light of the severity of Beckett's psychiatric symptoms, his literary achievement, which earned him the Nobel prize in 1969, testifies to his powers of endurance. Paradoxically, it is doubtful if Beckett could have produced his unique works if he had not been disturbed.

Wilfred R. Bion, who analyzed Beckett in London for over two years, starting in 1934 when Beckett was twenty-eight, states in his article "Emotional Turbulence"[2] that psychological growth involves making a choice and that such decision making activates emotional turmoil. Growth, change, discovery, and creativity all involve crossing a borderline and experiencing a psychological break or caesura. It is difficult if not impossible to effect a complete rupture with the past. Old solutions and integrations often stand in the way of restructuring the present, as is seen in resistance during analysis. Bion argues that turbulence is the price of psychological growth. It does not guarantee growth, much less creativity, because other factors are involved. In Beckett's case, for example, the conflicts of his formative years and the endless frustrations of his adult years could have led to defeat as an artist, to increased alcoholism, to chronic psychosis, or to suicide. Commenting on Beckett's state of mind shortly before he undertook analysis, Bair states: "He had gone through a period of rage, as evinced by the drunken scene in which he destroyed all the crockery and threw the pudding into the bushes. Rage gave way to panic when he realized that years were passing and he was still living at home, a wastrel son."[3]

Perhaps it was chance that saved Beckett from destruction. It was chance that led to the eventual publication of his obscure and difficult novels and the production of his unconventional plays, which had been turned down consistently for over two decades. It was chance that brought Beckett into contact with James Joyce, thus permitting him to enter one of the most important literary circles of his time. And it was chance that caused Suzanne Deschevaux-Dumesnil to wander by and give Beckett first-aid when he had been stabbed by a pimp and lay bleeding on a Parisian sidewalk in the middle of the night. Suzanne became Beckett's lifelong companion in 1938 and played a crucial role in tirelessly carrying his manuscripts to scores of potential publishers and producers at a time when Beckett was too dispirited to act on his own behalf. In short, there was nothing inevitable about Beckett's ultimate triumph as a writer; he might have been crushed by the turbulence within him and by the indifference of the external world.

Beckett's mother was a hostile, domineering woman, basically asocial although she entertained guests periodically because she felt her social position required it. She tried to keep her sons, Samuel and his older brother Frank, under her control throughout her life, working on their guilt feelings. She was apparently incapable of empathy or real warmth. Beckett's relationships were also marked by extreme coolness, the need for absolute control, and a compulsive need for privacy and seclusion. His social needs were met by drinking bouts with acquaintances and highly intellectualized relationships with colleagues in the literary and theatrical worlds. Even Beckett's closest relationships lacked intensity and directness. For example, Beckett's lifelong friend and confidante, Thomas McGreevy, was someone Beckett communicated with mainly through a voluminous, soul-baring correspondence. Beckett's mistress and (later his wife) Suzanne, shared his life on the basis of physical proximity only. Although Suzanne was an intelligent woman who had done some writing herself, Beckett did not confide in her, nor did she confide in him. Their relationship had started out as one in which Suzanne voluntarily devoted herself to caring for Beckett and furthering his literary career. Eventually, the essential character of this relationship came to the fore, with Beckett and Suzanne staying together but living separate lives. Suzanne resembled Beckett's mother in her tall, angular build and severe clothes. She took charge of Beckett's life in a calm and self-assured way, but she was as private a person as was Beckett. Beckett found in Suzanne the accepting mother-surrogate that he needed, but the relationship was asymmetrical: Beckett gave her nothing but the reflected glory of his success, when it finally came, whereas Suzanne worked diligently on Beckett's behalf. She did not succeed, however, in overcoming Beckett's depression, his cold anger, and his sense of separation from others.

Beckett is known for his silence, the opacity of his works, and his refusal to provide interpretations of his writing. This is because Beckett regards writing as a form of self-expression rather than as a medium for communication. He states: "I'm not interested in the effect my plays have on the audience. I simply produce an object. What people think of it is not my concern."[4] Beckett has not gone out of his way to be obscure. He is arbitrary and unaccommodating to his readers and viewers because he is powerless to be otherwise. The fantasies that Beckett projects into his writing have the quality of opacity because Beckett is split off from his deepest affects. These affects are terrible fears of physical and psychological helplessness, of enslavement and victimization, of mutilation, and of inescapable loneliness—but Beckett cannot confront them directly as his own terrors or talk about them as problems. The account of Beckett's analysis by Bion suggests that Beckett tried to intellectualize his difficulties: "The discussions . . . as often as not touched upon the abstract creative process as upon Beckett's personal problems."[5] This is all the more reason for turning to Beckett's writings as the mirror of his inner life and as a guide to the psychology of loneliness and depression.

The feeling of emptiness that borderline patients often express—and that Beckett frequently complained about in his letters—results from the inability to establish contact with one's own feelings. Beckett often communicates extraordinary boredom and emptiness in his fiction, with its monotony and verbosity. At other times he seems to inject sarcasm and gratuitous cruelty, even violence, to counteract the depression and hopelessness that permeate his work. In everyday life, too, Beckett alternated between sullen withdrawal and savage sarcasm. Beckett is either inert, blocked, or disgusted with life, or else he is furious. There is an isomorphism between his life and his work that is visible at every stage of his career. His literature is the literature of man in a borderline state between reality and psychosis, between the will to live (even to vegetate) and the compulsion to suicide, and between silent acquiescence and hostile response. As will be seen from the following summary of his life, Beckett has provided us with universal symbols for expressing the human condition, but he has done so out of the raw materials of his deep unhappiness.

Beckett was born in 1906 in a fashionable Protestant suburb of Dublin. His father William was a wealthy contractor with a hearty temperament, a love of sports, and an indifference to the life of the mind. His mother, May, a tall, angular spinster of thirty at the time of her marriage, came from a privileged background. She was an explosive, hostile person given to bouts of depression and sullen withdrawal. She was antagonistic toward her husband and her sons, especially Samuel. Samuel, in turn, grew up to be a sullen, stubborn child whom she frequently beat with great savagery, using a stick. He learned to endure the beatings in silence and contained his emotions in other situations, as well. Samuel resembled his mother physically to a striking degree, having inherited her gauntness and piercing blue eyes. The father taught Samuel and his brother Frank, four years Samuel's senior, to be highly competitive in sports. To avoid being with the mother, Beckett's father spent almost all his evenings at his club and was home only on weekends. The boys were so frightened of the mother that they often hid in their rooms when she was in one of her ugly moods. The mother suffered from tension headaches, insomnia, and the fear of ghosts. She prowled the house each night, listening for strange sounds and checking all the doors and windows while everyone slept. Sometimes Samuel would awake in fear, seeing his mother standing over him in his darkened room. When Samuel was eight, the family took in the three orphaned children of the mother's brother, two girls and a boy, and raised them as their own.

The children grew up in a large house that was staffed by servants and surrounded by ample grounds, including a tennis court. Apparently, there were no books on the premises. A formal religiosity permeated the outwardly well-ordered household, which Samuel found gloomy and oppressive. He was given to wild and dangerous, perhaps suicidal play activities, like jumping down spread-eagled from the top branches of tall trees, and stopping his fall on the lower branches. As an adolescent, Beckett drove motorcycles recklessly and survived several serious accidents without lasting injury. Like his brother before him, Beckett attended a private school in Northern Ireland for the sons of affluent Protestant families. He was an outstanding athlete and in his senior year at the age of seventeen he was captain of the rugby, cricket, and swimming teams. Beckett was a mediocre student, however. Self-centered and uncommunicative, he had no close friends but was widely known and respected for his athletic prowess. His attitude toward his teachers was generally one of contempt and his relationships with other students were cold and sometimes cruel and domineering. Samuel felt himself to be different and superior but was conscious of being unhappy and apathetic when he was not engaged in sports. He was tightly controlled at all times, often moody and remote like his mother, with much hostility barely beneath the surface.

Beckett attended Trinity College in Dublin, living at home during the first two years, a common arrangement. Once more he demonstrated athletic skill, becoming a member of the varsity cricket team. At first he was bored with his classes, was frequently absent, and had no clear sense of direction. During his third year, however, Beckett came under the influence of Professor Thomas Rudmose-Brown and began to study French literature and romance languages with great enthusiasm. Almost all of the students in his language classes were women, because it was unusual for male students to take an interest in foreign languages. Beckett's parents were pleased with his improvement academically but were puzzled by his new interests and fearful that he might not wish to enter the family business upon graduation. Beckett quickly became a prize-winning student and, upon graduation, was sent to the École Normale Supérieure in Paris as an exchange scholar. Before leaving for Paris, Beckett taught French briefly at a private school in Northern Ireland but was nearly discharged because of his harsh treatment of his students and his savage comments on their papers.

In Paris, Beckett came under the tutelage of Thomas McGreevy, a graduate of Trinity and his predecessor as exchange scholar at the École Supérieure. McGreevy, a Catholic and an Irish nationalist with literary interests, introduced Beckett to a wide circle of Irish expatriates in Paris, including James Joyce and his family. Beckett soon became Joyce's unpaid assistant and was almost like a second son. He modeled himself after his famous mentor, twenty-four years his senior, who was then working on the book eventually published as *Finnegans Wake*. Beckett even attempted to write like Joyce, but his need for precision and control and his desire for independence led him to develop his own style. During this period, when Beckett was still in his early twenties, he fell in love with his cousin, Peggy Sinclair, a beautiful and high-spirited girl raised in a bohemian atmosphere. Peggy apparently did not reciprocate Beckett's feelings. At about the same time, Joyce's schizophrenic daughter Lucia became infatuated with Beckett. After putting her off for a long time, Beckett finally told Lucia that he was not interested in her. Joyce and his wife Nora blamed Beckett for Lucia's subsequent deterioration and Joyce broke off his relationship with Beckett for a period of time.

Beckett won a literary contest in 1930 with his poem *Whoroscope*, based on the life of Descartes, as well as his ideas. Beckett was not well trained in philosophy but had begun to take a deep interest in Descartes' work. He was especially drawn to the idea that we cannot be sure of the reality of the external world but have to rely on our subjective understanding based on analytical reason. It was the emphasis on the inner workings of the mind and its ability to function independently of the world that appealed to Beckett, and which was given a magical interpretation in his later works, in keeping with his psychological needs. Beckett had also read with keen interest the works of Arnold Geulincz, a sixteenth-century follower of Descartes who argued that because we can control only our own mind we should not try to control the external world, including even our body. These ideas, with their emphasis on subjectivity and noninvolvement with the world, were to become the themes of Beckett's first novel, *Murphy* (1935). Shortly after his break with Joyce, Beckett wrote his study of Proust. Published in 1931, the book was well received by critics in England and sold reasonably well. Beckett's parents, who had been scandalized by *Whoroscope*, with its provocative title and Joyce-inspired linguistic experiments, were impressed by *Proust,* which they recognized as a scholarly book, although they could not understand it.

Beckett returned to Dublin in 1930 and was a French instructor at Trinity College. He had taken on many French affectations and felt superior to what he regarded as the provincialism of Dublin's cultural life. Teaching apparently terrified him and he concentrated on his development as a writer. Almost all of his students were young women who admired him initially for his youthful good looks and his obvious erudition. With the passage of time, however, Beckett found it increasingly difficult to prepare his lectures or to face his students. He appeared distracted in class, neglected his appearance, and became severely depressed. Beckett had equated Paris with personal and artistic freedom and felt trapped in Dublin. His symptoms took the symbolic form of feeling that he was choking and suffocating; he also suffered from painful boils. At the height of his depression, Beckett could not bring himself to leave his bed and would lie rigidly in a fetal position with his face to the wall and a blanket over his head. He began to improve when his parents decided to send him to stay with Peggy Sinclair's family, which was living in Germany at the time. Beckett resigned from his position at Trinity, having completed less than half of his three-year appointment. This decision, which greatly disappointed his sponsor, Professor Rudmose-Brown, and was a blow to his parents, was to be the cause of much guilt for many years thereafter.

After spending six months recuperating with the Sinclairs, Beckett finally felt well enough to go to Paris to resume his literary efforts. The year was 1931, and the next two decades, during which Beckett composed his major novels and plays, were to be years of poverty and frustration, intensified by the dangers and hardships of World War II. Between 1931 and 1933, Beckett composed a series of loosely connected short stories titled *More Pricks Than Kicks* (1934). This book was a revision of an unfinished episodic novel called *Dream of Fair to Middling Women,* which contained harsh satires of his family and friends. The protagonist of *More Pricks Than Kicks,* Belacqua Shuah, named after a slothful character in Dante's *Purgatory,* is a lazy young man who is pursued by various women but is afraid of sex. He is also depressed and has suicidal impulses, like Beckett. Belacqua's life is a series of comic disasters brought on by his waywardness. For example, in the story "Walking Out" Belacqua is revealed to be a voyeur who marries reluctantly, hoping that his wife will not make any sexual demands on him but will take a lover instead. His wife soon has an accident that makes it impossible for her to function sexually. During the next two years, until her death, Belacqua achieves happiness in a platonic relationship.

Belacqua's misadventures reflect Beckett's very real difficulties at this stage of his life. He could not find a publisher for his irreverent, somewhat scatological stories and sketches, and was dependent on his parents to send him small sums of money so that he could live in Paris. Beckett returned to Dublin in 1933 in a discouraged frame of mind and found himself under pressure from his mother to get a job. He vegetated at home for many months, refusing to look for a job. As his arguments with his mother became more acrimonious he began to drink heavily, became disheveled, and was shunned by acquaintances as a ne'er-do-well. Beckett again became depressed, suffered from interminable colds, recurring boils, inability to urinate, and pain in his joints and abdomen. His depression had an agitated quality and he was subject to nightmares and headaches. At this crucial point, Beckett's father died suddenly of a heart attack. Beckett's condition now took a turn for the worse. He was also deeply affected by the unexpected news that Peggy Sinclair had died of tuberculosis.

Beckett was devastated by his father's death, so much so that he had deteriorated to the point where his mother was convinced that he needed professional help. To avoid gossip about her son in Dublin, where the Beckett family aspired to social prominence, Beckett's mother agreed to send him to London for psychoanalytic treatment. Beckett responded well to his analyst, Dr. Bion, relaxed somewhat, and began to develop some insight into the depths of his rage, especially at his mother—and at himself. During this time, Beckett improved sufficiently to compose a collection of highly personal poems, *Echo's Bones* (1935), including a sensitive poem about his father's death, which he wrote with great difficulty. Also coinciding with his analysis, Beckett began to write the novel *Murphy* (1938), about an impoverished intellectual living with a prostitute in a run-down section of London. Beckett found that he was blocked and did not know how to develop the novel. He terminated his analysis despite Bion's warning that he had not worked through his neurotic relationship to his mother. Beckett once more returned to Dublin and fell into his old pattern of resentful dependency. As had been true in the past, he made no effort to find employment. He was now thirty years old and regarded his entire life, including his analysis, as a failure.

Beckett finally completed *Murphy* in 1937. Murphy contains in symbolic form the essential elements of Beckett's predicament. A brief summary of the plot may be helpful in this connection: Murphy, a broken-down, homely young man with a comical gait and painful feet (like Beckett), leaves his Dublin sweetheart, Miss Counihan, to seek his fortune in London. Failing to hear from Murphy, Miss Counihan sets out for London in the company, ironically, of her new lover, Wylie. Murphy's former teacher, Neary, has also gone in search of Murphy, who meanwhile has taken a job as a male nurse in a mental hospital. Murphy sought employment only after his London mistress, Celia, a prostitute, threatened to go back to streetwalking if he did not support her. Murphy's aim in the hospital setting is to achieve the impassivity and indifference to reality of the patients. In a bizarre chess game with Mr. Endon, one of the patients, Murphy realizes that he cannot give up his sanity even if he tries. He subsequently commits suicide by lighting a candle in a gas-filled room. In a note giving instructions for the disposal of his remains, Murphy had asked to be cremated and his ashes flushed down the toilet of the Abbey Theater in Dublin. Instead his ashes are spilled on the floor of a pub and swept out with the refuse. One of Murphy's foibles, it should be mentioned, was that he used to tie himself naked into a rocking chair and go into a trance in his darkened room, and was so occupied moments before he blew himself up.

Without going into great detail to interpret the story line, suffice it to say that the prostitute—who threatens to revert to her old ways if Murphy does not find a job—is reminiscent of Beckett's mother. May Beckett tried to be outwardly affectionate toward her troubled son each time he returned home penniless, physically ill, and intoxicated; but she would soon lose patience with his apparent shiftlessness and put pressure on him to find a job, screaming with rage. In *Murphy*, Beckett makes "everyone" go in search of his protagonist while Murphy courts psychosis, which he interprets as a completely subjective existence without ties or responsibilities. Unable to escape from the objective world and its demands, Murphy kills himself. Murphy's compulsion to tie himself into a rocking chair has onanistic as well as autistic overtones, but the central motif of the novel is the protagonist's desperate need to escape via regression and withdrawal. Beckett creates a "caring" pseudofamily for Murphy in the form of all the characters who have gone in search of him. He dooms Murphy to an ignoble end, very much as he felt doomed himself at this uncertain juncture in his life, when he seemed to be falling apart physically and mentally and his literary future was uncertain.

Murphy has much in common thematically with an earlier short story, "A Case in a Thousand" (1934). The protagonist, Dr. Nye, meets his old nanny, Mrs. Bray, whose son is hospitalized with a lung condition. To decide whether to operate, Dr. Nye stretches out full length beside the boy and falls into a trance. Dr. Nye, we are told, had loved his nanny as a child. She now sees him in a trance, but forces herself to look at her son, then shuts her eyes. Aroused from his trance, Dr. Nye is upset at being seen in this state and regrets that he has no candy to offer Mrs. Bray. He decides upon an operation that is carried out by a Dr. Bor and the boy dies. When Dr. Nye returns from a vacation, he learns that Mrs. Bray is keeping a vigil outside the hospital with an umbrella and shooting stick. Dr. Ney confronts her and the two declare that they have something to ask each other. Mrs. Bray relates something to Dr. Nye but the reader is not told the nature of this communication. Finally, Dr. Nye presents Mrs. Bray with a small box of peppermint creams, her favorite candy, and leaves to perform a Wasserman on an old friend. A brief interpretation: Mrs. Bray may be seen as a mother figure with erotic overtones and Dr. Nye as the bad son who is responsible for the death of the good son. Dr. Nye is the son who turns out a failure because of a wrong decision in life, in effect destroying himself or his double. The motive of appeasing the mother is present along with an inability to give her the gift of candy initially, to Dr. Nye's chagrin. In the end, by way of restitution for his failure, the bad son magically gives the mother the gift of candy. Is the candy an expression of love, a token of success, or merely a peace offering? The nanny's phallic umbrella and shooting stick indicate that she can be a formidable adversary. Will she punish the bad son for his failure, that is for destroying himself, or for something he merely did with himself while he was in a trance stretched out on the bed?

The composition of *Murphy* did not help Beckett to exorcize his ghosts. He was not even sure he should persist in pursuing a writing career, and he even entertained briefly the idea of becoming an airline pilot, something he knew nothing about. He continued to avoid looking for work in Dublin, then spent six months traveling through Germany (1936–1937), apparently oblivious to the Nazi dictatorship and insensitive to the plight of writers and artists who confided their fears to him. Beckett then spent another disastrous six months at home, drinking constantly and close to violence. Shortly after his brother married in 1937, Beckett left Ireland, probably to avoid being alone with his mother. He settled in Paris, which was now to become his permanent home and a symbol of the personal and cultural freedom that eluded him elsewhere. It was at this point in Beckett's life, in 1938, that he finally found a publisher for *Murphy* after forty-two rejections.

By this time Beckett had become reconciled with Joyce and was quickly drawn into Joyce's literary and social life. He had a brief affair with Peggy Guggenheim upon the latter's initiative, and then, under the benign influence of Suzanne Deschevaux-Dumesnil, his personality changed somewhat, according to his friends. Beckett's drinking diminished, he became less hostile and sarcastic, and he began to express an interest in other people. Apparently Beckett now felt more secure about his literary and financial future, although his income consisted of a small annuity and little else. Even his attitude toward his mother softened to a degree, reflecting his belief, at age thirty-two, that he would never again be dependent upon her for support.

Beckett returned to Paris from a visit to Dublin a few days after World War II broke out. He decided to stay in France even though most of his expatriate friends were preparing to leave. Through his friendship with Alfred Péron, whom Beckett had known ever since Péron had been an exchange scholar at Trinity College in the 1920s, Beckett was drawn into the French Resistance. His assignment was to translate messages into English and to relay information about German troop movements. He narrowly escaped capture in 1942 and fled with Suzanne to unoccupied France, hiding by day and traveling on foot at night. They were to spend the remaining war years in the village of Roussillon in the Vaucluse, along with numerous other refugees. Beckett lived in relative comfort in Roussillon, corresponding with his mother and brother and receiving money from them regularly. He felt immobilized in Roussillon and soon began to experience anxiety attacks, depression, and various somatic difficulties, including boils. At times Beckett was disoriented. He spent much time sleeping or taking long walks in the countryside, much as he had done in Ireland when he was under great stress. It is not clear if he experienced hallucinations or other psychotic symptoms during this period. He appears to have started writing the novel *Watt* to occupy himself. Toward the end of the war, Beckett was sufficiently recovered to accompany the local Maquis on night patrols and sabotage missions, apparently at their instigation because they had learned of his underground work in Paris.

Watt (1953) contains autobiographical features and also represents a conscious attempt to overcome Joyce's influence. Beneath its complex and baffling surface this novel contains many clues to Beckett's emotional problems and preoccupations. Watt is a servant in the house of a Mr. Knott. Like Murphy, Watt is intent upon escaping into an inner world divorced from reality. After working for Mr. Knott for a period of time, Watt, who experiences auditory hallucinations, makes his way to an institution of some sort where he becomes an inmate. He then relates the story of his quest for irreality to another inmate, named Sam, the narrator of the novel. Watt's search is unsuccessful because, like Murphy, he is ultimately unable to shut out the world around him. *Watt* is an absurdist novel filled with obsessive, often comical ruminations about concrete objects and events. Beckett's focus is almost microscopic as he locates his static characters in a world that affords minute sensory impressions and yields only ambiguous meanings, if any. Endless doubt and indecision beset Watt so that he can hardly be said to speak or move in a purposeful way. *Watt* lends itself to the interpretation that Beckett is exploring his own blocked emotions, inertia, and obsessive defenses against repressed hostility and guilt in relation to his mother. A French farmer who knew Beckett in Roussillon observed that Beckett had a sentimental attitude toward mothers: "Mothers of anything, dogs, cats, humans, anything!" When a neighboring laborer complained in Beckett's presence that he was loath to go to work because it meant leaving his old and ill mother alone, Beckett insisted on taking the man's place, declaring emphatically that "one should be with one's mother!" This attitude was clearly a reaction formation.[6]

A further interpretation of *Watt* is that Beckett, by placing Watt and Sam in a featureless world—in which there is no certainty about anything, no motion, no passion, and no human relationships—achieves absolute control of his fictional universe and can subordinate the objective demands of plot and characterization to his own ruminations. In this way Beckett achieves a sense of control over his life through fantasy. It is a magical control attained by abolishing the world outside the mind, except as an object for contemplation à la Descartes. It is also a control which results in objective failure to deal with life and its demands. A few years later, commenting on the difficulty of finding a publisher for *Watt*, Beckett said: "I'm not interested in stories of success, only failure."[7]

After the war Beckett spent some time in Dublin with his family and returned to Suzanne in Paris. Beckett's mother had never met Suzanne and never spoke of her or acknowledged her existence. In order to get back into France it was necessary for Beckett to volunteer for the Irish Red Cross. He was given the job of keeping records of medical supplies at a portable hospital in Saint-Ló. In 1946 he returned again to Dublin to straighten out his finances. While in Dublin Beckett fell in with a riotous group of English expatriates, the White Stags, many of them blatant homosexuals, and spent a few weeks in drunk and disorderly conduct, frightening and shocking everyone who knew him. It was during this bizarre interlude, a sort of last fling at the age of forty, that Beckett claims he suddenly found his literary direction. While standing half-drunk on a jetty on a stormy night, Beckett decided that henceforth he would write mainly in monologue form, concentrating on his own life, "digging up the detritus of my life and vomiting it out over and over again."[8]

After resuming his life with Suzanne in Paris in the summer of 1946, Beckett started to write *Mercier and Camier,* his first novel in French. It is not clear why Beckett began to write in French, but this change reflects his growing alienation from his old life. Suzanne now assumed the responsibility of supporting Beckett, working as a piano teacher and seamstress (Beckett had a small annuity). Suzanne deliberately avoided contact with Beckett's literary acquaintances. Beckett and Suzanne made no demands on each other, so that he was free to pursue his writing in a single-minded way. *Mercier and Camier* anticipates *Waiting for Godot* with its tramp protagonists, but Mercier and Camier are engaged in undertaking a journey of an unspecified and inconsequential character. Many of the obsessive features of *Watt* are present, along with Beckett's characteristic black humor, as in his description of a large, stout woman who has been hit by a car and lies bleeding in the gutter: "Ah, said Mercier, that's what I needed, I feel a new man. He was in fact transfigured. Let that be a lesson to us, said Camier. Never to despair, said Camier, or lose our faith in life." This passage conveys the sardonic tone of this work and of Beckett's later novels, notably his trilogy, *Molloy* (1951), *Malone Dies* (1951), and *The Unnamable* (1953). Beckett recalled in later years that writing these novels intensified his depression. A play written shortly after *Mercier and Camier* and titled *Éleuthéria* (freedom), was never produced or published. It was autobiographical and dealt openly with Beckett's struggle to free himself from the constraints of his family.

Molloy was begun in 1947 and completed in 1948. The protagonist Molloy is confined to his absent mother's room. His task is to write about himself, and his notes are picked up weekly. Molloy tells the reader about his quest for his mother, which started more than a year earlier. He had begun his journey on a bicycle, carrying a set of crutches with him. After running over a dog he is sheltered by the dog's owner, a woman called Lousse, who transfers her affections from her dog to Molloy. Molloy leaves her eventually and makes his way on crutches. At the seashore he gathers small stones, which he sucks. He now crawls on his belly, still in search of his mother. After falling into a ditch, he is at last taken to his mother's room and compelled to write about his quest, although it is not clear by whom or for what reason. A second character, Moran, a rather fastidious private detective, is dispatched to find Molloy. Like Molloy, Moran loses the use of his legs, which become stiff and paralyzed. While hiking in the forest, he clubs a man to death for no particular reason. Moran's son then transports him on a bicycle in search of Molloy, but the two quarrel and Moran's son leaves him in the lurch. Moran is ordered to turn back by a messenger named Gaber who has been sent by a mysterious figure called Youdi (French slang for Jew). Upon his return home, Moran finds everything in disarray. He eventually writes a report on his search for Molloy and decides to become a vagabond.

On the surface, it would appear that the paralyzed protagonists of *Molloy* were inspired by three of Beckett's relatives who had to have their legs amputated in their later years. On a deeper level, Molloy and Moran symbolize Beckett's paralysis of the will and his sense of helplessness. Molloy's search for his mother is consistent with Beckett's lifelong ambivalent attachment to his mother and his need to return to her at frequent intervals even though he could not stand to be with her. Moran's act of violence and the circumstances connected with it also point toward important conflicts. For example, while Moran was lying in the forest a man approached him and asked for a piece of bread. Moran gave him bread and asked to feel the weight of the man's stick. The following day Moran obtained a similar stick for his own use. A second man then appeared, one who looked very much like Moran himself, and asked if Moran saw an old man with a stick. Moran was engaged in poking his fire with his stick at this point and became very upset. All atremble, he ordered the man to leave and, when the latter refused, Moran killed him with his stick. Moran found that his stiff, paralyzed leg was flexible again, at least for the time being, and remarked that the slain man no longer resembled him.

Although there is a basis for interpreting this episode in terms of classical oedipal rebellion, Beckett's passive-aggressive attitude toward his mother and his positive feelings toward his supportive father suggest another line of reasoning, namely, that we are dealing with an allegory of incomplete resolution of the Oedipus complex. To the extent that resolution takes place it occurs through identification with the father's strength, that is, finding a stick as heavy as the old man's. Moran puts his newly acquired phallic strength to a perverse use, destroying the second man, who is his double. The act of self-destruction is here synonymous with Molloy/Moran's onanistic existence in which, trembling with guilt, he pokes his fire with his stick in the absence of a love object. This troubled existence relieves the protagonist of his paralysis temporarily because he finds he can now bend his leg. By implication, Beckett's self-centered style of life gave him a measure of mobility and freedom. The opening pages of the novel reveal, however, that Molloy's identification with his father is flawed and that he remains tied to his mother. In a brief confession, Molloy states that he has taken his mother's place in her room, occupies her bed, uses her chamber pot, resembles her more and more, and that all he needs now is a son. It would be a mistake to assume that this is a recital of perverse longing for the father, however. In effect, Molloy is telling us that he has identified himself with his mother on a regressive, preoedipal basis. The self-destructive nature of this identification is indicated by Molloy/Moran's decision, at the end, to give up his respectable life and become a tramp, not unlike Beckett's determination to avoid adult responsibility and emotional commitment at any cost, even if it meant tearing himself up by the roots and living in poverty and exile. As can be seen from Molloy's confession, Beckett wished to flee not only from respectability but also from enslavement by his mother.

Beckett's next novel, *Malone Dies,* is about a very old man who is bedridden and slowly dying. Equipped with a small pencil stub and some scraps of paper, he tries to make up stories to pass the time. The setting, like that of *Molloy,* is clearly Beckett's home district of Foxrock, outside Dublin. The narrative is also reminiscent of *Molloy:* The protagonist's thoughts are presented in obsessive detail, his attitude toward life is cramped and defensive, he is filled with guilt, doubt-ridden, and aware of his self-deceptions. Malone seems to take pride in the fact that his life is ebbing away, that he feels feeble and impotent, and that he has avoided deep involvement with other people, past or present. Beckett's savage sense of humor is rarely absent, but *Malone Dies,* like Beckett's other works, is fundamentally sad. His message is that death is a relief from living, which is the original sin.

Beckett next commenced the writing of his most famous work, *Waiting for Godot,* which was produced in Paris in 1952. Beckett was surprised at the success of *Godot* and regarded it as inferior to his labyrinthine novels. He has consistently denied that the play has metaphysical implications, or that his characters are waiting for God, redemption, or rebirth.[9] Beckett's motivation in writing *Godot* seems to have been the need to escape from the painful introspection of his highly personal novels. The play was inspired by traditional vaudeville routines in which two comic figures exchange one-line jokes. In this case the protagonists, Vladimir and Estragon (modeled after Laurel and Hardy, two of Beckett's favorite comics) engage in banter as they await a third person, Godot, who never arrives. They are visited by a seemingly affluent man called Pozzo and his servant Lucky (Beckett has said that Lucky was so called because he was "lucky to have no more expectations"). Otherwise, nothing happens and the play ends as it began with the characters resolved to go on waiting. The circularity of *Godot* is similar to the circularity of Beckett's novels, where there is no movement and the protagonists find themselves back at the starting point after much wasted effort. There are many references to feet and boots in *Godot* (Beckett has stated that the name Godot was suggested by the French slang word for boot, *godillot*).[10] Beckett was very self-conscious about his feet. Ever since childhood he had walked with stiff legs and his feet turned out. His feet had always given him great pain, as well. This is not to say that *Godot* is about feet or boots; it is about waiting and enduring and is an expression of the futility of life, in keeping with Beckett's other works.

While Beckett was looking for someone to produce *Godot*, he composed *The Unnamable*, the last of the trilogy that includes *Molloy* and *Malone Dies*. This novel, or antinovel, carries Beckett's compulsion toward minimalism to a further extreme. The account is of a featureless creature sitting in tatters in limbo or possibly hell. The creature relates a series of disjointed tales of terror and despair. Beckett makes it clear that this spokesman represents his own voice, which he has found at last after needlessly hiding behind his fictional characters. He explains his compulsion to spill out his thoughts as one that can end only with his mother's death: "I'm looking for my mother to kill her, I should have thought of that a bit earlier, before being born."[11] Beckett's aim appears to have been to produce a novel with minimal content but stylistically faultless. As always, the nihilistic tone is pervasive.

In the play *Endgame* (1956), Hamm, who is blind and confined to a wheelchair, shares a shabby, desolate room with Clov, a sort of servant with a spirit of independence. Clov's disability is that he cannot sit down. In the same room are Hamm's elderly parents, Nagg and Nell, who live in two garbage cans. Some of the dialogue bespeaks the unhappy relationship between Hamm and his parents and is filled with bitter reproaches; for the rest, the play is an account of Hamm's life. Clov at last prepares to leave his blind master, telling him that there is a child outside who may take his place. Hamm is afraid of being abandoned, just as Clov is reluctant to leave. Because the title *Endgame* suggests the final stages of a chess game in which only the two kings and a few pawns remain, critics have speculated that Hamm is a symbol of man making his last meaningless moves before he is checkmated by death. Also, there are hints in the play that the outside world has become impoverished, or transformed in some malevolent way—perhaps it, too, is dying. Beckett denies any universal implications for *Endgame* or for any of his other works. Instead, he has intimated that Hamm and Clov represent himself and Suzanne and their strained relationship at this point in their lives.

Krapp's Last Tape (1958) is highly autobiographical and communicates a degree of emotional intensity. The play is almost sentimental in evoking people and places out of Beckett's Irish past, as its aged, clownlike protagonist plays tape recordings that describe the highlights and trivia of his life. Krapp emerges as one who always drank too much and was torn between sentimentality and cynicism, even in the face of his mother's death. Beckett makes use in this play of the incident in his life in which he watched from outside with a mixture of sadness and relief as the window shade was pulled down in his mother's room in a nursing home, signifying her death (in 1950). The protagonist also plays back the tape recording the end of his last love affair, a relationship abandoned apparently so that he could devote himself single-mindedly to writing. As Krapp contemplates his life, he concludes that he gave up everything that really counts in exchange for nothing of value.

How It Is (1961) is not a novel in the usual sense but is rather a long unpunctuated monologue that records the nameless narrator's slow progress crawling in darkness through endless mud, dragging a sack after him. He recalls his old life painfully and, like Krapp, relives an old love affair. The protagonist finally encounters another person called Pim, who lies prostrate in the mud. The narrator, now calling himself Bim, spends much time conditioning Pim to make certain simple responses by administering painful stimuli to him, such as prodding him with a can opener. In the last part of *How It Is*, the narrator recalls how, before he met Pim, he himself had been cruelly tormented by someone called Bem. In the future the protagonist expects to revert to his status as a victim, this time at the hands of a person named Bom. In *How It Is* Beckett has stated his harsh philosophy of life with an economy of means, intensifying the note of sadomasochism present in his earlier novels. In the final pages the reader learns that there is only the narrator after all, alone in the slime with his memories of his former existence (which correspond to Beckett's life in many details, including his relationship with Suzanne). That relationship had been deteriorating for some years, and by the early 1960s Beckett and Suzanne lived together uneasily, even though Beckett had married her in 1961 to make sure that she would inherit his estate. Suzanne had become increasingly resentful of Beckett as his fame increased, feeling that he had not made public the important role she had played in advancing his career. She also felt that she was no longer indispensable to him as he grew in independence and self-confidence.

The play *Happy Days* (1961) is about a middle-aged couple named Winnie and Willie living a dull, empty existence. Winnie, who is buried up to her neck in a mound of earth, spends all her time being compulsively cheerful and optimistic, while Willie remains silent, reading a newspaper. In the last moments of the play, Willie, who can only crawl, finally approaches his garrulous partner and looks her directly in the face. It is not clear whether he intends to shoot her (a gun is visible close by) or whether his intentions are friendly. Whether Beckett is expressing his hostility toward women in general or toward Suzanne in particular— or is stating that life is dull and devoid of love—is not clear.

In general, Beckett's later works were shorter and less ambitious than his earlier works. The tenor of such works as *Play* (1963), *All Who Fall (1956), Eh Joe* (1966), and other short pieces is somewhat more domestic than in his early works, but the familiar motifs of conflict, loneliness, and futility persist. In expressing his own nihilistic outlook Beckett seems to be writing about the spiritual condition of modern man. Man is psychologically on a trash heap, but unlike Job on his dunghill, he shows no sign of raising himself up. Beckett tells us that man has almost exhausted his small capital of hope and endures only out of animal instinct.

The loneliness and helplessness that most men fear, repress, and then deny by a show of determined adequacy, Beckett permits to take possession of his literary imagination. The phrase "lingering dissolution," spoken by the aging Mrs. Rooney in the radio play *All That Fall* expresses Beckett's deadly sense of life. True to his own psychic needs, he allows his characters only one form of control over their otherwise formless existence. He turns them into anal compulsives who count every step they take and hoard the minutes of their lives even though they have no constructive means of filling time. They hoard their very boredom, stretching it to the limits of endurance, just as Beckett pushes his readers to the limits of patience. Their goal is to crawl into bed and stay there, conserving their energy for no particular purpose, and defying the world to make them bestir themselves, very much like Beckett himself for much of his life. Their minds operate like a computer that has gone wrong, producing seemingly random messages, repeated with endless variations.

Some will object that this account does violence to the lucidity of Beckett's mind. Although his characters can deal with reality solely in terms of probabilities, as if everything were chimerical and uncertain, Beckett is an introspectionist with remarkably clear vision. He notices the most minute details of the outer world and records the most subtle nuances of his thoughts. In so doing, he makes of every fleeting image a microcosm of logical, spatial, philological, metaphysical, scatological, and comical speculation. Is he not a successful, indeed an intrepid explorer of consciousness? The problem is that Beckett, like Sartre, is a Cartesian, aware only of the cognitive processes of the mind but ignorant of the identity of the thinker. This is why Beckett's protagonists, though generally not nameless, have no real identity, no essential particularity, no specific graces or vulnerabilities. They are cogitating machines, calculating what they have left in the pocket of an old raincoat, or reasoning that if a lost object is not in one place then it must be in another. These are the author's defenses against depersonalization, against the fear of disintegration, the classical obsessive-compulsive defenses against destructive rage. With verbal magic Beckett dissolves human emotions, so that the reader is left entirely in the dark about the true passions, if any, of his characters. He obliterates the human attributes of love, courage, tenderness, concern, and independence to create a new form of art, of antiliterature and antitheater. At the same time, by allowing the return of the repressed, and exploring negative affects with complete candor, Beckett searches for radical freedom from the constraints of the external world. Starting with *Murphy*, he has located this zone in the subjective world, only to find it populated with terrors of its own. Beckett has faced these terrors with courage, and like his beloved Dante has taken us on a tour of the nether regions that exist in the human mind. But he has payed a price for being our guide through hell, for revenging himself against the human spirit and the flesh, and for mocking life. Beckett has taught us a lesson in mortality and has humbled human pride. But in the process of creating an inhuman landscape and exploring it with an infinitely expanded mind, Beckett has suffered a contraction of the heart, and has left us with nothing to oppose the menace of death.

In the light of Beckett's pessimism, how is it possible to explain how he has turned pain into art and failure into success? Perhaps a simple borderline diagnosis obscures more than it reveals, because it does not disclose the springs of creativity. Nor does it clarify the means by which regression in the service of the ego can result in art of the highest order, reflecting ego strengths not normally associated with borderline conditions. I believe these questions can best be answered by reference to Beckett's dependence on alter egos to stabilize and motivate him. One must not underestimate the ego support Beckett derived from his father, his intensely loyal brother, Professor Rudmose-Brown, Thomas McGreevy, James Joyce, and Suzanne Deschevaux-Dumesnil, who simply saved his life and nurtured his talent until he was strong enough to stand on his own feet. These alter egos accomplished more than the mere preservation of Beckett's ego and his escape from psychosis. Joyce, in particular, provided a context in which Beckett, as his personal secretary and protege, was placed at the center of a cultural revolution, the very heart of twentieth-century modernism in literature. The conjunction of Beckett's special psychic needs with the empathic response of his alter egos was crucial for stabilizing his identity, alleviating his disabling symptoms, and enabling him to become a writer of the first rank.

Chapter 10

HAROLD PINTER

Ego Development and Psychological Space

Harold Pinter's dramas, like all good theater, stimulate the imagination by means of evocative stage settings. These settings are in the minimalist tradition, but their effect is to evoke compelling images of loneliness, conflict, and insecurity. The basic element in Pinter's stage settings is a room that invariably suggests ominous possibilities of desolation and trauma. As Jerome Singer has suggested, the "crystallizing potential" of our ability to form mental images can provide us with metaphors that point to the deepest layers of experience.[1,2] Along these lines, Pinter potentiates a type of imagery in his audiences that carries its members into the recesses of their own private experience. Most dramatic plays stimulate objectification in the viewer, focusing attention on the immediate scene on the stage. Pinter's plays operate on a subjective principle, impelling the viewer to supply his own complementary images. The fantasies enacted on Pinter's stage radiate out into a thousand private lives. There they bring to the surface matching fantasies that are experienced as cathartic even when they evoke the terror of life.

That the effect of such shared fantasies can extend beyond catharsis has been maintained by investigators such as Reyher[3] and Singer[4] who have tried to demonstrate that imagery associations can be a valuable tool of psychotherapy, overcoming defensiveness and bringing to the surface repressed materials. At the same time, the therapist can enter into the patient's experience empathically by producing corresponding images of his own.[5]

This is not to say that viewing one of Pinter's plays can be therapeutic. Rather, the visual images suggested by Pinter's sets, and the vivid visual memories that his characters articulate, permit Pinter to make contact with his audiences with the smallest possible number of words. Like Beckett, Pinter brings into play a strategy that is outwardly reductionistic. His characters engage in repetition and incantation, always with the same spare vocabulary, until the audience begins to see beyond the stage and to literally visualize the characters' obsessions, which are localized in rooms, basements, pubs, buses and other places experienced in the past. In effect, the stimulation of place imagery by Pinter throws the theater audience back upon itself, forcing it to confront its own suppressed desires, including its nostalgia for the lost stasis of the past and the seeming security of childhood.

Seen from this perspective, the past that Pinter's characters try to recapture consists above all of visual imagery that has been cathected for compelling reasons. By combining these images of the past with spent emotions and obsessive ideation, Pinter creates fictional characters who exist in the round. These protagonists are conceived as cognitive-affective-perceptual beings with whom the audience can empathize and through whose eyes it can contemplate its own inner landscape. In this connection, Singer draws attention to the challenge during psychotherapy of helping the patient integrate the revived images of his childhood with his present life. If such integration is to strengthen the patient's hold on reality, it must involve abreaction and working through of the original affective charge associated with retrieved imagery. It is no small part of Pinter's power as a dramatist that the affect-laden images his characters dredge up out of their past are not always sentimental and regressive. When these images are not revived for the purpose of bolstering a character's fragile ego they have the power to move audiences for all the right reasons—namely, because they restore the sharp and painful edges of reality that selective memory has blunted. Meichenbaum, in this regard, links imagery-based psychotherapy with behavior modification, through the patient's learning to monitor and interrupt images that lead to maladaptive behavior. Pinter similarly highlights for his audiences the association between his characters' disturbed behavior and their bondage to pathogenic images. The theater audience can share the images that Pinter's characters recapture from their past, but they are in a position, by virtue of their relative detachment, to see how this imagery has stunted the psychological growth of the characters. By extension, Pinter succeeds in sensitizing his audiences to the relationship between their own imagery that refers to the past and their current existential dilemmas.

Pinter's use of remembered images goes beyond the past and the present, and points to the future by demonstrating the adaptive, problem-solving potential of directed imagery. As Shorr[6] has argued, directed imagery can be used in psychotherapy not only to investigate an individual's personality and conflicts, but also to permit the exploration of new possibilities by integrating the actual self with the ideal self. Shorr points to the interpersonal implications of achieving greater harmony between fantasy and reality through the play of imagination. Pinter's characters, by contrast, often evoke the past by recalling visual images of idealized harmony and security for regressive or compensatory reasons, and not to understand themselves better. The playgoer, however, is made to understand that the fictional character is self-deceiving. Pinter highlights the difference between regressive fantasy and images of positive action by demonstrating how people seal themselves off from new possibilities for growth. They do so by clinging to magical images of the past that have the effect of confirming them in their powerlessness. There are no therapists in attendance on Pinter's stage to guide his self-deceived protagonists, or to inspire them with a vision of their potential. These characters are literally boxed in and have neither the strength nor the will to break out of their claustrophobic existence. The members of the audience, however, can serve as their own therapists, applying to themselves the lessons that the characters on the stage will never learn.

The central image in Pinter's plays is that of a contested shelter, the analogue of a remembered room or house in which the protagonist once found the illusion of security, often by seeking protection behind the skirts of the mother. Pinter's stage sets are ambiguous shelters, the possession of which constitutes the major source of dramatic conflict. Often an external object intrudes itself to pose a challenge, or as if to prevent retreat into the womb—or, more accurately, into regression and dependency. Pinter's rooms are actual spaces that belong to the realm of the good/bad mother, but they are spaces she is powerless to protect, either against external threats or the internal pressure of the protagonist's infantile aggressive drives. The symbolism of insecure space in Pinter's plays may be viewed, in Melanie Klein's[7] terms, as a projection of the preoedipal child's destructive impulses toward the mother, and the associated fear of retaliation. The presence of the failed mother/wife in many of Pinter's dramas helps to explain the symbolic meaning of his rooms. The room emerges as an affect-laden symbol of the nongratifying mother, as well as a vehicle for the fantasy recovery of the mother as love object. Indeed, Pinter's rooms represent the protagonist's striving for the physical reparation of the mother's "destroyed" body, destroyed by the child's aggressive impulses.

Pinter's rooms are therefore settings in which the force of projected malice is pitted against the vain hope of redemption. The usual fictional formula of redemption-through-love does not apply in these contests. Pinter's antiheroes struggle ineffectually and half-heartedly to redeem themselves from the regressive mode of existence into which they have sunk, in which the mother/wife is at once overprotective and inaccessible. The outcome of their efforts is problematic because they cannot recreate the lost mother as internalized object, or integrate the internal with the external world. Even Pinter's fictional aggressors attempt to falsify the past in relation to the mother, conjuring up impossible images of an idealized childhood. Their needs are no different from his antiheroes' need to sustain themselves by illusions, but Pinter's aggressors are active agents whom the playwright has intuitively cast as the embodiment of infantile rage. Pinter's aggressors resemble his antiheroes in another respect insofar as they are involved in the destruction of a symbolic security system. Whereas Pinter's antiheroes allow their infantile hatred and guilt to destroy their world through projection, his predators mete out punishment for aggression against the mother. Antiheroes and their tormentors alike represent the divided self, and the latter act on behalf of an archaic, preoedipal superego. But what basis is there for assuming that the self-destructiveness of Pinter's protagonists is the result of arrested ego development traceable to the very earliest stages of life?

In an article titled "The Prerepresentational Self and Its Affective Core" Robert Emde[8] speaks of the self as consisting of an *affective core* that begins to crystallize at the age of one-and-one-half years (when children are able to recognize themselves in a mirror), but which undergoes new levels of integration throughout the life cycle. Emde's position is that the evolution of the self begins even before the age of fifteen months. One of Emde's observations is particularly useful for understanding Pinter's use of the concept of time. Citing numerous studies that point to the infant's power of memory, Emde hypothesizes that "the relevant context for memory enhancement will be shown to be social and affective."[9] Memory, reinforced by affect, serves as a link connecting the different stages in the development of the ego, and provides a basis for the continuity of a sense of self. The affective core contributes to the child's growing ability to relate to others. Emde's argument is that affective continuity is a function of the emotional availability of caregivers and of parental responses to *referencing* behavior in the infant. By *referencing*, Emde means asking for help or reassurance in an affect-arousing, unfamiliar situation. Referencing is therefore an important part of an emotional signalling system.

For our present purpose, the relevance of Emde's studies becomes apparent when it is noted that Pinter's characters are not vulnerable because of any recent trauma or frustration in their lives. Their inadequacy is lifelong and is traceable to early defects of ego development. The symbolism of contested life space needs to be referred to the absence of a stable referencing system in the lives of Pinter's characters. His characters, for example, rarely answer each other or even look at each other, but instead speak past each other, so that they do not obtain veridical, much less empathic feedback. Whatever tenuous security they have found is based on holding on to familiar surroundings—in fact, any four walls—rather than being based on long-term human relationships. Pinter's much-noted and justly admired ability to compress his characters' thoughts and feelings into tersely lyrical statements reinforces the impression that their anomic and emotionally isolated existences are due to their stunted ego development. Only the four walls that they inhabit tell them that they have an identity; it is a barely human identity that is not buttressed by love. Often the rooms to which Pinter's characters cling are the sites of their final humiliations. It is no less clear that at no point in their lifetimes have Pinter's characters flourished in the ambience of their rooms. Instead, these enclosures are problematic sanctuaries providing a kind of external ego not unlike the external soul that ancient man took to be the envelope of his identity. Just as the destruction of the mythical giant's external soul, hidden in an egg, signifies his physical and spiritual death, so too the expulsion from one's room, or homelessness, denotes the death of Pinter's childlike antiheroes.

It is a measure of the extent to which the inadequate protagonists in Pinter's plays have relinquished their claim to the good will of others, and to love objects in general, that they do not try to enlist others in their unequal struggle against fate. One of the rare exceptions to this rule is the tramp Davies in *The Caretaker* (1959). This is a play about a trusting, partially recovered schizophrenic, Aston, who provides shelter for an old tramp. The latter, upon learning that his young benefactor is a formal mental patient, seeks to displace him from his house, a structure that, significantly, is in a state of permanent ruin and incompletion. To accomplish his aim, Davies tries to align himself with Aston's sadistic brother, Mick, against Aston. We learn also that Davies, though pathetic in many ways, is not entirely lacking in ego strength and is ready to defend himself with a knife when threatened by Mick. But Davies is different from Pinter's other losers because he has never had a haven of any sort, even an insecure one. The other protagonists run the risk of being turned out and losing the precarious security of the good/bad mother, as symbolized by a room or a house. Davies' strength derives from his conflict-free acceptance of the world as bad, like the unequivocally bad mother who has no room for her irredeemably bad son.

One of Pinter's earliest literary productions, the short story "The Black and White," written in 1954, reveals Pinter's early concern with the theme of homelessness. "The Black and White" presents the thoughts of two homeless elderly women—bag ladies—who discuss how they manage to get through each day riding on all-night buses, sitting around pubs, and evading the police and various predators. That this subject should have engaged Pinter at the age of twenty-four is not accidental. Apart from his early dislocations due to the wartime bombing of London (Pinter was separated from his parents and evacuated to the countryside), the fear of homelessness signifies a deeper apprehension, namely, fear of abandonment by the mother. In "The Black and the White," the mother figure is herself bereft, deprived of home and family. As such, she cannot be a source of nurturance. Weak mother figures play an important role in Pinter's plays, whose helpless protagonists exist mainly in relation to a mother figure who is outwardly supportive but ultimately disappointing, if not treacherous. These antiheroes are not oedipal losers in the usual sense because they do not put up a struggle against father figures for the possession of a woman. Instead, they are rejected or devastated completely because they are perceived as weak. In The Birthday Party (1957), for example—a play about a failed young musician who lives an idle, phobic existence in a shabby boarding house until he is physically removed by two menacing figures, Goldberg and McCann—the protagonist, Stanley, caves in without a real struggle. In surrendering to Goldberg and McCann, who will either kill him or take him to an institution, Stanley abandons his symbiotic relationship with his motherly landlady. Stanley's capitulation results from two conditions. First, he has already been debilitated and rendered impotent by his life as a childlike, sheltered man locked into a parasitic relationship with an incestuous mother figure, his landlady. Second, Stanley is powerless to resist his own destruction because Goldberg and McCann, who confront him with his weaknesses and pretensions, are personifications of his cruel superego, upbraiding him for his self-indulgence and failure in life. Significantly, Stanley does not respond to the overtures of Lulu, a sexually attractive girl who ends by giving herself to Goldberg, a powerful oedipal father figure.

A similar pattern of oedipal-defeat-without-a-battle is seen in the play *The Homecoming* (1964). This play involves the return of a college professor son and his attractive wife for a visit to the London house of the young professor's father. The father, Max, an elderly widower, shares the large, barely furnished house with two ummarried young sons, Lenny, a pimp, and Joey, an aspiring boxer who works as a laborer. The professor, Teddy, who has been living in America with his wife and children, has not seen his father or brothers for many years, and their resentment of him is obvious. Max and his sons join in humiliating Teddy, first by Max's declaring repeatedly that the wife, Ruth, a former "model," is in reality a tart. The father then proposes that Ruth move in with him and his sons and support all of them by becoming a prostitute. At the play's end Teddy prepares to return to America without Ruth, who is locked in a sexual embrace with one brother while the other prepares to join them, and the father begs for her sexual favors as well. Teddy, like Stanley in *The Birthday Party,* acquiesces without a struggle to the victory of his oedipal rival. Teddy, in fact, has long since removed himself from a world in which people act on vital impulses; he, too, is a weak son whose wife/mother is taken away from him because he is infantile, fixated at a pregenital level, and therefore unworthy of a woman's love.

Esslin is partially correct in interpreting *The Homecoming* as an oedipal wish fulfillment in which the sons come into possession of the mother—their sister-in-law Ruth—while their father is reduced to begging her for a few crumbs of affection.[10] Esslin has not taken into account, however, that Teddy has been shut out of his family home and deprived of his wife, who has agreed to become a prostitute. Because Ruth is portrayed as a woman with a shady past, who might even have been a London call girl before her marriage, indicates that she is a bad mother who, in addition, betrays her weak son by consenting to be the father's whore. Teddy is manifestly the loser in this play, and the victory of the hostile father and brothers is understandable only in the light of Teddy's humiliation. In view of Teddy's predicament, it is not possible to say that the sons have won a victory over the father. The crude, abusive father—a retired butcher—and his menacing younger sons serve the same function as Goldberg and McCann in *The Birthday Party* insofar as they are projections of Teddy's cruel superego, punishing him for his passivity, and perhaps even for his neglect of his wife because of his arrested emotional development. The fact that Teddy has fathered three children does not alter the situation because it is Ruth who is manifestly the Shakti, or active sexual principle in their lives.

There are no unambiguous oedipal winners in Pinter's work, in which uncertainty is all-important, as Pinter has stated.[11] Pinter's drama can be understood only from the standpoint of the victim or antihero, who is rendered homeless or motherless not because society is evil (Pinter makes it plain that he is not concerned with social or political issues), or because other people are insensitive, but because of his own infantilism and lack of desire. Pinter belongs to the fraternity of Beckett and Ionesco, whose male protagonists are beyond the reach of maternal love, romantic passion, or even human charity. These antiheroes are defeated from the start. If Pinter's female characters appear now as nagging, overprotective mothers, dissatisfied wives, or cynical whores, it is because they represent the frustrating mother, who cannot love her son enough to make a man of him. Out of this failure of nurturance emerges the intense rage that Pinter's males feel toward the world at large, and particularly toward women, whom they wish to humiliate in the manner that Albert, the momma's-boy protagonist of *A Night Out* (1959), revenges himself for his impotence with a prostitute by making her lace his shoes for him. It is not coincidental that the genteel, garrulous, and controlling prostitute resembles Albert's possessive mother in her behavior, and that the act of tying his shoelaces is what a mother might do with her small child. Albert obviously has displaced his anger from his mother (whom he was about to hit with a clock earlier in the evening) to the prostitute. In a sense, all of Pinter's frustrated, angry men are like Albert.

They associate home with a destructive wife/mother, but yearn for a room of their own, symbolizing the elusive good mother. The rage that these protagonists feel grows out of the central conflict between the need for maternal love and the dread of rejection. Although Pinter gives us formidable, indeed overpowering father figures in the guise of Goldberg in *The Birthday Party* or Max in *The Homecoming*, they are merely symbols of the harsh, uncomprehending world that confronts the pregenital antihero, and which reflect his own hostile projections.

Melanie Klein assumes that the infant achieves a *depressive position* during the second half of the first year, after an initial *paranoid position* based on projection of innate aggressive drives onto the mother. The depressive position results from the child's effort to integrate the images of the nurturant good mother and the frustrating bad mother, and its dysphoric tone is said to derive from nascent guilt feelings. However, abnormal and persistent guilt feelings may attend failure to fuse the disparate images of the mother, thus producing depressive trends. If the paranoid component remains dominant, Klein speaks of consequent *persecutory anxiety,* occasioned by the child's fixation on the bad mother, the prototype of a world perceived as menacing. Pinter's characters are singular in that they combine depression with anticipatory dread. His married couples, for example, preside over the bitter residue of their burnt-out marriages. The stereotypy of their words and gestures and their deafness to each other are symptoms of their underlying sadness. Usually, these failed relationships are threatened by an external force, the projection of their own repressed rage. Their anger at an unresponsive love object translates into persecutory anxiety; their morbid guilt leads to pervasive depression.

Following Klein's lead, D.W. Winnicott views normal depression in infants as indicating a capacity for guilt, along with a tendency to want to make amends to the mother.[12] Pinter's antiheroes, acting in the capacity of the betrayed and abandoned son, still want to make restitution to the discredited mother. The act of restitution is usually beyond the resources of Pinter's antiheroes, but sometimes the playwright acts on their behalf, as in the play *A Slight Ache* (1958). This play is about a middle-aged couple who have retired to a country home, and whose lives are boring and empty. The husband, who is presumably working on some vague scholarly project, is arrogant and insecure and barely able to contain his diffuse anger. The wife, aptly named Flora, is absorbed in her flower garden but leads a stultified, sexually repressed existence. A mute old matchseller holds vigil outside their home, standing motionless day after day. When Flora finally invites the silent old man into the cottage, his arrival signals the blinding, and then the collapse of the husband, a man whose strategy for survival was essentially regressive: "Sometimes, of course, I would take shelter, shelter to compose myself. Yes, I would seek a tree, a cranny of bushes, erect my canopy and so make shelter. And rest. And then I no longer heard the wind or saw the sun. Nothing entered, nothing left my nook." The entry of the matchseller indicates a new lease on life for Flora, who is starved for love. The matchseller, who is perceived as "extraordinarily youthful," as well as old, is the ambiguous son/lover who has returned to redeem the mother from her bondage to the "bad" father, who is left in a blinded, symbolically castrated condition. For once, the son has stood his ground, but his mute and bedraggled condition reveals that some of the hostility directed toward the mother has been displaced against the self. Nevertheless, a "rescue fantasy," in Melanie Klein's terms, has enabled the son to carry out a symbolic act of reparation.

In the final scene of *A Slight Ache* Flora hands the matchseller's tray of matches to the prostrate Edward, indicating that the two men are about to exchange roles. In terms of satisfying Flora's needs, the matchseller is, however, no improvement over Edward, and is even more lifeless and unresponsive. Presumably, it will now be Edward's turn to wait outside until Flora has had enough of the matchseller, and is ready to share the house with her husband. Clearly, the house is the woman's domain, and the man's foothold is precarious. Critics who have interpreted Pinter's fictional battles for possession of a room as exercises in territoriality have not understood what is at stake in these preoedipal contests. Rooms and houses belong, above all, to the women in Pinter's plays, a circumstance that is strictly in keeping with psychoanalytic theory. In *The Homecoming*, it is Ruth, the daughter-in-law, who takes possession of Max's household, while her husband departs, defeated by his own lack of vitality. In *The Room* (1957), a play about a middle-aged, working-class couple who live in a run-down room, it is the woman, Rose, who remains in possession of the room after her husband, Bert, beats up a mysterious visitor who urges her to depart with him. In *The Birthday Party*, Meg, the landlady, remains the presiding spirit of her rooming house after the half-blinded Stanley is led away to his doom. In *The Basement* (1966), two men alternate in their possession of a room, but it is Jane, the young woman who is the mistress of each man in turn (perhaps like Flora in *A Slight Ache*), never relinquishing her connection with the room, who remains in control. In *The Tea Party* (1963), Disson, a nouveau-riche industrialist, ends up in a catatonic stupor, his eyes open but unseeing, while his upper-class wife Diana and her brother Willy appear to take possession of Disson's business. Although women do not figure in all of Pinter's plays, they are clearly central to his major themes. Their ability to endure, even though they are weak and treacherous, and to remain in charge of the domestic hearth, is as important as the tendency of Pinter's antiheroes to be blinded, Oedipus-style, for the sin of incestuous attachment to a mother figure.

In this regard, one cannot exclude Riley, the blind black man, who is savagely beaten, and perhaps killed, by Bert in the last scene of *The Room*. What was Riley's offense? Perhaps his error was to remind the sixty-year-old Rose, "Your father wants you to come home." This message, coming from a black man who had been living obscurely in the remote cellar of the house, suggests that he is a messenger of death summoning Rose to the underworld. Rose responds positively by touching Riley's eyes, the back of his head, and his temples just as her husband enters the room. Was Bert's outburst, then, an act of sexual jealousy, or the act of a dependent son (he is ten years younger than Rose), panicking at the thought that his wife/mother might be taken from him by death? The latter interpretation is consistent with the way Pinter ends *A Slight Ache*, in which Flora rejects her husband in favor of their mute visitor. Although I have suggested that the matchseller in *A Slight Ache* is a reparation for the bad father, the old-young man is an ambiguous gift because he can be seen as Death himself, like Riley in *The Room*. Death is preferable to Edward in *A Slight Ache* because Edward is antilife, exulting in having trapped a wasp in a jar of marmalade, just as he has ensnared Flora in his deadly round of life, with its bourgeois pretences.

Esslin observes that the hostility of Pinter's protagonists toward women results from their sexual impotence. This is not the whole explanation, however. Pinter's frustrated and defeated antiheroes are indeed impotent, but their hostility toward women antedates their sexual disability and is a consequence of their hatred of the bad mother who plays such an important role in Pinter's dramas. The theme of displacement from one's home, which Pinter has developed with obsessive intensity, points to the feared removal of infantile emotional support. Pinter has created a dramatic cycle of maternal-overprotection-as-reaction-formation, hostility and dependency on the part of the son, and consequent impotence and generalized helplessness. For this reason, oedipal interpretations of Pinter's plays do not tell the whole story. There is also a tragic dimension to Pinter's characters, male and female alike, which has implications that go beyond the oedipal drama, and which involves the vicissitudes of the developing ego in its instrumental aspect. I say tragic, rather than pathetic, because Pinter's characters have dreamed of self-realization but have lacked the strength to pursue their visions. Stanley in *The Birthday Party*, for example, once had hopes of becoming a concert pianist. Spooner, a tramplike character invited into the home of a successful literary man in *No Man's Land* (1974), boasts of a once-elegant style of life and claims to be a poet and a patron of poets—in sharp contrast to his seedy appearance and menial employment in a pub. Beth, in *Landscape* (1967), who was a housekeeper for a wealthy, aristocratic man, reminisces about an idyllic love affair with a man of exceptional sensitivity, who might have been her husband in his youth (before he became crass and brutal) or her late employer.

Like the heroes of classical tragedy, Pinter's antiheroes are defeated by their own defects of character, in which self-pity and self-indulgence are equally balanced. But unlike true heroes, Pinter's antiheroes have developed a defensive, life-denying orientation, attesting to fixation at early levels of ego development, or, at best, a pattern of regression. The source of their self-defeating attitude is a sense of guilt, which has transformed their aggressive wishes toward the bad mother into masochism. As Freud[13] argued in "A Child Is Being Beaten: A Contribution to the Study of the Origin of Sexual Perversions," masochism derives from sadism that has been directed toward the self after being displaced from an erstwhile love object. The imagined scene in *The Birthday Party* in which Stanley is beaten—or browbeaten—into total submission by Goldberg and McCann is in striking accord with Freud's treatment of the fantasy "a child is being beaten." Freud's interpretation of the fantasy is that it is a symptom of repressed hostility and fixation at the anal sadistic stage. It is worthy of note that Stanley is mute and like a complete automaton after his tormentors have finished with him, and that he has been blinded by the loss of his glasses. This cruel transformation is consistent with the motive of self-punishment for guilt-inducing hostility.

In spite of Stanley's degradation in *The Birthday Party*, it would be a mistake to assume that there are any true oedipal victors in Pinter's plays. The play *The Collection* (1961) illustrates the impossibility of conflict resolution in Pinter's oedipal, or, rather, pseudooedipal contests. In *The Collection*, a presumably homosexual young man, Bill, is accused of adultery by a half-irate, half-fascinated husband, James. It turns out that it is far from clear as to whether anything took place between Bill and James' wife, and that it is possible that the wife, Stella, made the whole thing up. Bill's homosexual partner, an older man named Harry, finally convinces the husband that nothing transpired between Stella and Bill, but the play ends with the reality of the situation still in doubt, at least as far as James' role is concerned. Stella has succeeded in remaining enigmatic from start to finish. Although *The Collection* contains some of the sadomasochistic elements that are present in most of Pinter's dramas, its salient pattern resembles that of *A Slight Ache*, namely, the love-triangle motif presented in more or less explicit form. If one sets to one side for the moment the division of the cast into homosexual and heterosexual couples, it is apparent that the hidden agenda of the play is a conflict between James, a man in his thirties, with Bill, a younger man, for the love of

Stella, who is in her thirties. In this oedipal constellation, Stella appears to have planted the seeds of suspicion in James' mind and has instigated the rivalry between her husband and Bill, who are attracted to each other. But Pinter's resolution of the conflict is less clear-cut than in *A Slight Ache,* in which the wife chooses the ambiguous father figure in preference to the husband/son. In *The Collection,* the conflict seems to be oedipal on the surface, but there is one difficulty with this interpretation; namely, that Bill, the son-challenger, is a homosexual. There is, in fact, no conflict resolution in Pinter's oedipal duels because the son, fixated at a pregenital level, is capable only of a mimesis of sexual rivalry with the father figure. The wife/ mother/mistress in Pinter's dramas engenders father-son conflict because of her incestuous needs, but Pinter's fictional sons are not equal to these demands because of their infantile dependency. The seeming victory of the husband/son, Bert, in *The Room,* in which the blind and bedraggled father figure, Riley, is beaten up by the son, is a Pyrrhic victory because the wife/mother is blinded too.

Pinter's fictional women endure, unlike the males, who are either destroyed or deceived. This is all the more remarkable because the women are weak and unreliable. One may conclude that their endurance is a wishfulfillment of his dependent protagonists. The play *Landscape* illustrates this quality of endurance. The monologues delivered by its two characters, Duff, the former estate chauffeur and handyman, and his wife Beth, the former housekeeper, disclose their separate yet joined destinies. The two characters, who have inherited the estate of their former employer, live in separate worlds, with Beth absorbed in her idealized memories of the past, and Duff confined to the present. As mentioned earlier, it is not clear whether Beth was the mistress of their employer, Mr. Sykes, or whether her romantic, lyrical images of the past represent an earlier phase of her relationship with her husband. Pinter himself, when he wrote *Landscape,* was uncertain as to the identity of Beth's earlier lover. Although Beth and Duff have survived their employer and now possess his fine home, it is apparent that only Beth, with her fine sensibilities, is fully identified with her beautiful surroundings and is the presiding spirit of the place. She is truly the mistress of a great house, though it is empty of guests because Duff, ill at ease with his new possessions, cannot bring himself to invite his working-class companions of the pub to share his good fortune.

The identity of woman and house is underscored by Beth's having formerly worn a housekeeper's chain around her waist, with her keys, a scissors, and a thimble—symbolic objects that Duff tore off angrily and scattered over the floor after Mr. Syke's death. Who, then, is the romantic figure of Beth's recollections? One reason for thinking of him as Duff is the interpretation that he is the idealized lover in the guise of the beloved son, the son that might have been. The figure in Beth's daydreams is the son's wish fulfillment, the son-and-lover who shared the mother's splendid house, shutting out the actual husband, Duff, in his crudeness and insensitivity. The son/lover also shares open spaces with Beth on the beach and countryside. Unlike the other sons trapped in Pinter's symbiotic relationships, this fantasy son has emerged briefly from the claustrophobe gloom of an enclosed space and has been energized by the sun's rays. Unfortunately, most of Pinter's characters are not fated to enjoy the freedom of an idealized past, when they experienced a mother's love, or the spontaneity of the present moment, which is shadowed by the intrusion of destructive fears and hatreds.

In one of his more recent works, *Betrayal* (1978), Pinter has begun to move away from his main preoccupations, but he remains deeply concerned with the symbolic meanings of home and family. Told in a series of flashbacks, *Betrayal* is the story, in reverse chronological order, of an extramarital love affair. The play begins with the final dissolution of a long-standing adulterous relationship and proceeds back in time to trace the gradual waning of the affair. The play centers on Emma and Jerry, who have been betraying Robert, Emma's husband and Jerry's best friend. Evidently, Robert has been aware of the affair for a number of years but has continued to be friendly with Jerry. Emma confessed her infidelity to Robert only after she learned that Robert had been betraying her with various women. The play ends with a reenactment of the initial meeting between Emma and Jerry at a party, where the liaison began almost casually and in a mood of drunkenness. Although the play has been faulted by critics for the superficiality of the love relationships depicted, Pinter's point is to reveal precisely the hollowness of such relationships, inside and outside of marriage.

Whatever the faults of the play are from an artistic standpoint, Pinter has demonstrated that the same emotional forces that are at work in his earlier plays operate under the seemingly smooth surface of upper-middle-class life. The affects involved continue to be those of apathy, boredom and forced responsiveness, with strong undercurrents of rage and sadism. Pinter is still dealing with failed relationships, the futility and duplicity of married life, and the resentments that flow from these failings.

In *Betrayal* and the other late plays, such as *The Collection,* or *The Lover* (1962) (a play about a married couple who pretend that they are lovers engaging in illicit sex), the home is no longer a symbol of the failed or absent mother. Now the symbol is replaced by the actuality of the failed wife/mistress who can no longer arouse her husband/lover. Stella, in *The Collection,* may have deliberately planted the suspicion of her infidelity in her husband's mind to reawaken his interest in her. Richard, the husband in *The Lover,* reaches a point where he requires his wife to behave like a prostitute in order to evoke a sexual response from him.

The male protagonist, too, in Pinter's recent plays, is a failure in his relationship with his wife/mistress rather than in relation to the world at large. Viewed superficially, a great psychological distance separates the infantile, passive-aggressive Stanley of *The Birthday Party* from the cool Robert of *Betrayal,* who does not care enough for his wife to want to put a stop to her infidelity. But there are important similarities, as well. Like Teddy in *The Homecoming,* Robert accepts the loss of a once-cherished love object with philosophical resignation, if not relief. Perhaps Pinter has meant to say that his antiheroes relinquish the wife/mother as a love object because of the insufficiency of her love, as well as the passivity of the male. The symbol of the psychologically absent mother in *The Homecoming* is a large, empty living room with a wall knocked out. Here, where all the action of the play takes place, the mother has long since departed.

The theme of the mother-absent home is repeated in another recent play, *No Man's Land,* in which, as I have mentioned, a wealthy and successful writer, Hirst, invites a down-at-the-heels poet, Spooner, into his home. Hirst is a heavy drinker and is apparently under the care of two menservants, Foster and Briggs, who are hostile toward Spooner and treat him as an interloper. There is no real movement in the play and no dramatic climax as the two old men reminisce—perhaps confabulate—about their pasts. The characters appear to be frozen in a no-man's-land, a sort of land of the dead in which no growth or change is possible. Spooner is in fact an upgraded version of the tramp Davies in *The Caretaker.* He is a homeless and loveless man seeking sanctuary, but he is wily and not willing to surrender his pretensions. Like Pinter's other failed protagonists, Spooner has been rejected by the significant others in his life: "I have never been loved. From this I derive my strength. . . . I looked up once into my mother's face. What I saw there was nothing less than pure malevolence. I was fortunate to escape with my life." Spooner blames himself for his mother's rejection of him, adding that it occurred when he was twenty-eight. Hirst guesses the reason: "You'd pissed yourself."[14] *No Man's Land,* a wordy, static play that is amusing but seems to be pointless, does make a point. It portrays the empty lives of men without women and without love. Whether Hirst's household is really a homosexual menage, as some critics have speculated, is less important than its elegant bleakness. Hirst's mansion is no improvement over the ramshackle house that Aston presides over in *The Caretaker.* It is a bleak home, whose only stage prop is an elegant bar, and the men who inhabit it, including Spooner, are motherless, orally deprived children. Hence, the mood of depression and lifelessness.

This atmosphere of paralysis, scarcely concealed by the wit and sarcasm of the characters, makes it possible to relate *No Man's Land* to several other Pinter plays that are entirely static. These plays are, on the surface, different from his menacing, violent plays, such as *The Room, The Birthday Party, A Night Out* or *The Dumb Waiter* (1957), in which two hired gunmen prepare to kill someone. *No Man's Land* belongs with a series of retrospective plays characterized by obsessive doubt and ambiguity about the past. These "inert" plays include *The Dwarfs* (1960), in which one of three friends destroys the trust that the other two have in each other; *Landscape,* a mood piece in which a woman and the two men in her life recollect the past; *Old Times* (1970), which is about a middle-aged woman, her husband, and her roommate of twenty years ago, who give conflicting accounts of their past involvements with each other. *No Man's Land* and the other plays that explore the ambiguity of memory reveal a side of Pinter's characters that is merely implicit in the acting-out plays. I refer to their ruminative, doubt-ridden existence, in which directed activity is blocked by obsessive fears. The past is fearful because it has undergone distortion in the service of the destructive infantile wish; as a result, it is a treacherous foundation for future action. As for the present, it is already a lost cause, given over to inertia and a nostalgia that does not ring true.

Now we can understand why Pinter's most dramatic plays are filled with tension and sudden eruptions of violence. Pinter's characters can break out of their paralysis only by means of a violent gesture, thereby releasing their pent-up rage. When they are unable to summon up anger because of inhibiting guilt feelings, repression takes over and they become intellectualizers, meditators, people who play with words, and also poseurs. Because both Hirst and Spooner strike a pose in *No Man's Land,* this play is partly a vehicle for satirizing pretensions to gentility and intellectuality; it is also a study of burnt-out lives, without the hope of release from futility. In this play, Pinter's characters can only pretend that their lives possess meaning, but they are unable to act on their own behalf. Their past lives were equally empty, and Pinter's satirical treatment of Spooner's mendacity and sycophancy may be seen as the moral equivalent of the kind of diffuse anger that permeates his more violent plays. When one places the violent plays beside the meditative ones (bearing in mind Pinter's satirical orientation) it becomes clear that Pinter uses acting out and obsessive inaction as reciprocals. In neither type of play does Pinter permit his characters to exercise control over their lives, except through their fantasies. They can retain the illusion of control over their past lives by pretending that they at least displayed promise, even if they did not achieve fulfillment. When these pretensions are carried too far, as in

Night School (1960), in which a petty criminal exaggerates how tough and dangerous he is, he loses the girl he has sought to impress. Love relationships are doomed from the start in Pinter's plays because of the innate weaknesses of his protagonists, whose affect hunger can never be appeased.

Pinter's rooms, like his failed love relationships, are linked with regression to a past that was as emotionally deprived as is the present. These rooms were never associated with real security, much less with joy or youthful idealism, as is true of the playroom in Philip Barry's comedy *Holiday,* in which a daughter associates the playroom with her loving mother. By contrast, Pinter's rooms evoke an ambiguous past, at best. Pinter's characters are creatures of their past, which has deformed them for reasons that are left to the theater-goer's imagination, and which is unalterable in its effects. The starkness of Pinter's stage is more than a device of stagecraft, because it denotes the emotional wasteland that his characters occupy; at the same time, it points to a future that threatens to fulfill the unspoken portents of the wasted past. The question as to why Pinter chose to invest his stage rooms with so much surplus meaning, transforming objective space into contested psychological space, is an intriguing one. In a sense, if the room, or home, is bound up with the symbolism of mother, can it not be said that Pinter's failed sons represent the prodigal son, who returns home as an intruder, more dead than alive, and guilt-ridden because he is a failure in life? He is met with parental rage and incomprehension and is repudiated for his unacceptable (in the parents' eyes) style of life. Is this a fantasy, or is it a reality based on the playwright's choice of the profession of acting as a career when he was still in his teens?

Chapter 11

THE ELOQUENCE OF PAIN

Based on the evidence gathered in this volume, it is difficult to avoid the conclusion that pathology is inseparable from the production of great works of fiction, drama, and poetry. Nor is the role of pathology confined to providing the motivation for literary creativity. The choice of themes, delineation of character, and development of crystallized literary styles cannot be separated from pathology. By *pathology* I mean severe emotional disturbance or profound characterological defects—and not merely anxieties and insecurities of mild or moderate severity. I realize that these conclusions, which I have accepted reluctantly, will be most unwelcome to all those who regard literary creativity as the outcome of productive thinking: a blend of imagination, cognitive restructuring, and controlled affect that has only an incidental relationship to the psychic conflicts of the author. But I find it impossible to separate the life of an author from his or her work.

It could be argued, of course, that great writing transcends the sufferings and confusions of the author and represents the achievement of new heights, where craftsmanship and inspiration overshadow the personal factor. In the same vein, it could be said that great writing replaces the personal and idiosyncratic with universal symbols and meanings. Inferior writing, in turn, could be characterized as showing all the seams that went into its composition, including the psychic scars of the author. But these arguments in favor of the essential normality of great writing are the result of wishful thinking, rather than being based on a careful study of the relationship between biography and literary creativity. Such a study reveals that great literary art is a synthesis of technical skill with tremendous fear, rage, or other powerful emotions, and that the fundamental character of great writers reveals significant failure along developmental lines, that is, a basic lack of maturity.

Whether there is a connection between certain kinds of pathology and the ability to produce literary works of distinction is a question that must await more systematic study. It is conceivable, for example, that writers whose psychological problems are of preoedipal origin produce literature that is fundamentally different from that of writers who are more mature. For example, writers such as Byron, J.M. Barrie, D.H. Lawrence, Faulkner, W.H. Auden, Tennessee Williams, and Beckett, who failed to achieve separation from the mother in early childhood, or were traumatized in the separation process, seem to be preoccupied with problems of self-preservation in their writings. Their fictional protagonists are vulnerable children menaced by the bad mother, or, in Barrie's case, lost boys in search of an elusive, idealized good mother who exists only as a ghost out of the past. In a more general sense, these fictional figures are overwhelmed by life's demands. By contrast, Hawthorne, William Carlos Williams, Hermann Hesse, Hemingway, Nabokov, and Eugène Ionesco have produced characters and situations that approximate the classical norm of oedipal rebellion and fear of retaliation by the father.

These are only hypotheses, of course, and it must be admitted that oedipal motifs are by no means absent in the writings, say, of E.T.A. Hoffmann, D.H. Lawrence, Sartre, and Georges Simenon. The precise balance between ego-preservative and oedipal motifs in the writings of a particular author has to be worked out. I suspect that most writers will show a predominance of one set of motifs over the other, but this supposition is not well grounded at the present time. Freud's[1] discussion of "danger-situations" in "Inhibitions, Symptoms and Anxiety" (1926) drew attention to the role of signal anxiety as an anticipatory response to the threat of being rendered helpless through separation from the mother. Although signal anxiety in relation to the mother comes into play before castration anxiety, which belongs to the phallic stage, the two dangers constitute a similar, though not identical challenge to the self-preservative functions of the ego.

If separation anxiety refers to the dread of losing a narcissistically valued love object in the form of the mother, castration anxiety, broadly conceived, denotes something in addition to fear of losing a narcissistically valued organ. The threat of castration is simultaneously a threat that the phallic son will never be united with the mother, and that his ties with the father will be sundered, as well. Viewed in this way, it becomes possible to understand oedipal rivalry, including the Electra complex, as an extension of the fear of losing the love of one or both parents. At the preoedipal level, where the danger consists of the fear of losing the object itself, the child is faced with the prospect of being thrust into a state of "psychical helplessness," as Freud puts it. At the phallic level, when the ego is stronger, the danger consists of losing the object's love, rather than the object itself—a less devastating possibility, but one that does not remove the danger to the ego. Unlike the preoedipal child, the phallic child has at his disposal a variety of ego defenses against anxiety, including sublimation upon the resolution of the oedipal crisis. Although the preoedipal and oedipal child are alike dependent on the mother, it is consistent with the main line of Freud's thinking to conclude that the child who is traumatized at the preoedipal level is placed in a more precarious situation. The fantasies that might arise from fear of object loss would, of necessity, be different from those occasioned by fear of losing the love of a permanent object, and would involve different coping strategies based on different levels of ego organization.

If we think of literature as resulting from—among other things—the effort to evolve ego-preservative strategies in fantasy or on the symbolic level, it follows that the solutions will vary along several dimensions, reflecting different degrees of ego strength. An overview of Thomas Hardy's novels, for example, shows a transition from purely ego-preservative, externally produced solutions based on accident, to self-initiated oedipal victories by the male protagonist, to a final relapse into psychical helplessness reflected in pessimism and defeat. In *Desperate Remedies* (1871), Hardy's first published novel, Manston, the evil oedipal rival of the young protagonist Springlove, conveniently commits suicide in prison after having murdered his wife. The young suitor, Dick Dewy, in Hardy's second novel, *Under the Greenwood Tree* (1872), does not have to exert himself any more than does Springlove in order to win the hand of the pretty ingenue Fancy Day. It is the female protagonist who chooses Dick Dewy in preference to an older rival, the Reverend Maybold. These effortless oedipal victories by the good son come to an end with Hardy's third novel, *A Pair of Blue Eyes* (1873), in which the female protagonist comes close to marrying her young suitor, Stephen Smith, but ultimately marries Lord Luxellian, a man of much higher status. As if to punish the heroine, Elfride, for marrying Lord Luxellian, an older man and a widower—hence a father figure—Hardy causes her to die of a miscarriage. Although the oedipal son, Stephen, was clearly defeated, the oedipal father won only a hollow victory. Elfride's father, the Reverend Swancourt, also won an empty victory over young Stephen by blocking his marriage to Elfride on the grounds that Stephen was of humble origin. Parenthetically, Hardy had been courting his first wife, Emma Gifford, at this time, and had been rejected by her father as an unsuitable choice for his daughter, primarily because the father was a snob.[2]

Far From the Madding Crowd (1874), composed during the final months of Hardy's four-year courtship of Emma, still features a male protagonist who is destined for oedipal defeat, but who triumphs by accident. The victory of Gabriel Oak over his two rivals in love, Farmer Boldwood and the malevolent Sergeant Troy, was not the result of his own strength. If Farmer Boldwood had not shot Troy in a psychotic rage (thereby eliminating himself as well as Troy from competition for the hand of Bathsheba Everdene), Gabriel would have remained an oedipal loser. Gabriel is depicted as being inherently a victim who succeeds against all expectations because his rivals stumble. Four years later, Hardy, now married to Emma, who collaborated closely with him on most of his literary work, was still unable to produce a resourceful male protagonist in *The Return of the Native* (1878). Although the female protagonist, Eustacia Vye, is a passionate, restless woman, and a rebellious spirit, her husband, the idealistic Clym Yeobright, is a guilt-ridden, mother-fixated man who cannot cope with life. In the end, Hardy frees Clym from the unfaithful Eustacia by the expedient of drowning her and her lover. It is possible that Eustacia's fate represented a wish fulfillment by Hardy in relation to Emma, but there is nothing in his autobiography or in her published recollections to indicate that the marriage had begun to go bad at this point.

Hardy's method of resolving conflict between his characters in *The Return of the Native* was arbitrary and magical, because the defeated characters did not fall of their own weight, that is, by virtue of their flawed character. There is a strong resemblance between Hardy's solution and Nathaniel Hawthorne's gratuitous destruction of the bad father, Pyncheon, in *The House of Seven Gables*. In both instances, the reader is provided with good protagonists who are too weak and dependent to deal resourcefully with their powerful, manipulative adversaries. It remains for the author to rescue his fictional creations from psychical helplessness. In this context, an external, potentially devastating threat is confronted with a magical, preoedipal solution, the effect of which is to relieve pressure on an ego that is too weak to act in its own behalf. In this regard, S. S. Furst[3] has linked psychic trauma with overstimulation of the ego, resulting in the replacement of ego functions by more primitive mechanisms of adaptation. Hardy's good characters are traumatized by his bad ones because of the great disparity in their strength. The bad characters, embodiments of cruel and destructive id impulses, overwhelm the good characters, mobilizing their guilt and forcing them into childlike passivity. No doubt part of the appeal of *The Return of the Native* resides in the destructive vitality of Eustacia and her lover, Wildeve, who overshadow the lesser characters in the same degree that Milton's Satan outshines the other angels by his malign brilliance.

The Mayor of Casterbridge (1886), Hardy's next major novel, at last reveals an author who is strong enough, at least in fantasy, to attempt to resolve a fictional conflict by creating a self-reliant protagonist who triumphs over a seemingly formidable oedipal rival. I refer, of course, to Farfrae's humiliation of the bad father, Henchard, the mayor of Casterbridge. Farfrae's victory, and his marriage, first to Henchard's erstwhile mistress Lucetta, and then to Henchard's step-daughter, Elizabeth Jane, represent the mastery of an external menace in the form of a powerful oedipal rival. For this reason, the climax of *The Mayor of Casterbridge* belongs psychologically to a stage midway between *The Return of the Native*—with its helpless oedipal "sons," Clym and Diggory, and its vulnerable ingenue, Thomasin (as in Thomas Hardy?)—and Hardy's last important work, *The Dynasts*, completed in 1908. *The Dynasts*, with its thoroughgoing sense of life's futility, projected Hardy's depressive thoughts onto a world-historical dramatic stage. In *Tess of the D'Urbervilles* (1891), Hardy has begun to move away from self-assertion through his fictional characters, and to emphasize the motif of victimization. Although Tess is victimized by Alec, her seducer, she nevertheless has the power to destroy her nemesis by stabbing him to death. Hardy has once again provided an arbitrary solution, but it is less gratuitous than the accidental drowning of Eustacia and her lover in *The Return of the Native*. In contrast to Tess, who struggles against her harsh fate, her husband Angel Clare, like Clym in *The Return of the Native*, is a passive, masochistic individual—a true oedipal loser.

Jude the Obscure (1894), Hardy's last novel, was also his most pessimistic. To an even greater extent than *Tess of the D'Urbervilles*, it is a story of victimization and helplessness. At age fifty-four, Hardy had ceased to be on good terms with Emma. He was now a literary lion, wealthy, and inclined to reciprocate the affection bestowed up on him by a series of attractive young women with literary aspirations. Perhaps his guilt feelings toward Emma, who had remained entirely devoted to him, and whom he was to praise repeatedly in his poems after her death in 1912, contributed to the depressive tone of *Jude the Obscure*. The protagonist is a Job-like character who is abandoned by the two women he loves, bereft of his children, and left to die in misery. Jude is the quintessential victim of forces beyond his control. From this story of pathetic failure to the depiction of the equally meaningless failure of collective human experience was but a short step for Hardy. Hence the production of the long epic poem, *The Dynasts,* with its Olympian view of the madness of the Napoleonic wars. Hardy had experimented with conflict resolution based on the strength or weakness of his characters, as well as with solutions based on the force of circumstance. Hardy's tendency to blame social forces and other situational factors for the failure of his protagonists makes it difficult to recognize the inherent weaknesses of these characters, especially the long list of antiheroes. *Jude the Obscure* went as far as Hardy could go in writing novels about failure and defeat. In the end, Hardy had to return to desperate remedies of ego preservation although he was capable, for a brief moment in his literary career, of creating characters who were not afraid of life.

In comparison with such later writers as Kafka, Beckett, or Ionesco, Hardy was far from being a thoroughgoing pessimist, if for no other reason than his belief that an imperfect society could somehow be redeemed by reform measures. But Hardy's characters already carry the seeds of their own destruction within them in the form of characterological defects, masochism, dependency, and helplessness. He is a transition figure on the road to twentieth-century fiction. The outlook of twentieth-century authors is indeed different from that of the most despairing of nineteenth-century writers, including Dostoevsky, who held out some glimmer of hope for human redemption through the self-sacrifice of such noble souls as Sonia in *Crime and Punishment* or Alyosha in *The Brothers Karamazov.* By contrast, a sense of irredeemable loss permeates the imaginative writing of our time. Is it despair resulting from the loss of traditional values and familiar sources of security grounded in unexamined assumptions or ancient folkways? Perhaps the problem is compounded by new modes of perception created by the breakdown of traditional aesthetic conventions. The restless aesthetic experiments of twentieth-century literature from Joyce onward reflect altered ways of looking at the world, but they are emblematic of a wider crisis of modernism. I speak, above all, of the loss of cherished objects of devotion.

What is missing in twentieth-century literature of the first rank is the ability to idealize love objects. The fictional characters of the nineteenth century can still experience unconflicted love for their fellow creatures, even if it is tinged with pity or inspired by a sense of duty. Writers such as E.T.A. Hoffmann, Gustave Flaubert, Tolstoy, and George Eliot, like Hardy, could still imagine wholehearted human relationships, but even their most integral characters show signs of unraveling, of drawing into themselves, and of becoming destructive. Twentieth-century fiction can provide us only with split-off atoms, or fictional characters whose central cores are gone, and who, moreover, cannot form real love relationships. To describe these fictional creations as alienated is to leave them unexplained. Similarly, to say that characters in modern fiction are more complex than their nineteenth-century predecessors is not entirely satisfactory. Instead, it is necessary to search out the causes of alienation in the lives of modern writers, and to trace their gift for complexity to their inner conflicts.

Hardy anticipates these developments without acknowledging that his protagonists are in the process of losing their ideals. Like Hardy, the atheist who could still participate in the religious life of his community, and who still had a strong emotional attachment to the liturgical, architectural, and atmospheric features of the Church of England, his characters still have one foot in the world of tradition. Their lack of conviction, however, adds to their vulnerability. They are aware, like Clym, of the existence of a world of unattainable ideals, but they gaze out at a remote, deterministic universe with the knowledge that their roots in the earth and in a special place have been partly severed.

Hardy's nineteenth-century protagonists (unlike his fictional chorus of peasants) are alienated from a changing and increasingly unfamiliar world. But the existence of this new universe does not invalidate their ideals, it merely emphasizes the difficulty of fulfilling them. By contrast, Joseph Conrad's fictional creations tell us that the meliorative goals that still meant something to an idealist like Clym Yeobright, or to a man of reason like Angel Clare, have all but lost their meaning by the start of the twentieth century. Conrad's antiheroes are destined not only to lose love, nurturance, and loyalty, but also the very objects of their devotion—swept away from them by death or by the force of circumstance. Conrad's novels are much closer in spirit to *Jude the Obscure* than to Hardy's earlier works because they take place in a world in which the protagonists are profoundly insecure, lost, and without roots. Conrad's Lord Jim or Axel Heyst are men who value truth, goodness, courage, and honor in a world that has abandoned all absolute values and is as likely to reward good as evil. It is a world in which evil can turn into good and in which good can turn into evil. Society itself is powerless to separate the forces of good and evil, so they penetrate each other and traditional decencies are corrupted by the evils of opportunism. We are no longer among Hardy's hills of Wessex, where an intact folk culture still exists side by side with a corrosive outer world. Conrad's universe of seas and ships and remote islands is an uncharted hell in which a few good men wander about aimlessly, barely sustained by an innate sense of decency that cannot preserve them from destruction. Evil men are all around them and treachery is a way of life.

Conrad's tragic heroes and heroines are forerunners, as we will see, of Hemingway's code hero, and are motivated by similar though not identical compulsions. Conrad's protagonists, for example, still believe in altruism and feel pity for those who suffer from injustice. For Hemingway's code hero, the noble act is also a gratuitous and useless gesture and is not intended to help anyone, its nobility consisting only of stoical courage. In his autobiography, *A Personal Record*, Conrad professed to believe that the universe is not an ethical universe at all, but is rather a "spectacular universe" in which it is man's duty to use his senses and imagination to the fullest, and not to despair, because life itself is precious. This contradiction may be at the bottom of the discrepancy noted by Christopher Cooper,[4] between the morality of Conrad's major protagonists and the overall morality of his books. Conrad's tales unfold in an amoral world where men normally can be expected to behave selfishly, but where a few men and women take it upon themselves to live up to a higher standard of conduct, usually with disastrous consequences.

Winnie Verloc, for example, the female protagonist of *The Secret Agent*, demonstrates by her love for her retarded brother

Stevie that she is a caring, devoted person. She is otherwise relatively indifferent to moral considerations, and helps her husband in his pornography business, a front for his activities as a spy—indeed, a triple agent. Like Stevie, Winnie is not guided by formal moral principles as much as by an instinctive need to alleviate suffering. Although she ultimately kills her unscrupulous husband in revenge for his having caused Stevie's death, her violent act is the result of her outraged sense of justice. Winnie's suicide is representative of the fate of Conrad's protagonists. They do not meet Heinz Hartmann's[5] criteria of successful adaptation to the external world, because the ego, in their cases, does not serve their long-range goals of survival. The failure of Conrad's protagonists is not caused by the pressure of overpowering id impulses, but by pressures exerted on them by unexpected environmental demands. This failure often takes the form of flight from society and avoidance of close human relationships by escape into a hermitlike existence. Hartmann's[6] concept of *regressive adaptation* is useful in suggesting that such escapism is not pathological in itself, or a sign of pregenital fixation. It is the failure to use "regression in the service of the ego" to achieve a higher level of adaptation, or, to use Hartmann's terminology, to attain "secondary ego autonomy," that is, sublimation, that results in the eventual victimization of Conrad's protagonists. His implicit formula is: To be good is to be destroyed. Hence, the impulse toward altruism is dangerous, and flight from the risks of intimate involvement is to be preferred to pursuing a relationship to its possibly fatal conclusion.

Intimacy also poses the danger to Conrad's characters of losing the love object, the way Conrad lost his tubercular mother when he was seven years old and his father at eleven. He had been brought up in exile, almost completely bereft of the companionship of other children, and in a household clouded by his mother's lingering illness and his father's helplessness and grief. After his father's death, Conrad was raised by his relatives, but by the age of fifteen, inspired by adventure stories he had read, he resolved to go to sea. His guardians protested vigorously, and his tutor called him "an incorrigible, hopeless Don Quixote."[7] Within a short time, Conrad made his way to

England and began his career as a merchant mariner, eventually becoming a sea captain distinguished by his high standards of craftsmanship. Until his marriage at the age of thirty-nine, he led a wandering existence, corresponding with relatives but otherwise careful to avoid emotional entanglements for over twenty years. There was one exception, a brief but intense love affair that culminated in Conrad's apparent suicide attempt in 1878, when he was 21.[8] Several of Conrad's protagonists commit suicide. In addition to Winnie Verloc, as I have mentioned, Captain Whalley, the planter of Malata, Martin Decoud in Nostromo, and Axel Heyst in Victory take their own lives.

Conrad gave up his career as a sea captain abruptly in 1894, only a few months after the death of his uncle and guardian, Thaddeus Bobroski, whom Conrad had loved and respected, according to his letters. He had been unable to find a new assignment at sea and decided to finish Almayer's Folly, his first novel, which he had started in 1889. The novel was finally published in 1895 and Conrad commenced a second career as a writer. A year later, he married Jessie George, a twenty-one-year-old Englishwoman whom he had met six months earlier. The wording of his marriage proposal, which Conrad made while the couple were taking shelter from bad weather in the National Gallery, was as follows: "Look here, my dear, we had better get married and out of this. Look at the weather. We will get married at once and get over to France. How soon can you be ready? In a week—a fortnight?"[9] The proposal captures something of the impersonal tone of Conrad's interactions with the people who knew him in England, and suggests as well a degree of inequality between the thirty-nine-year-old aristocrat and the young secretary, one of nine children and the product of a more humble background.

Conrad was to endure eighteen years of financial failure and literary obscurity in his career as a writer. Works such as The Nigger of the Narcissus (1898), Lord Jim (1900), Heart of Darkness (1902), Nostromo (1904), The Secret Agent (1907), and Under Western Eyes (1911)—Conrad's best novels—brought him scant recognition. It was not until the publication of Chance in 1913 that Conrad achieved popular success and financial security, but by then his literary powers had begun to wane. This decline reflected an intensification of earlier psychological defenses, the tendency to "shrink from actualities when it came to face suffering," as his wife expressed it in her memoir.[10] Conrad's best work included fictional characters, such as Lord Jim, who suffered precisely because they could not blind themselves to the discrepancy between their lofty ideals and the actuality of their conduct. In such later works as Chance, Victory, The Shadow Line, and The Rescue, the protagonists have lost their capacity for feeling guilt or self-doubt, and have ceased to be complex. They have even lost their horror of death, and, like Renouard in "The Planter of Malata," prefer suicide to living without a love object. Conrad's later antiheroes no longer suffer from the terror of life, but surrender to their own passivity, like Lingard in The Rescue, who dreams only of spending his life at the feet of his beloved, soothed into a "World-embracing reverie." There is a marked loss of intensity in these characterizations, as if Conrad had come to terms with himself. All along, Conrad had combined naturalism with an aestheticism that was highly subjective and had also probed the motives of his protagonists, pitting them against their own weaknesses. Captain Giles in The Shadow Line continues to express this philosophy: "A man should stand up to his bad luck, to his mistakes, to his conscience, and all that sort of thing. Why—what else would you have to fight against?"[11] But the narrator, to whom Giles has directed his remarks, has no answer, having already declared that he feels old and tired, even though, in comparison to his earlier mood of emptiness and despair, he is on the road to recovering his spirits.

The loss of dramatic tension in Conrad's later works is more than a reflection of the author's growing complacency, but is nevertheless related to the enervating effect of success. Conrad's deficiencies are associated with an increased use of the defense of splitting, as well. Now his characters begin to be divided into those who are absolutely good—Conrad tells us that they are honorable and courageous, like old Peyrol in The Rover, rather than showing us their inner qualities—and those who are absolutely bad. Hitherto, self-doubt had generated the dynamism in Conrad's best work, the anguish of his protagonists reflecting the insecurity of the neglected author. Once Conrad's characters are deprived of their capacity for unconscious duplicity, all that remains is the unequal struggle between a virtuous protagonist and the destructive people who surround him, such as Mrs. Fyne, the caricature of a power-seeking feminist in *Chance*. Even the sea recedes in Conrad's later works, taking with it much that is elemental and moving in Conrad's earlier productions.

These deficiencies are bound up, of course, with Conrad's aging process. They are also reminders of the psychological distance that Conrad had always maintained from his created characters and situations. Conrad's narrators who report events they have learned about second-hand, and his fictional love relationships, vapid and impersonal, such as that between Lingard and Mrs. Travers in *The Rescue*, are indicative of Conrad's difficulty with fictional object relations. Conrad was more successful in cathecting his fictional characters and describing them in depth when he was hard-pressed and almost despairing of popular and critical recognition. He was at his best under stress, when his imagination was fueled by frustration and the fear of failure. Success weakened Conrad's creative powers by making it unnecessary for him to identify himself with his antiheroes. In this sense, whatever had been pathogenic in his early life combined with the desperation of his apparently failed literary career (until the success of *Chance* in 1913) to produce a gallery of sympathetic and believable victims. Financial security, prestige, critical acclaim, a happy family life—all the ingredients of a normal, fulfilled existence—conspired to defeat Conrad as a writer.

If we use a developmental frame of reference, it can be argued that Conrad, at the peak of his creative ability, had to cope with two kinds of threat. On the one hand, he was faced with the task of neutralizing instinctual pressures of a sexual and aggressive type. These pressures, shaped by unfulfilled and apparently repressed dependency needs in Conrad the orphaned child, led to their neutralization and their effective use in the development of ego functions, including those of problem solving in reality and fantasy. The process of sublimation involved Conrad in a series of defensive adaptations consistent with his history of traumatic object loss. This process entailed distancing himself from people, first through his career as a seaman who held himself aloof from his fellow officers, and later, through his writing, in which he characteristically tried to hold his characters at arm's length. Paradoxically, the result of these ego-defensive strategies, particularly when Conrad dealt with his own frustration and despair through his fictional characters, was the production of powerful works of fiction.

The second source of threat to Conrad emanated from the external world, or what Hartmann[12] labels the *conflict-free sphere*, as distinguished from intrapsychic conflict. Conrad's environment posed a series of difficult challenges to him. As the child of exiled, defeated parents who were visibly wasting away from tuberculosis, and who did not conceal their deep depression from their only child, Conrad started life with few emotional supports. Later, as the orphaned dependent of his extended family, Conrad lacked a secure home base, and had already begun to cut himself adrift emotionally from the people around him. As a sailor, he suffered from loneliness and "lived like a hermit with my passion" (for the sea), as he expresses it in his Author's Note to *The Mirror of the Sea*. As a British subject, he had to cope with an unfamiliar culture in which he never felt fully at home. As an impoverished and unsuccessful writer for most of his literary career, Conrad had to struggle with a language he never learned to speak with perfect fluency, without a marked foreign accent. Even his health, seriously impaired by his hardships as a seaman, added to his problems. Thus, the real world of object relations was hardly free of stress for Conrad, and continued to the end to make demands on him that exhausted him. But the true source of exhaustion was not hardship, illness, or old age. Conrad's depletion as a creative artist is traceable to his victory over poverty and neglect; the tightly coiled spring relaxed and lost its tension, and Conrad ended his career as a writer who was satisfied with himself.

I have described Hardy as a nineteenth-century writer who still believed in life-affirming ideals. At the same time, his deep insight into man's self-destructive drives made him pessimistic about the future of mankind. Hardy can be described as a naturalist with modern psychological insights resembling Hawthorne's guilt-consciousness. Nevertheless, he does not belong in the ranks of twentieth-century postsymbolists such as

Joyce or Proust. The latter had placed themselves at a distance from their characters even while dwelling in detail on their most minute perceptions and reflections. The moral perspective is still too strong in Hardy to classify him as a true modern.

Conrad, too, stands at the threshold of the modern age in literature because his fictional antiheroes are still aristocratic in their rectitude and bourgeois in their moral earnestness. They live and die, however, in a world that resembles the anomic landscape of twentieth-century fiction. Like Hardy's fictional idealists, they know they are on the side of virtue, but they have begun to doubt their ability to be true to themselves. Thus, Hardy is a modern insofar as he creates weak but noble men who are easily destroyed by deterministic forces operating in a still-familiar rural landscape. Conrad, by comparison, is a modern because he sketches a world that is far more amoral and primitive than the traditional folk culture that forms the backdrop for Hardy's fiction. In this semibarbarous universe, with the heartless and mindless sea as a constant reminder of man's smallness and vulnerability, Conrad's protagonists are doomed to sink to the bottom. Strangely enough, they still believe in a type of brave code hero not unlike Dominic Cervoni, Conrad's real-life mentor in the ways of the sea.

What really gives Hardy and Conrad their modern tone, even though they are not quite twentieth-century in their persistent attachment to positive values, is that they have all but given up on the objective world. Their protagonists cannot fulfill their ideals in this world. In fact, they can barely survive in this world, let alone salvage their self-respect as they are buffeted about by external forces or betrayed by inner weaknesses. The stage is set for Edmund Wilson's cast of twentieth-century newcomers, namely, William Butler Yeats, Paul Valery, T.S. Eliot, Proust, Joyce, and Gertrude Stein. As we shall see, Hemingway, as well, belongs with this cast of characters by virtue of his pessimism and his compensatory preoccupation with style. These writers not only have much in common, as Wilson makes clear in *Axel's Castle*, but are the ideological forerunners of Nabokov, Beckett, and Ionesco.

Hemingway's bleak view of society, like that of Yeats or T.S. Eliot, or any of the others, is the reciprocal of their emphasis on stylistic innovation. The greater the disenchantment with the manmade world, the greater the corresponding emphasis on *form*—sometimes, as in Gertrude Stein's case, at the expense of content. Yeats was not only concerned with form, but he even tried to substitute the landscape of a fairyland for the gritty contents of the real world, at least in his early writings. His heroes, for example, find the real world a depressing place and try to escape to an ideal realm of imagination, complete with its own magical people. These fictional characters—Oisin, Red Hanrahan and others—resemble Conrad's antiheroes who abandon the land for the sea, where they can be alone with their thoughts and safe from society's corruption.

The cultivation of subjective experience is based on the assumption that the objective world has nothing left to give but sensory impressions, which can serve as raw materials for reflection. As seen through the eyes of Proust or Joyce, the old ideals that inspired men to try to change the conditions of life are dead. In their place, the senses awaken to a life of their own. The life of the senses has nothing to do with solving problems or reforming the world, but is valid in its own right. For these writers and kindred spirits, the senses are the gates of imagination, and everything outside these gates is the world of inert matter. In fact, when we turn our attention to Hemingway, we see that the imagination has been all but eclipsed by the senses, which are linked not only with literal description, but with a self-validating hedonism as well.

With Hemingway, modern literature takes another step toward the depiction of an existential universe in which there is nothing of substance that an honest person can believe in. All that remains, once the senses have been given their due, is the bitter satisfaction that one has tried to live one's life with style, that is, so as not to offend the senses by a false or clumsy gesture. Hemingway even went so far as to try to discipline himself to write only about immediate experience, in the belief that it was a valid substitute for reflection. In so doing, he sought to evade the broad implications of his radical skepticism. As interpreted by Hemingway, Conrad's gentlemanly virtues of courage and dignity are translated into the compulsion to maintain good form, or grace under pressure. The same tendency pervades his strategy of literary composition, with its emphasis on absolute fidelity to sensory impressions and avoidance of "unmanly" elaboration or reflection.

In a universe without apparent meaning, Hemingway followed Conrad's lead in singling out the man whose essential decency consists of his stylistic integrity. Such men are not guided by substantive values, such as belief in justice or human freedom, but by the imperative to meet life-threatening challenges with grace and determination, and to endure pain without whimpering. Although Hemingway's code hero appears to be capable of idealizing love objects, he is fundamentally narcissistic and unconcerned with the fate of others. Instead of pursuing ethical goals, Hemingway's code-hero concentrates on style, on the perfection of method, on fighting or hunting or dying gracefully and in accordance with a set of aesthetic norms. When Hemingway's code hero is drawn into conflict with forces in the external world, his adversaries are hardly more than projections of id impulses in the form of wild animals, bulls, enormous fish, and an occasional gangster. I am not forgetting the fascists in *For Whom the Bell Tolls,* but then, by the time Hemingway was through with this novel, he had done a much better job of damning the Loyalists and their partisan allies.

As was true of the symbolists and their twentieth-century successors generally, Hemingway's main concern was aesthetic. He was aware that his fictional heroes were without a cause, and were mere ritualists hunting, boxing, and soldiering for no other reason than to maintain their stylistic purity and to keep in shape. It did not concern him that his heroes were out of touch with social and political realities, nor did he try to convince his readers that his heroes risked their lives for high stakes. The essential quality of Hemingway's heroes is their ability to *endure,* but to endure the way an artist handles the frustrations associated with the practice of his craft, conscious of his need to strive for the perfection of form. Ironically, Hemingway's manly heroes, projections of his inordinate need to be strong and unsentimental, are engaged in a graceful dance of life. They endure, conscious that they are striking a pose, and knowing that it is absurd to endure. It is the gratuitous act par excellence to appear to remain unmoved in extreme situations, knowing that the outcome makes no difference in a world in which all values can be summed up by the word *nada*—nothing, zero, emptiness. Hemingway's strategy as a writer is to try to replace lost illusions with a defensive posture, which he shares with his fictional protagonists. This posture reflects the "separate peace" that Hemingway made with his conscience, namely, to look at life egocentrically as a series of dangers to be met by cultivating a particular frame of mind in which the best defense is the aesthetically perfect mortal wound to the adversary.

Hemingway's self-centeredness made his writing an exercise in subjectivism disguised as the objective reporting of sensory impressions and the faithful recording of dialogue. His fears, hatreds, enormous vanity, and defensiveness—as well as his enthusiasms—colored everything he wrote. Always selective in his perceptions, Hemingway saw and felt only what was relevant to his defensive needs. The result was that his imagination was constricted, and his invented characters, such as the protagonists of *The Sun Also Rises,* are in many ways less interesting and less complex than their real-life prototypes. Hemingway's celebrated apprenticeship to Gertrude Stein and Ezra Pound, which sensitized him to the problems of form, merely confirmed his egocentricity and made it more difficult for him to free himself from the constricting influence of his destructive needs.

This criticism applies not only to Hemingway, but also to many writers of our time. Although Hemingway's defects as a writer were exaggerated by his egocentricity, they were the product of his cynicism as well. The collapse of traditional values and beliefs has made it difficult for creative artists to interpret human experience as if it had any significance. Hemingway's concern for purity of form, in this connection, has much in common with Pablo Picasso's search for new and distinctive art forms. In both cases there is a break with convention and an implied criticism of society, accompanied by an affirmation of life on the experiential level. This affirmation, which is playful at its best, makes no moral judgment, and lapses into self-indulgence at its worst. Similarly, Hemingway's commitment to form-in-lieu-of-faith resembles Joyce's need to effect an oceanic elaboration of form, in the absence of a coherent philosophy of life. D.H. Lawrence mingled the sex drive with the will to power to produce his own alternative to a life of meaning and purpose. Kafka, that master of the futile gesture, elevated suffering and isolation to the status of an art form, as in "The Hunger Artist," and consoled himself with the reflection that if life is devoid of human significance, perhaps it all adds up to something in the opaque mind of God.

Like a poor motherless child, the best writers and artists of our time cry out in their several ways, or turn their love inward, or hallucinate a reality of their own. It is no wonder that their antiheroes are destroyed from within and from without. It is a truism to say that modern society provides little nurturance for the life of the mind or the spirit, but we are dealing with more than the indifference of popular culture to serious art. Democratic and totalitarian societies alike are in the process of contracting the life space of writers and artists, and eventually ending their independent existence. If this prognosis seems alarmist it is only because we have assumed all along that serious fiction, poetry, and drama are perceived as performing a valuable and unassailable function in society. But these cultural activities are coming under increasing pressure under the conditions of mass society. In response to these conditions, art ceases to be a sublimated act based on the neutralized energy of instinctual drives. Instead, it becomes a compulsion that employs a set of symbolic defenses erected by the beleaguered ego in the face of a hostile cultural environment. The ideal of beauty, however defined, has no necessary place among these strategies of ego-preservation. The hostile conditions of which I speak are all the more threatening because they are not based exclusively on the exploitation of man by man, or by the state, but involve something new, namely, the growing irrelevance of the aesthetic side of life.

There is no evidence, of course, that beauty is a necessary condition of life, or even of civilization. The ability to create beauty, however, reflects the wish to transcend the limitations of everyday life, or at least to enhance objects of everyday use by imbuing them with some special distinction. Even the condemned of Terezin in the midst of the Holocaust continued to write poems, make drawings, and stage musical performances while awaiting deportation to the death camps. Were they conscious that their efforts were an affirmation of life? Surely they were aware of the irrelevance of their artistic productions to the designs of their executioners, or to the concerns of the embattled world around them. Yet there is a similarity between this art produced under the threat of extinction and modern art in general. The similarity consists of the artist's finding himself in an extreme situation, life-threatening in the first instance, and soul-crushing in the second. Under these conditions, art ceases to be a sublimation of sexual or aggressive drives. The prisoner who is being systematically starved to death has no need to neutralize his nonexistent libido; the modern artist who lives in a sexually permissive society is under no compulsion to redirect his sexual energies to sublimated activities. If they choose to create art, it can only be to signify their attachment to life or to express their resistance to the inhumanity of the world around them. When the aggressive drive cannot be expressed through open defiance, the artist is compelled to resort to indirection. The danger that blocked aggression will be turned against the self is very great. If humor, wit, satire, or parody are sublimated forms of aggression, as Freud maintained, then compulsive self-maceration, including self-ridicule, is also displaced hostility, but without sublimation. In the absence of neutralization of affect, the full force of the artist's bitterness makes itself felt through the metaphors and images of art.

I believe that aggression that is compulsively turned against the self underlies much of the best writing of the nineteenth and twentieth centuries. It is a dominant strategy of creation in such chroniclers of victimization and self-destruction as Dostoevsky, Hawthorne, Melville, Hardy, Henry James, D.H. Lawrence, Kafka, Faulkner, F. Scott Fitzgerald, Hesse, Tennessee Williams, Nabokov, Beckett, Ionesco, Simenon, and many other writers of the modern era.

These writers are caught in an inner struggle between the forces of life and death. Often, their life-affirming impulses are obscured and even hidden from themselves by their sense of decay and corruption. They provide catharsis neither for themselves nor for their readers. They can resolve neither the conflict between dependency and separation vis-à-vis their love objects, nor the conflict with the oedipal father. The playfulness of Barrie or H.H. Munro or Ionesco is less an expression of the pleasure principle than it is a cry of pain. Although Freud has made the search for sublimated sexual pleasure a basis for object cathexis and aesthetic achievement, it is evident that the most important writers of the modern period are motivated neither by the pleasure principle nor the quest for beauty. Their object choices in life as in art are narcissistic and their egocentricity drives them to create fictional protagonists in their own image. In addition, their expenditure of psychic energy in defense of the vulnerable ego fails to produce equilibrium either for the writer or his reader. Instead of tension reduction, something else takes place, namely, the reactivation of obsessive concerns reflecting excessive inner stimulation.

I agree with the formulation presented by Jack Spector in *The Aesthetics of Freud*[13] when he states, "A major problem of arriving at a workable psychoanalytic aesthetics comes from its undue weighting of pleasure in its implied definition of beauty." Freud's idea of beauty, as Spector notes, is also tied up with the concept of psychic integration, in which the ego achieves a balance between conscious and unconscious processes in the creation of a work of art. The literature of our time—leaving to one side the literature of popular culture—does not yield pleasure, and its implicit definition of beauty is as far removed from sublime tragedy as it is from the contemplation of the harmony of the cosmic spheres. The literary works described in the foregoing chapters convey pathos and lay bare the ugliness of the human comedy as perceived by contemporary writers. Nor is the ego always able to impose coherent artistic form on the emotions churned up out of the writer's unconscious. The reader of fiction or poetry and the play-viewer have accepted a new set of aesthetic conventions that makes room for unpleasure—disgust, despair, unrelieved fear, unredeemed failure, helplessness, loneliness, and lovelessness. Thus, the writer and his audience have come to share a common set of expectations about the function of art. If art, then, ever had a healing function, or provided people with a sense of harmony and beauty, this is no longer the case.

What is the function of modern art? It provides no haven from the everyday world, makes no effort to inspire people, provides no role models with whom the young can identify

themselves in a life-affirming way, and does not permit catharsis. But it seeks out the truth intuitively and on the basis of
empiricism, and therefore occupies a position somewhere between science and religion. Should we condemn the best writers
of our time if they present us with unpleasant truths, and if
these truth possess neither the rational properties of scientific
thought nor the uplifting beauty of religious ritual? There is
such a thing as the aesthetics of truth, in which beauty consists of
the conquest of illusion, no less than in the creation of illusion
that bespeaks an underlying truth. Modern literature has freed
itself of the false idealism praised by Frederick Schlegel in his
History of Literature Ancient and Modern,[14] in which he speaks of
idealism as "the system of those who recognize ideas as superior
to sensation." The importance of Beckett or Kafka or even
Hemingway is that, in the absence of certainty, they start at the
beginning, with sensations, with the flux of mental images, with
the sound of waves. The reader is entirely free to draw his own
conclusions, although they can hardly be very consoling. The
aesthetics of truth can move us, nevertheless, by presenting us
with those facts of life we have repressed in order to maintain a
counterfeit serenity. Art-based-on-truth will not allow us to steal
away from the world or to hide from ourselves. If psychoanalysis
as a theoretical system has failed to convince some people of the
duplicity of the human heart, the best literature of our time
cannot be brushed aside as easily. Its truths, which have been
shaped by art, strike us with a powerful impact. We try vainly to
evade the force of these unwelcome insights, and clap our hands
as if to summon the reassuring gods of textual criticism or some
other mode of exegesis. But the gods of reason, order, romantic
idealism, social criticism—or of any of the other intellectual
traditions—do not respond. Instead, demons appear and knock
on the door with the haft of a knife, like the old man described
by Laurence Sterne in *A Sentimental Journey Through France and
Italy,* who banged on the table to summon the members of his
family to dance after supper. They are the demons of truth,
flushed out by Freud and other demon hunters. They summon
us to the dance of life, but we must not be afraid to move in
rhythm with the music, even when it jarring, or so soft that all we
can hear is our own ominous heartbeat.

REFERENCES

CHAPTER I

1. Freud, S. "Delusions and Dreams in Jensen's *Gradiva*," in *The Standard Edition of the Complete Psychological Works of Sigmund Freud* (SE), Vol. 9. J. Strachey (Ed. and Trans.). pp. 7–95. London: Hogarth Press, 1959.

2. Kris, E. *Psychoanalytic Explorations in Art*. New York: Schocken Books, 1964.

3. Hoffman, F. J. *Freudianism and Literary Mind*. New York: Grove Press, 1959.

4. Hartmann, H. *Ego Psychology and the Problem of Adaptation*. New York: International Universities Press, 1958.

5. Kris, op. cit., p. 318.

6. Erikson, E. *Adulthood*. New York: Norton, 1978.

7. Schafer, R. *A New Language for Psychoanalysis*. New Haven: Yale University Press, 1976, pp. 3–15.

8. Ibid., p. 187.

9. Ibid., p. 183.

10. Rothenberg, A. *The Emerging Goddess: The Creative Process in Art, Science, and Other Fields*. Chicago: University of Chicago Press, 1979.

11. Lacan, J. *Ecrits.* Paris: Editions du Seuil, 1966.

12. Schwartz, M. M. "Shakespeare Through Contemporary Psycho-analysis," in *Representing Shakespeare.* M. M. Schwartz & C. Kahn (Eds.). Baltimore: Johns Hopkins University Press, 1980.

13. Ibid., p. 24.

14. D. W. Winnicott. *Playing and Reality.* New York: Basic Books, 1971, p. 103.

15. Holland, N. "Hermia's Dream," in *Representing Shakespeare,* loc. cit.

16. Ibid., p. 19.

17. Holland, N. *Poems in Persons: An Introduction to the Psychoanalysis of Literature.* New York: Norton, 1973.

18. *Ibid.,* p. 85.

19. Lesser, S. O. *Fiction and the Unconscious.* New York: Vintage, 1962.

20. Slochower, H. *Mythopoesis: Mythic Patterns in the Literary Classics.* Detroit: Wayne State University Press, 1970.

21. Kaplan, M., & Kloss, R. *The Unspoken Motive: A Guide to Psycho-analytic Literary Criticism.* New York: Free Press, 1973.

22. Mordell, A. *The Erotic Motive in Literature.* New York: Boni & Liveright, 1919.

23. Eissler, K. R. *Goethe: A Psychoanalytic Study.* Detroit: Wayne State University Press, 1963.

24. Eissler, K. R. "Psychopathology and Creativity," *American Imago,* 1967, *24,* 35–81.

25. Eissler, K. R. "Remarks on an Aspect of Creativity," *American Imago,* 1979, *35* (1–2), 59–76.

26. Kaplan & Kloss, op. cit., p. 193.

27. Crews, F. *The Sins of the Fathers: Hawthorne's Psychological Themes.* New York: Oxford University Press, 1966.

28. Kleinschmidt, H. "On Psychoanalysis, Art, and Creativity 1964–1976," *American Imago,* 1979, *35* (1–2), 45–58.

29. Rangel, L. "The Creative Thrust: A Psychoanalytic Theory," *American Imago,* 1979, *35* (1–2), 27–44.

30. Kris, op. cit., p. 302.

CHAPTER 2

1. Faulkner, W. *Uncollected Stories of William Faulkner.* Joseph Blotner (ed.). New York: Random House, 1979.

2. Blotner, J. *Faulkner: A Biography* (vol. 1). New York: Random House, 1974, p. 178.

3. Ibid., p. 179.

4. Ibid., p. 630.

5. Carpenter, M., & Borsten, O. *A Loving Gentleman: The Love Story of William Faulkner and Meta Carpenter.* New York: Simon & Schuster, 1976.

6. Blotner, op. cit., p. 79.

7. Federn, P. "The Ego as Subject and Object in Narcissism," in *Ego Psychology and the Psychoses* E. Weiss (Ed.) New York: Basic Books, 1952, pp. 283–322.

8. Faulkner, W. *Light in August.* New York: Random House, 1959, pp. 78–79.

9. Wilson, E. *Classics and Commercials.* New York: Vintage, 1962, p. 461.

10. Faulkner, op. cit., p. 334.

11. Collins, C. "The Interior Monologues of *The Sound and the Fury*," in *Psychoanalysis and American Fiction.* Irving Malin (Ed.). New York: Dutton, 1965.

12. Ibid., p. 225.

13. Kazin, A. *On Native Grounds.* New York: Doubleday, 1956, Chapter 14.

14. Sartre, J. P. *Literary and Philosophical Essays.* New York: Collier, 1962.

15. Beckett, S. *Proust.* New York: Grove Press, 1931, pp. 2–3.

CHAPTER 3

1. Adler, A. *Individual Psychology.* Paterson, N.J.: Littlefield, Adams, 1959.

2. Hellman, L. *An Unfinished Woman.* Boston: Little, Brown, 1969, p. 280.

3. Ibid., p. 43.

4. Ibid., p. 44.

5. Wright, W. *Lillian Hellman, The Image, The Woman.* New York: Simon & Schuster, 1986, pp. 403–414.

6. Hellman, L. *Maybe.* Boston: Little, Brown, 1980.

7. ———— *An Unfinished Woman,* loc. cit., p. 53.

8. ———— *Pentimento.* Boston: Little, Brown, 1973, p. 154.

9. Ibid., pp. 34–35.

10. Hellman, L. *An Unfinished Woman,* loc. cit., p. 29.

11. ———— *The Collected Plays.* Boston: Little, Brown, 1972, p. 126.

12. Wright, W., op. cit., pp. 164–167.

13. Hellman, L. *Scoundrel Time.* Boston: Little, Brown, 1976, p. 113.

14. ———— *The Collected Plays,* loc. cit., p. 747.

15. Buttinger, M. G. *Code Name Mary.* New Haven: Yale U. Press, 1983.

CHAPTER 4

1. Kernberg, O. F. *Internal World and External Reality.* New York: Jason Aronson, 1980, p. 125.

2. Ibid., p. 127.

3. Nabokov, V. *Tyrants Destroyed and Other Stories.* New York: McGraw-Hill, 1975, p. 198.

4. Vergote, A. "Foreword," in Anika Lemaire's *Jacques Lacan.* London: Routledge & Kegan Paul, 1977, p. xxi.

5. Alter, R. "*Invitation to a Beheading:* Nabokov and the Art of Politics," in *Nabokov: Criticism, Reminiscences, Translations and Tributes.* A. Appel, Jr. & C. Newman (Eds.) Evanston, IL: Northwestern University Press, 1970, pp. 41–59.

6. Amis, M. "The Sublime and the Ridiculous: Nabokov's Black Farces," in *Vladimir Nabokov: A Tribute.* P. Quennell (Ed.). New York: Morrow. 1980, p. 76.

7. Nabokov, V. *Speak, Memory: An Autobiography Revisited.* New York: Putnam, 1966, pp. 288–293.

8. Leith, W. C. *Sirenica.* London: Lane, Bodley Head, 1916, p. 17.

9. Pifer, E. *Nabokov and the Novel.* Cambridge, MA: Harvard University Press, 1980, Ch. VII.

10. Ehrenzweig, A. *Psycho-analysis of Artistic Vision and Hearing.* New York: Braziller, 1961.

11. Bullough, E. *Aesthetics: Lectures and Essays.* London: Bowes & Bowes, 1957, p. 21.

12. Nabakov, V. *Lectures on Literature.* F. Bowers (Ed.). New York: Harcourt Brace Jovanovich, 1980.

13. Ehrenzweig, op. cit., p. 151.

14. Nabokov, V. *The Eye.* London: Weidenfeld & Nicolson, 1966, p. 103.

15. Ibid.

16. Nabokov, V. *Laughter in the Dark.* New York: New Directions, 1960, p. 58.

17. Grunberger, B. *Narcissism.* New York: International Universities Press, 1979, p. 153.

18. Trilling, L. "The Last Lover: Vladimir Nabokov's *Lolita*," *Encounter,* 11, 1958, October.

19. Pifer, op. cit., p. 71.

CHAPTER 5

1. O'Connor, F. *The Habit of Being.* S. Fitzgerald (Ed.). New York: Farrar, Straus, Giroux, 1979, p. xxi.

2. Cheney, B. "Miss O'Connor Creates Unusual Humor Out of Ordinary Sin," in *Flannery O'Connor.* R. E. Reiter (Ed.). St. Louis, MO: Herder, 1968, p. 43.

3. Tolstoy, L. *What Is Art?* Indianapolis: Bobbs-Merrill, 1960, p. 138.

4. Joselyn, Sister M. "Thematic Centers In 'The Displaced Person,' " in *Flannery O'Connor,* loc. cit., p. 89.

5. O'Connor, F. *The Habit of Being,* p. 307.

6. O'Connor, F. *Mystery and Manners.* London: Faber & Faber, 1972, p. 17.

7. Ibid., p. 21.

CHAPTER 6

1. Giovacchini, P. L. *Psychoanalysis of Character Disorders*. New York: Jason Aronson, 1975.

2. Radó, S., "The Problem of Melancholia," *International Journal of Psycho-Analysis*, 1928, *9*, 4–20.

3. Kernberg, O. F. *Object Relations Theory and Clinical Psychoanalysis*. New York: Jason Aronson, 1976.

4. Williams, T. *Memoirs*. Garden City, NY: Doubleday, 1975.

5. Meissner, W. W. *Internalization in Psychoanalysis*. New York: International Universities Press, 1981.

6. Kernberg, O. F. *Borderline Conditions and Pathological Narcissism*. New York: Jason Aronson, 1975.

CHAPTER 7

1. Kohut, H. *The Analysis of the Self*. New York: International Universities Press, 1971, p. 308.

2. Cheever, S. *Home Before Dark*. Boston: Houghton-Mifflin, 1984.

3. Ibid., p. 6.

4. Ibid., p. 32.

5. Cheever, J. *The Wapshot Chronicle*. New York: Harper & Row, 1957.

6. ———— *The Wapshot Scandal*. New York: Harper & Row, 1964.

7. ———— *Bullet Park*. New York: Knopf, 1969.

8. ———— *Falconer*. New York: Knopf, 1977.

9. ———— *The Stories of John Cheever*. New York: Random House, 1981.

10. ———— *Oh What A Paradise It Seems*. New York: Random House, 1982.

11. Kohut, H., op. cit., p. 27.

12. Cheever, J. *Bullet Park,* loc. cit., p. 146.

13. Ibid., p. 220.

14. Ibid.

15. Ibid., p. 216.

16. Ibid., pp. 146–147.

17. Sartre, J. P. *No Exit and Three Other Plays.* New York: Vintage, p. 47.

18. Cheever, J. *Falconer,* loc. cit., p. 175.

19. _____ *Oh What A Paradise It Seems,* loc. cit., p. 97.

20. _____ *The Stories of John Cheever,* loc. cit., p. 40.

Chapter 8

1. Bell-Villada, G. H. *Borges and His Fiction.* Chapel Hill: U. of N. Carolina Press, 1981, pp. 262–268.

2. Borges, J. L. *Other Inquisitions 1937–1952.* New York: Simon & Schuster, 1965, p. 74.

3. Freud, S. "The Uncanny," in S.E., Vol. 17, 1955, pp. 219–252.

4. Rank, O. *The Double.* Chapel Hill: University of North Carolina Press, 1971.

5. Smith, J. H., Pao, P.-N., and Schweig, N. A. "On the Concept of Aggression," in *The Psychoanalytic Study of the Child, Vol. 28.* New Haven: Yale University Press, pp. 331–46.

6. Eigen, M. "Creativity, Instinctual Fantasy and Ideal Images," *Psychoanalytic Review,* 1982, 69(3), 317–39.

7. Christ, R. J. *The Narrow Act: Borges' Art of Allusion.* New York: New York University Press, 1969.

8. Noy, P. "Form Creation in Art: An Ego-Psychological Approach to Creativity," *Psychoanalytic Quarterly,* 1979, *48*(2), 229–56.

9. Eissler, K. R. *Discourse on Hamlet and HAMLET.* New York: International Universities Press, 1971.

10. Capell, M. D. "Passive Mastery of Helplessness in Games," *American Imago,* 1968, *25*(4), 309–32.

11. Rappaport, E. A. "Notes on Blindness and Omniscience: From Oedipus to Hitler," *Psychoanalytic Review,* 1976, *63*(2), 281–90.

12. Kris, E. *Psychoanalytic Explorations in Art.* New York: International Universities Press, 1952.

13. Niederland, W. G. "Psychoanalytic Approaches to Artistic Creativity," *Psychoanalytic Quarterly,* 1976(45), 2, 185–212.

14. Eissler, K. R. "Remarks on an Aspect of Creativity," *American Imago,* 1978, *35*(1–2), 59–76.

15. Borges, J. L. *Borges: A Reader.* E. Rodriguez Monegal & A. Reid (Eds.). New York: Dutton, 1981, p. 279.

16. Borges, J. L. *Ficciones.* New York: Grove Press, 1962, p. 80.

17. Jurado, A. *Genio y Figura de Jorge Luis Borges.* Buenos Aires: Editorial Universitaria de Buenos Aires, 1964.

18. *Borges: A Reader,* loc. cit., p. 29.

19. Borges, J. L. "Hawthorne," in *Other Inquisitions 1937–1952,* loc. cit.

20. *Borges: A Reader,* loc. cit., pp. 266–67.

21. Wheelock, C. *The Mythmaker; A Study of Motif and Symbol in the Short Stories of Jorge Luis Borges.* Austin: University of Texas Press, 1969.

22. Rothenberg, A. *The Emerging Goddess: The Creative Process in Art, Science, and Other Fields.* Chicago: University of Chicago Press, 1979, p. 55.

Chapter 9

1. Bair, D., *Samuel Beckett: A Biography.* New York: Harcourt, Brace, Jovanovich, 1978.

2. Bion, W. R., "Emotional Turbulence," in *Borderline Personality Disorders.* P. Hartocollis (Ed.). New York: International Universities Press, 1977.

3. Bair, op. cit., pp. 178–179.

4. Ibid., p. 577.

5. Ibid., p. 177.

6. Ibid., p. 324.

7. Ibid., p. 349.

8. Ibid., p. 352.

9. Ibid., p. 382.

10. Beckett, S., *The Unnamable.* New York: Grove Press, 1958.

CHAPTER 10

1. Singer, J. L. *Imagery and Daydream Methods in Psychotherapy and Behavior Modification.* New York: Acadenic Press, 1974.

2. Singer, J. L., & Pope, K. S. (Eds.). *The Power of Human Imagination: New Methods in Psychotherapy.* New York: Plenum Press, 1978.

3. Reyher, J., "Free Imagery: An Uncovering Procedure," *Journal of Clinical Psychology,* 1963, *19,* 454–459.

4. Singer, J. L., "Imagery and Daydream Techniques Employed in Psychotherapy: Some Practical and Theoretical Implications," in *Current Topics in Clinical and Community Psychology,* Vol. 3. C. Spielberger (Ed.), New York: Academic Press, 1971.

5. Frank, S. J., "Empathy Through Training in Imagination," in *The Power of Human Imagination: New Methods in Psychotherapy,* J. L. Singer & K. S. Pope (Eds.), New York: Plenum, 1978.

6. Shorr, J. E. *Psychotherapy Through Imagery.* New York: Intercontinental Medical Book Company, 1974.

7. Klein, M. *Our Adult World and Other Essays.* New York: Basic Books, 1963.

8. Emde, R. N. "The Prerepresentational Self and Its Affective Core," in *The Psychoanalytic Study of the Child,* Vol. 38. A. J. Solnit & R. S. Eissler (Eds.). New Haven: Yale University Press, 1983, 165–192.

9. Ibid., p. 177.

10. Esslin, M. *The Peopled Wound: The World of Harold Pinter.* Garden City, NY: Doubleday, 1970, p. 163.

11. Pinter, H. "Introduction," in *Harold Pinter: Complete Works,* Vol. 1. New York: Grove Press, 1977.

12. Winnicott, D. W. "The Depressive Position in Normal Emotional Development," *British Journal of Medical Psychology,* 1955, *28,* 89–100.

13. Freud, S. "A Child Is Being Beaten: A Contribution to the Study of Sexual Perversions," (1919), in SE, Vol. 17, 1955, p. 177.

14. Pinter, H. *Harold Pinter: Complete Works,* Vol. 4, New York: Grove Press, 1977, p. 26.

Chapter 11

1. Freud, S. SE, Vol. 20, 1959, p. 130.

2. Kay-Robinson, D. *The First Mrs. Thomas Hardy.* New York: St. Martin's, 1979, p. 77.

3. Furst, S. S. "Psychic Trauma: A Survey," in *Psychic Trauma.* S. S. Furst (Ed.). New York: Basic Books, 1967, pp. 3–50.

4. Cooper, C. *Conrad and the Human Dilemma.* New York: Barnes & Noble, 1970.

5. Hartmann, H. *Essays in Ego Psychology.* London: Hogarth, 1964, pp. 4–18.

6. Ibid., p. 60.

7. Jean-Aubry, G. *The Sea-Dreamer.* Garden City, NY: Doubleday, 1957, p. 52.

8. Gurko, L. *Joseph Conrad: Giant in Exile.* New York: Macmillan, 1962, pp. 25–6.

9. Jean-Aubry, op. cit., p. 213.

10. Conrad, Jessie. *Joseph Conrad As I Knew Him.* London: Heinemann, 1926, p. 2.

11. Conrad, Joseph. *The Shadow Line,* in *A Conrad Argosy.* Garden City, NY: Doubleday, 1942, p. 661.

12. Hartmann, op. cit., p. 107.

13. Spector, J. J. *The Aesthetics of Freud.* New York: Praeger, 1973, p. 140.

14. Schlegel, F. *Lectures in the History of Literature Ancient and Modern, Vol. 2.* Philadelphia: Dobson, 1818, p. 307.

INDEX